CROSS-COUNTRY SKIING:
Building Skills for Fun and Fitness

MOUNTAINEERS
OUTDOOR EXPERT
series

CROSS-COUNTRY SKIING:
Building Skills for Fun and Fitness

Steve Hindman

THE MOUNTAINEERS BOOKS

THE MOUNTAINEERS BOOKS
is the nonprofit publishing arm of The Mountaineers Club,
an organization founded in 1906 and dedicated to the exploration,
preservation, and enjoyment of outdoor and wilderness areas.

1001 SW Klickitat Way, Suite 201, Seattle, WA 98134

First edition, 2005

Published simultaneously in Great Britain by Cordee, 3a DeMontfort Street, Leicester, England, LE1 7HD

Manufactured in the United States of America

Acquiring and Project Editor: Mary Metz
Copy Editor: Cindy Bohn
Cover and Book Design: The Mountaineers Books
Layout: Jennifer Shontz
Illustrations: Brian Metz
All photographs by Susan Cottrell Hindman unless otherwise noted.

Cover photograph: *Striding out at Washington Pass above the Methow Valley, Washington*
Frontispiece: *Touring the Callaghan Valley, British Columbia, near the 2010 Olympics cross-country ski trails*
Backcover photograph: *Keep your eye on the ball.*

Text on page 218 adapted from "Skin Your Way to the Top to Prevent a Hairy Slide to the Bottom" by Scott McGee in *The Professional Skier,* Winter 2003, and used with permission of the Professional Ski Instructors of America Education Foundation.

Figure 13.1 on page 208 reprinted with permission from *Avalanche Safety for Skiers, Climbers & Snowboarders* by Tony Daffern.

Library of Congress Cataloging-in-Publication Data
Hindman, Steve, 1957–
  Cross-country skiing : building skills for fun and fitness / Steve Hindman.— 1st ed.
    p. cm.
  Includes index.
  ISBN 0-89886-862-9
  1. Cross-country skiing. I. Title.
  GV855.3.H56 2005
  796.93'2—dc22
                            2005006148

Contents

Part I: Skiing for Fun

CHAPTER 1

Learning to Ski

CHAPTER 2

Basic Ski Skills

Part II: Skiing for Fun and Fitness

Part III: Skiing for Fun and Adventure

CHAPTER 14
Parallel and Telemark Turns

Preface

Do you remember the last time you rode a sled down a snowy hill? Or how much fun it was to ride a bike when you were a kid? Feel that way again on cross-country skis.

Do you exercise inside each winter so you can play outside each summer? This winter, stay in shape outside in the crystalline air instead of in the dank and sweaty gym.

Cross-country skiing offers freedom and fun wherever you find snow. When the country is covered in white you can go wherever you please on cross-country skis. You're not restricted to the marked trails of summertime or the designated slopes of an alpine ski resort. Veer off familiar paths this winter and discover secrets in your own backyard or hidden treasures at more distant ski destinations.

Cross-country skiing offers the most adventure for the least time and effort of any other sport. All you need is a snow-covered hill close to home. Put your skis on and zigzag to the top. Have lunch. Relax. Rest a spell. Then ski back down. There you have it—just possibly the first ascent and descent on skis of that particular piece of earth.

Remember when? (Photo: Steve Barnett)

Acknowledgments

I always thought an endless list of acknowledgements to be ridiculous, but that was before I knew how much help I would need and what it takes to write a book.

Thanks from the bottom of my heart to my wife, Sue, the principal photographer, for her patience with my pursuit of just the right image. Thanks also to Mary Metz and all the others at The Mountaineers Books who accommodated my work schedule, guided me through inexperience, and tolerated my perfectionist tendencies.

The following folks contributed to the learning process that produced this book. Thanks to them all and to those I missed.

Strummin, Brent Harris, and Alan Millar hooked me on free-heel fun. Kirk Flanders, Ben Thompson, Morrie Trautman, and Dick Zagelow gave me a start in the ski business. My fellow team members over the years on the PSIA National Nordic Demo Team helped develop my skiing and teaching skills. My editors at *The Professional Skier* gave me the opportunity to write and then the feedback I needed to develop my writing skills.

Nordic sages Don Portman and Dickie Hall continue to joyfully share their knowledge of skiing and teaching with me. Todd Eastman's gentle coaching and suggestions have influenced my skiing, teaching, and this text to a large degree, and kept me fit through a year of long hours at the writing desk.

Old friends, new friends, and others I have never met contributed quotes, text, and their time to this project. The following made time to talk to me on the phone or via email: Peter Ashley, Jeffrey Bergeron, Tor Brown, Susan Burak, Sandy Cook, Norm Crerar, Fred Griffin, Dick Hall, Leslie Hall, Michael Jackson, Stephen King, Bert Kleerup, Louisa Morrissey, Bruce Ronning, Mary Jo Tarallo, and Sue Wemyss. Thanks for the thoughts and ideas that you shared.

Chris Frado and Missy Lackey of the Cross Country Ski Areas Association (CCSAA) went out of their way to help, and Chip Chase and his family treated me like an old friend when I visited their Whitegrass Touring Center in West Virginia.

Thanks to the following authors who contributed excerpts from their own writings: J. D. Downing, Mark Harfenist, Scott McGee, Mitch Mode, John Mohan, Don Portman, Gregg Rinkus, Steve Walker, and Sue Wemyss. Chris Frado, Roger Lohr and Jonathan Wiesel are also quoted in the text. Your contributions add wisdom and perspective that I could not provide alone.

Thanks to the many members of the CCSAA and others who submitted photos in response to my requests and those of Chris Frado. Images from the following photographers appear in these pages: Tor Brown, Middleton Evans, Kate Carter, Don Portman, Phillip Savignano, David Smith, Tom Stillo, Don Svela, and Don Weixl. The National Capital Commission of Canada, Fischer Skis, Silver Star Mountain Resort, and xczone.tv have also supplied photographs. Steve Barnett deserves special recognition for access to his archives that chronicle cross-country skiing in North America over four decades. Without the contributions of these photographers, Sue and I would have been unable to illustrate the diversity and beauty of cross-country skiing.

Thanks to Peter Ashley of Fischer Skis, Mike Hattrup with K2 Telemark, Oliver Steffen of G3, and Dane Stephenson of Swix who provided much of the equipment that appears in the photos and for their support and encouragement over the years.

Teaching Children to Ski, written by Asbjörn Flemmen and Olav Grosvold, and translated by Michael Brady, has been an inspiration and guide for me. Thanks to the authors and translator for such an insightful and timeless text.

A NOTE ABOUT SAFETY

Safety is an important concern in all outdoor activities. No book can alert you to every hazard or anticipate the limitations of every reader. The descriptions of techniques and procedures in this book are intended to provide general information. This is not a complete text on cross-country skiing technique. Nothing substitutes for formal instruction, routine practice, and plenty of experience. When you follow any of the procedures described here, you assume responsibility for your own safety. Use this book as a general guide to further information. Under normal conditions, excursions into the backcountry require attention to traffic, road and trail conditions, weather, terrain, the capabilities of your party, and other factors. Keeping informed on current conditions and exercising common sense are the keys to a safe, enjoyable outing.

—The Mountaineers Books

Cross-Country Skiing—Fun, Fitness, and Adventure

What exactly is cross-country skiing? The simple answer is that cross-country skiing is play. Of course, there are people who use skis in their line of work, but for most of us getting out on skis is a way to relax or rejuvenate, get some exercise, connect with nature, or engage in the thrill of competition.

Skiing was just emerging from its utilitarian roots in the late 1800s when Norwegians and other Scandinavian immigrants brought their skis and their culture to the snowy regions of North America. When they found they could cover greater distances more easily on these strange contraptions, hunters, miners, railroad workers, mail carriers, and others soon replaced the wood and skin snowshoes they had adopted from the Native Americans with what they called "Norwegian snowshoes." By the time John Muir was describing a late 19th-century outing above Lake Tahoe as "lusty reviving exercise on snow-shoes that kept our pulses dancing right merrily," the New World had discovered that skiing could be as much fun as it was practical.

Mechanical ski lifts began to appear in the 1930s, eliminating the need to keep the heel free for climbing hills. Locking the heel to the ski made for better control, and specialized bindings for this new and distinct branch of skiing soon became available. These developments split skiing into two branches—Nordic or cross-country skiing and Alpine or downhill skiing.

Today, cross-country skiing itself has split into several branches, offering even more ways to play in the snow. Other than using equipment that keeps the heel free, there are no rules for what it is or is not.

Cross-country skiers themselves use different terms to describe what they do,

Track skiing in the Methow Valley, Washington. (Photo: Don Portman)

Ski touring. (Photo: Steve Barnett)

including Nordic skiing, cross-county skiing, skinny skiing, ski touring, track skiing, skate skiing, classic skiing, telemark skiing, and backcountry skiing.

They ski in backyards and fields. They ski to work through parks and along the medians when sudden snowstorms make it possible. They ski on snow-dusted golf courses early in the morning before the greens-keepers arrive to chase them off. They ski in the winter on summer hiking and biking trails. They ski in the summer on snowfields and glaciers.

Some ski on skis as thin as your wrist on specially prepared tracks, while others use skis as wide as any downhill ski to ski up steep mountains and then back down.

Some boots look and feel like slippers or running shoes, others like square-toed hiking boots, and the burliest boots for going up and then back down look like something a futuristic riot cop might wear to work.

For simplicity, the varieties of cross-country skiing can be grouped into three categories: ski touring, track skiing, and backcountry skiing.

SKI TOURING—SKIING FOR FUN

This is the broadest category, with roots stretching directly back to skiing's origins, when outdoor workers donned skis to keep doing what they wanted or needed to do when there was snow on the ground. Skis, boots, and poles suitable for ski touring are versatile and affordable. Although acquiring some advanced skills and technique make ski touring easier and more enjoyable, you can get by with just the basics if you choose good snow conditions and a gentle path. Ski touring is "skiing out your back door" and it appeals to those who like to watch nature, walk, jog, hike, or ride their bikes on quiet roads, gravel paths, and smooth trails.

FLOGGED

I am a passionate wild turkey hunter, and my pursuit of America's grandest game bird transcends the hunting season. No matter what time of year, you can find me hiking, mountain biking, and, yes, even cross-country skiing to learn more about wild turkeys.

One perfect January morning, I was cross-country skiing near my home in northwestern Pennsylvania with Lakota, my chocolate Lab. The temperature hovered in the teens, several inches of soft, dry snow had fallen overnight, and it was remarkably clear and calm.

In near silence, I was gliding swiftly down an old logging trail beneath a canopy of Eastern hemlocks. Rounding a sharp bend, I was suddenly enveloped in a flurry of beating wings and a cacophony of squawks, clucks, and other sounds the likes of which I had never heard. I had skied smack dab into a flock of what seemed like a hundred wild turkeys. It seemed like all the demons of the forest had unleashed their fury against me, and I found myself sprawled on the ground amidst a maelstrom of beating wings and scurrying bodies—legs, feet, and sharp spurs lashing out in all directions. A couple of birds had gotten tangled up in my skis and thrashed me all the harder until they escaped.

There were probably only a dozen or so birds, but eastern turkeys can weigh 15 to 20 pounds and getting slapped around by these powerful birds is something I'd rather not repeat.

Hearing my startled cries, Lakota came on the run. Seeing me splayed out in the snow like a beaten welterweight, she thought I wanted to play and proceeded to pounce on me with all her 80 pounds. I quickly calmed her down and took stock of my condition. Except for a few scratches I was none the worse for wear, although the stench was horrible!

On my journey home I wondered what my family would say when I told them my strange tale. My wife Patty met Lakota and me at the garage. One whiff of that repugnant smell gave her no choice but to believe that this turkey hunter had been flogged by a flock of avian thugs.

Gregg Rinkus, outdoor writer and avid hunter

Kick and glide in Crested Butte, Colorado. (Photo: Tom Stillo Photography)

TRACK SKIING—SKIING FOR FUN AND FITNESS

Skiing on marked trails that are machine groomed is the most specialized category of cross-country skiing. Groomed ski trails provide a flat, firm surface in the middle of the trail for ski skating with parallel grooves pressed into the snow on each side of the trail for the traditional diagonal stride.

Many skiers use touring and back-country skis on groomed trails, but the glide and grace made possible by all this snow grooming can only be unlocked with lighter equipment and some time spent learning how to use it. However, if you are just learning, groomed trails can make your first day or two more successful no matter what type of cross-country equipment you are using.

Track skiing on groomed trails appeals to runners, road bikers, mountain bikers who like to ride single-track trails, and others looking for an exciting and fun wintertime workout. Easy groomed trails also appeal to those seeking a gentle and predictable skiing option reminiscent of walking or cycling on a gravel bike path through town. Regardless of what attracts you, reliable snow conditions, interesting trails, the camaraderie of others, plowed parking, day lodges, and other amenities all conspire to make skiing a pleasurable experience at groomed-trail areas.

BACKCOUNTRY SKIING—SKIING FOR FUN AND ADVENTURE

Backcountry skiing lets you step outside of the lines and beyond the boundaries to make your own tracks in the snow. Backcountry skis are generally wider than

BALLOON BIATHLON IN THE DARK

Things change when the lights go out. One Saturday night the Kongsberger Ski Club hosted a race at their lodge on the east side of Snoqualmie Pass, near Seattle. The race consisted of a Le Mans start (everyone starts on foot, runs to pick up their skis, puts them on, and then proceeds), followed by a classic race (skating not allowed) on a short loop lit by lanterns, then a balloon biathlon competition, and finally a loop around the course skiing backwards.

A friend who was a member invited me to join in, and although the club had a reputation for being serious about competition, I figured that this was all about fun. It didn't take me long to realize that perhaps I was wrong.

When I sprinted to where I had left my skis, I discovered they had been moved and jumbled with many other pairs. As if by magic, however, the club's race sharks found their skis instantly. Everyone quickly double poled onto the course and began striding mightily—at least until we turned the corner beyond the first pool of light cast by the lanterns. Then the sharks broke into lusty skates and continued in their forbidden activity until they reached the next lantern and could once again be seen. Not wanting to be left behind, I followed suit.

For the next part of the competition, balloons had been affixed to the railing of the lodge's porch and each racer had to use his or her pole as a spear to pop three balloons from fifteen feet away. It soon became clear that perhaps there had been some pre-race festivities of which I was unaware, as many contestants could barely see the balloons, much less hit them with their poles.

Now came the backwards portion of the race, in which skating was permitted. Once again the lead skiers were a bit less than fastidious about the rules—spinning around to skate facing forward in the darkness between the lanterns. Getting into the swing of things, I did the same, and as the finish line loomed in the light of the final lantern, I spun around and skated backwards into third place.

Once the awards committee became aware of my non-member, non-Scandinavian status, however, I was stripped of my medal, which was passed on to someone of purer Nordic blood. I was just a tiny bit miffed, since I felt that I had earned my finish fair and square by quickly learning how to cheat like a good Norwegian.

I was soon distracted from my disappointment by the spectacle of folks at least twice my age flying into the dark of night off a jump in front of the clubhouse. Not only were they doing this on light and skinny racing skis, but in between each jump they quenched their thirst with swigs from what looked like a bottle of Aquavit (of course, it *could* have been a sports drink). Any thoughts that I was cheated and deserved a medal quickly vanished. There was no way I belonged in the same club as these crazies!

touring or track skis, the boots are higher, and the bindings are more durable. This category spans the spectrum, from traveling without a marked trail through gentle country to climbing up and skiing back down a mountain peak.

Skill and experience are needed, but a day or so spent ski touring or track skiing should be sufficient to prepare you for your first well-chosen backcountry ski day.

Backcountry skiers tend to be those who like to trail run, backpack, day hike, or mountain bike on remote and challenging trails. Many alpine skiers and snowboarders turn to backcountry skiing to escape the crowds and to ski on uncrowded slopes full of fresh snow.

TELEMARK SKIING

This specialized subcategory of backcountry skiing uses skis and boots that are often as wide and as heavy as alpine skiing equipment. Most backcountry skiers are also telemarkers, but not all telemark skiers venture into the backcountry. Telemark skiing focused exclusively on going downhill is increasingly done at lift-served resorts and will not be covered in this book.

Backcountry skiing

SERENDIPITY

The first rule of cross-country skiing is to take your skis with you everywhere. Don't leave home without them in the wintertime. Serendipitous skiing opportunities are endless. Some of my most memorable skis have been spur-of-the-moment tours on the way to somewhere else.

Thirty years ago when wooden light-touring skis were about all you could buy, my wife and I took these beautiful pine-tarred boards up mountains, over frozen lakes, and across a snow-covered golf course or two.

One of our greatest little tours was at Strawberry Pass in Utah. We parked the car at the side of the road, waxed the skis with green hard wax, skied uphill through a beautiful aspen forest, and then turned around and enjoyed making parallel turns in perfect powder all the way back to the car. The total round trip took just an hour and yet the memory of those sweet turns has lasted a lifetime.

On another trip, crossing the Continental Divide from Montana into Idaho, we stopped just past Monida Pass. It was springtime and there was no snow anywhere except for a thin ribbon deposited by the wind on the lee sides of the rolling hills—continuous for as far as we could see. So off we went. Once we were out of sight of the road, we could have been in Mongolia.

Sometimes, of course, we ended up following boring roads to nowhere, but most of our serendipitous tours have been fabulous.

Don Portman, a founder of the Methow Valley Sport Ski Trails Association, and owner of the Sun Mountain Ski School, located near Winthrop, Washington

Part I: Skiing for Fun

CHAPTER 1

Learning to Ski

It takes some effort to achieve the relaxed joy of gliding over the snow on skis. While reading this book can help, you cannot truly understand the descriptions of what skiing is and how to do it until you actually get out on the snow. Once you're out there, give skiing a couple of days or more of your time to get the hang of it. Give it time to sneak up on you. Keep at it and you will soon find that moment when you stop trying, when you stop practicing, and you simply ski, riding on skis as you would a bike, startled by the clarity of the winter air as they carry you forward.

Learning to ski is a never-ending process. Long-time skiers constantly investigate new things to do on skis and new ways to do old things. Finding a mentor, taking a lesson, reading this book, and watching others and yourself on video are great learning tools. One of the best ways to learn is to find other skiers in your community and ski with them. Camaraderie always accelerates learning: faster skiers will benefit from the balance and technique challenges presented by slowing down, while slower skiers will learn just by trying to keep up.

As you play around with different ways to ski, be inquisitive. Do something slow. Then do it fast. Then do it somewhere in-between. Be sure to do it long enough to get tired and let your body take over from your brain. This process happens naturally as children play. Adults have to learn to let go.

THE TRUTH ABOUT TECHNIQUE

When you go out intending to play on your skis and have fun it will be hard to do something "wrong." But if you try to ski like you think you should or how somebody else thinks you should, it can be easy to have no fun at all. Approaching learning to ski like a child going out to play is half the battle. Kids don't worry about doing it right or even knowing what the right way is. Fears vanish when skiing is play. Make your time on skis into play and you will learn quickly. Focusing on the right or wrong way to ski is silly, and counterproductive.

While it is true that new techniques are always developing as new situations and new ski equipment come along, that is not anything to worry about. It is skiers who create ski technique and not coaches or instructors or writers. You will create your own personalized technique as you play on skis. Use this and other resources only as a guide.

FINDING A GOOD COACH

A good coach or instructor can accelerate your learning as you continue to play. They know *what* you need to do to and can help you with *how* to do it.

Author and ski instructor Mitch Mode advises new skiers to "Take a lesson. Most people don't; most people should. Find a reputable instructor and spend the money. It'll pay dividends immediately and set you on the path to long-time enjoyment of the sport."

When you are looking for a good instructor or coach, ask others who have taken a lesson for their recommendations. In the absence of local contacts, the easiest place to find a qualified instructor is at a PSIA (Professional Ski Instructors of America) or CANSI (Canadian Association of Nordic Ski Instructors) member ski school. In Europe,

look for a member of ISIA (International Ski Instructors Association).

But the most important thing is to find an instructor who is willing to understand your needs and has the ability and desire to meet them. The organization they belong to and the certifications they possess are not as important. When you talk to a potential ski teacher, look for a good listener who is interested in your questions. A good coach wants to know why you have sought them out and what you want to accomplish. With this information, they can customize the lesson just for you.

OK, now try it like this!

WHAT I LEARNED IN NORWAY

- Herring is not good anytime before lunch.
- Aquavit is good anytime after lunch.
- Coffee can't be found anywhere before 8 a.m.
- Coffee out of a machine can actually be good.
- Don't worry when old ladies pass you on the ski trails—you'll catch up when they stop for their next cigarette break.
- Always wear clean undies while skiing—if it gets hot, you'll need to ski in them if you want to fit in with the locals.
- If you see a view while driving or on the train, enjoy it—you will soon be in another mile-long tunnel.
- If you see hot food while traveling, eat it. By the time you are hungry, all the restaurants will be closed.
- Every white liquid at a breakfast buffet is not necessarily what you want to put on your cereal or into your coffee.
- If you are a vegan, good luck.
- If you do not like to look at, ski on, or drive around lakes, do not go to Norway.
- Norwegians love to jump—on skis, while folk dancing, and from the rafters while drunk.
- Reindeer really do exist.
- If you see water in the mountains, you can drink it—unless it is in one of the years when all the reindeer die off.
- There is almost always a gentle ski route to where you want to go in the mountains—even in areas with big peaks, steep slopes, and spectacular cliffs.
- Beer really can cost $10 a glass.
- Roadside kiosks do not sell Mexican food. What looks like burritos are reindeer sausages wrapped in lompers (or lefse), flatbread made from potatoes.

Often the only way to hire a specific person is to take private lessons. Although the hourly rate is higher, the value of the time is greater. If you can form your own group composed of similar skiers, a "group private" will provide many of the advantages of a solo private lesson at a reduced cost.

When you find a good candidate conduct a job interview because what you are hiring is an employee. In return, be ready with a good job description so that your prospective employee understands what you expect. If you are not having fun at any time during a lesson, it is important to stop and ask why.

Women now make up more than half of the cross-country skiers in North America but most instructors are still male. This is unfortunate, and it may be worth your

Euro snacks at Torfinsbu, Jotunheimen, Norway

time to make the effort to seek out a female coach. As Jonathan Wiesel opines in his book, *Cross-Country Ski Vacations,* "Female instructors are seldom afflicted with 'egoitis' and frequently are more versatile in the types of lessons they'll willingly give."

TAKING A LESSON

When you do go out with a friend or an instructor, ask what gear you will need. If they suggest that you rent different gear, give the recommendation serious consideration. If you do rent, reserve the day before, or arrive an hour early to pick up your equipment so you are ready and relaxed when the lesson starts.

Remember to ask for what you want in the lesson, and be specific. Be sure your coach hears you. He or she should state your goals and desires back to you. If your instructor only tells you *what,* be sure to ask *how.* If you need to know *why,* ask more questions. If you need to *see* it, ask for a demonstration or inquire about seeing yourself on video. If you need to *feel* it, ask to move more.

Good instructors know that everyone learns differently, so they teach in a variety

Learning by doing

of ways. Some may work for you, others may not. When something you have learned clicks, you will know it. Be sure to use it often until you can claim it as your own. When you are not "getting it," ask for more clarification, a different approach, or simply let it go and forget about it! Keep in mind that the goal of a good lesson is to learn something useful about skiing, not to learn how to do a drill correctly. A willingness to feel uncomfortable, awkward, and even confused when you try something new or different will increase your ability to learn.

If you find that you tend to learn in one way to the exclusion of any other, you may be able to achieve more by trying a different approach. If you typically need to know everything before you try a move, try doing it first, and then analyze it. If you find yourself standing back and watching all the time, for a change jump in and check out how a movement feels before watching others.

Recognize what you are doing well, and cut yourself some slack. Thinking you are no good at something has a way of becoming true if you convince yourself of it.

If you see, feel, or understand one or two new things during your lesson, then you and the instructor are doing great. Do not worry about the things you missed, or that missed you. People often find that a confusing tip or a drill that seems useless at the time becomes valuable when remembered a day, a month, or even several seasons later.

Like a good lesson with a good coach, some approaches and ideas in this book may work for you, while others may not. If you do not understand something, skip it and come back later. If that doesn't work, forget about it!

HOW I BECAME A CROSS-COUNTRY SKIER

I started downhill skiing as a kid in Pennsylvania, and in 1976 I packed up my Chevy Vega and headed west to become a ski bum, taking it on faith that the snowy slopes of the Continental Divide, which I had only seen in magazines, were real. When Pikes Peak came into view on I-70, I pulled onto the shoulder, got out of my car, and stared. The picture was real, so I stayed.

I ate Thanksgiving dinner in Telluride, Colorado, and stayed on for the winter—or what passed for a winter that year. Day after day of sunshine, with nary a snowflake to be seen, and all the ski lifts idle.

I knew there was snow on the higher peaks, and I became determined to ski there, even though this involved lugging my heavy downhill skis and bulky boots up the slopes. I'd been at this for a few months when a long-haired, bearded gnome skied by me on a pair of narrow wooden skis wearing wimpy little boots. Although he slowed to talk, he couldn't resist mocking my ill-adapted gear. Maybe it was sheer exhaustion, but shortly thereafter I acquired some skinny skis and floppy boots of my own, and soon found myself on this flimsy gear in all the places where I thought I needed downhill gear. But that is another story.

CHAPTER 2

Fresh tracks, fresh face. (Photo: Middleton Evans)

Basic Ski Skills

This chapter presents the basics of going up, down, and across on skis. If you are standing on your skis with this book in hand and just want to know what to do, succinct instructions are highlighted at the beginning of each section.

GETTING STARTED

Everyone needs to know how to crawl before they can walk. Take a few minutes to prepare before hitting the trails.

CONDITIONING
Walk around the block every day for a few weeks before you go cross-country skiing.

Cross-country skiing can be a gentle, low impact form of exercise, but it is still exercise. You'll have more fun on skis if you get your blood moving in more familiar surroundings beforehand. Before you head out onto the snow walk around the block every day for a few weeks or take the stairs instead of the elevator at work.

A more extensive conditioning program will help you have even more fun, but there is no need to get too serious about it. Check with your doctor before embarking on any significant change in your activity level and use your head when you start to use your body in new ways.

EQUIPMENT
Rent when you start out so you can try cross-country skiing before you invest in equipment.

Most rental skis are wide and slow, but that's OK. Wider skis make balance a little easier and slow skis that provide reliable grip on the snow are more important at first than skis that glide easily. After a day or three of skiing on basic skis, or one lesson, find some rental equipment that offers more performance and that is matched to where you are skiing and what you want to do.

As you learn more, you may want to continue to rent different types of equipment to try the different types of skiing before you decide on what to buy. Find out more about equipment in Chapter 3.

WHEN AND WHERE TO LEARN

To choose the best learning conditions apply the Goldilocks rule: Choose snow that is not too soft and not too hard. Choose skis that are not too wide and not too narrow and not too slow and not too fast. Choose terrain that is not all flat but not too hilly.

Doing anything new is tiring, so choose a time when you are feeling fresh and excited. Snow conditions are important—if it is too hard, a fall will feel like hitting the pavement. If the snow is thick and deep, skiing will be as grueling as walking through knee-deep water. It may be better to wait for another day if conditions are too gnarly.

A freshly groomed beginner area or a beginner trail at a Nordic center is an ideal place for your initial outings. The snow there should be smooth but not icy, with mostly flat terrain and gentle hills to play on. A warm place to change, indoor plumbing, and a cup of hot soup for lunch in the lodge are all an added bonus.

If groomed trails are unavailable, a wide, gentle logging road, or a field or meadow will do just fine. The ideal location includes a gentle hill to one side that ends in another flat area.

PUTTING ON YOUR SKIS

Getting your skis on can be confounding at first, but with practice it will quickly become routine.

Find a flat spot where the snow is firm or make one by stamping out an area with your feet. Place your skis on the snow side by side and determine what type of bindings you have (read more about binding choices in Chapter 3). You have three-pin bindings if they stick out beyond the sides of your skis. If that is the case, you need to determine which is your left and right ski by inspecting the graphic stamped into the binding itself. Place your skis on the snow in the proper position and open the bail (the wire or metal bar hinged to the sides of the toe piece).

Three-pin Bindings. Support yourself with one pole and clean all the snow off the bottom of one boot, then slide the boot's square toe into the toe piece beneath the upright bail. Press down with the ball of your boot to push the three pins into the three holes in your boot. You may have to jiggle your foot from side to side to get the holes to align with the pins. Do not force the boot into the binding—this may turn your three-pin boot into a six-pin boot. When the boot is properly aligned the bail should be easy to push down and clamp to the plate.

System Bindings. If you have system bindings (they look streamlined and do not stick out beyond the sides of the skis) then either ski will fit on either boot. Some system bindings are automatic and some are manual. Pull up on the toe piece—if it

A.   Mate the three holes in the sole of the boot into the three pins of a three-pin or 75 mm
     binding. Place the bar into the slot behind the raised hood of a manual system binding.

B.   Both bars in the boot sole need to mate with their respective slots with the SNS Pilot boot
     and binding system for skating. For automatic system bindings, push the bar into the slot
     behind the raised and rounded piece on the front of the binding. The slot is just behind the
     thin white piece in the photo.

opens, it is a manual binding, if not, you have an automatic or step-in model. If the toe piece lifted up, leave it up.

Support yourself so you can lift one leg and rotate your foot upward so you can see the sole of your boot. Remove all snow from around the bar beneath your toes and note where the bar is in relation to the very front of the sole. Now place the bar into the slot on the binding, which is just behind the open toe piece (manual system) or behind the raised and rounded part (automatic system). If you cannot see this slot, put your foot down and pick up your ski to locate the slot.

It is important to push down with the ball of your foot and not just with your toes to force the bar beneath your toes into the slot. If you have automatic bindings, you should hear and feel a soft click as the binding captures the bar. With manual bindings,

reach down and close the toe without lifting your heel. The toe piece should close easily when the bar is in the slot. If the bar will not go in, you are either lifting your heel, there is snow caught in your sole, or you are not aligning the bar with the slot.

After putting on either type of binding shake your skis to make sure they are firmly attached. Check the alignment of your heels on the ski to make sure you have the right binding on the right foot if you have three-pin bindings.

FIRST STEPS

Slow, gentle movements are the best way to find your ski legs and the best way to warm up your body.

Once you have your skis on securely, take your first steps on skis with the attitude of a toddler learning to walk—tentative perhaps, but unconcerned with the outcome and with no expectation of instant success. Walk around a bit on your skis before you try anything fancy.

Start out gently as you investigate sliding on skis. Don't worry about doing any fancy warm-ups. It is better to do your stretching after you've finished skiing, when your muscles are warm and they can stay loose and relaxed.

If you are not at an area with groomed trails, create your own learning tracks by simply walking back and forth over a flat area as you get to know your new and longer feet. Shuffle forward on your skis in as straight a line as you can manage with your skis shoulder width apart. Turn around after a hundred yards or so or when you run out of flat terrain. Shuffle back and forth several times, staying in your original tracks as much as possible. If you fall down or deviate from your original path, do not worry about it. To prepare a gentle hill for learning, place your skis across the hill and step sideways up and down the hill to pack the snow into a firm, smooth surface.

FALLING DOWN
Falling is a part of skiing. Get over it.

Toddlers spend as much time on the floor as on their feet while learning to walk. The big difference between a toddler and an adult learning to ski is that the toddler doesn't berate herself for being such a hopeless walker, or wonder why she's not getting

An intentional fall onto your side is preferable to a headlong slide.

it as fast as her buddy each time she falls. There will be times when you feel you are in the snow more than on your skis. That's OK—developing balance on skis takes time.

Once you start to go down, do not fight it. Trying to regain your balance or avoid embarrassment is not worth a pulled muscle or a strained ligament.

An intentional fall to the side is better than a headlong dive. Check for rocks and

TO GET UP AFTER YOU FALL

Keep your legs straight and hinge forward from your toes to get your chest over your skis. This is possible since your heels are not locked down. Come up on one knee, then stand up.

1. Roll onto your back like a dead bug and stick your limbs, skis, and poles in the air to untangle them.

3. Keeping your legs extended, slide your hips towards your tips until you are beside your skis (if you are on a hill)

2. If you are on a hill, place your skis on the snow below you and across the hill.

4. or until your chest is on your skis (if you are on flat ground).

stumps if you can, then simply sit down to one side or the other of your skis. Avoid falling onto your knees and resist the urge to stick out your hands.

To stop yourself when sliding after a fall, keep your legs below you and press your skis into the snow. Curling up will not slow you down, but it may spin you around into a headfirst slide. Wait until you have come to a stop before you try to get up.

CHANGING DIRECTIONS

If you want to go in a different direction, lift your ski and step in the direction you want to go. To practice, do this when you are not moving.

When you begin to tromp around on skis, you will need to change directions. The simplest way to do this is to stop and, one ski at a time, pick up either the front of the ski (the tip), the back of the ski (the tail), or the entire ski and turn it in the direction you want to go. Then repeat with the other ski.

5. *Come to one knee.*

6. *And stand up!*

- To pick up just the tip, lift your toes against the top of your boot, flex your foot up toward your shin, and lift your knee toward your chest.
- To pick up just the tail, curl your toes down against the sole of your boot and bring your heel to your butt while keeping both knees close together.
- To pick up the entire ski at once, bend your knee and bring it forward as you lift your heel toward your butt.
- To go to the left, pick up the left tip and move it in that direction. Then pick up the right tip and move it alongside. This may seem obvious, but new skiers often lead with the foot opposite to the direction they wish to go.
- Take a lot of small steps instead of a few big ones. Move your tip only a foot or two in the new direction with each step.

A LITTLE DISCO

A fun way to turn around at the end of your practice area is the kick turn. This looks fancy, but once you catch on it is a snap. You will need your poles for this. Practice away from an audience for the first few times.

To kick turn, follow these four steps:

2a. Swing the leg of your front ski back and then forward.

1. Turn so that your shoulders make a straight line with the tips and tails of your skis. Place your poles behind you, one basket planted behind both tips and one basket planted behind both tails of your skis. Flex your legs and sag slightly onto your poles.

2b. As it swings forward, lift and open your knee to swing the tip around 180 degrees to point in the opposite direction.

POLES

Use your poles if they help, set 'em aside if they are a bother.

If you are brand new to skiing, you may wonder what to do with your poles. If you are an alpine skier, you may wonder why they are so long. If you are a snowboarder, you probably want to get rid of them.

At this point, feel free to set them aside or to keep them to push and balance with. Either way, relax and swing your arms naturally as you ski. Balance over your feet and not on your poles. We'll get back to the poles in a bit.

3. Step your weight onto that ski, and then repeat step 2 with your other leg.

4. Bring your shoulders back into normal alignment and your pole baskets to either side of your feet.

STANCE
Slouch like a juvenile delinquent on the street corner.

Check your stance. Gut in, chest out, eyes straight ahead is not a good position for skiing. Instead of the Marines, think about hanging out on the street corner.

- Imagine that you have an air valve on your body. When you're on skis, let out some of the air so that there is flex and bounce in all your joints. Don't be such a stiff.
- Keep your pants pockets closer to the ground than you would while walking.
- Resist your mother's voice telling you to stand up straight. She's not looking, and if she is, tell her I said it was OK.

To stay slouched over your skis as they slide over the snow you can't completely relax, you'll have to maintain some tension. A cat stalking prey is an example to emulate. Resist any force or other authority that tries to wrestle you out of this teenage slouch.

KEEPING YOUR BALANCE
Move your belly button in the direction you want to go before moving your feet.

Most of your weight is centered somewhere near your belly button (more for some than for others!)—this is known as your center of gravity. To maintain your balance, keep your hips and upper body centered over your skis as you glide forward. When you want to change direction, move your belly button before you move your feet. Balance on skis is not static. To keep your balance you must constantly shift your center of gravity forward and toward where you will be in the future.

MOVING FORWARD

If the ground is flat, and you are careful, you can walk on skis without them sliding forward, but what's the point of that?

Walking, jogging, or running on skis is a bit different from doing the same thing on dry land, because skis are slippery.

MASTERING THE GLIDE

To keep up with your skis while you glide, you need to tilt forward as if you were skiing into a strong wind.

Gliding requires you to keep up with your feet in much the same way as running. See for yourself. Get up and walk a few steps. Notice how your foot gets out in front of you during each step? Imagine what would happen if you stepped onto something slick like a ski with your leading foot. Now pick up the pace and jog for a few strides. See how you tipped forward from your ankles to keep your balance, keeping your body centered over or ahead of your feet?

Tipping forward from the ankles puts your body in motion and falling forward before your foot is there to catch you. Do this when skiing and your skis will glide more with each stride. That may make you feel a bit unsteady at first, but slouch, stay relaxed, and you'll be fine, mate. You don't have to actually run or jog all the time you are on skis, but you do need to keep up with your feet. When you want to move more slowly, shift from ski to ski as if you were jogging on the moon to keep your forward tilt.

GET A GRIP

To grip the snow and move forward, push down through the middle of your ski, not back. Imagine you are running
on a beach and gripping the sand with your toes.

The magic of skiing is in the glide, but without grip you would have no way to create glide. In traditional or classic cross-country skiing, the main technique used to get your skis to both grip and glide is called the "diagonal stride" or the "kick and glide."

Skis slip backward about as easily as they glide forward (some would say more easily). Their ability to grip the snow and still glide comes from a "grip" or "kick" zone centered beneath the ball of your foot in the middle of the ski where special wax or a mechanical pattern makes the ski stick to the snow when you press down. This center part of the ski is stiffer than the tip and tail sections, which enables it to support a portion of your weight and reduce the pressure in the grip zone so you can glide.

All glide and no grip is a recipe for a pratfall. To make the magic grip zone work for you, imagine you are jogging barefoot on a sandy beach, your toes gripping the sand as you run. Mimic this motion on skis and grip the snow with your toes through the soles of your boots. Feel the ski grip the snow with each stride. Ah, smell that suntan lotion!

JUMP THE CREEK

Get more grip by moving from ski to ski as if you were jumping over small creeks running across the trail.

Skis grip the snow better when all your weight is on one ski as you press the grip zone into the snow. To feel how this works, pretend a creek has opened up across the trail in front of you. Put all your weight on one ski, then lift the unweighted ski and jump it across to the other side. Transfer your weight to that ski as it lands and glide with it as it surges forward. Don't drag your feet through that imaginary creek or you'll have to go back to the car and change your imaginary boot and sock to avoid freezing your foot off! If you have to slap the other ski down to recover your balance, then your imaginary creek may be too wide or you may be leaping up instead of across the creek. Adjust the width of the creek to make your leap less heroic.

As balance and confidence improve you can take larger leaps, but try to land as softly and quietly as you can. The goal is to move forward with each stride and not to hop like a kangaroo.

RHYTHM AND RELAXATION
Relax and glide during each stride.

Many skiers rush the rhythm of their stride, moving from one ski to the next too quickly. Slow down, relax, and ride the glide. This is the pause that refreshes.

Get your rhythm by taking three quick strides and then stretch the fourth one into a long glide. 1, 2, 3, g-l-i-d-e, then repeat, followed by 1, 2, g-l-i-d-e, then one stride and a g-l-i-d-e, and finally g-l-i-d-e, g-l-i-d-e, g-l-i-d-e. R-e-l-a-x and imprint the rhythm of the stride into your body.

POLING

Learning to ski inevitably creates a little bit of tension that can lead to a death grip on the poles. Although poles are an aid to balance, you shouldn't be using them to support yourself. Holding the pole correctly and learning how to adjust the strap is crucial to getting your poles to work for you.

Every pole adjusts differently, so investigate (preferably indoors) how to tighten and loosen the straps on your poles before using them. Look at how the strap emerges from the handle to determine if your pair has a left and right. If the two poles look different, keep the strap that comes out on the top toward the inside to get the correct pole on the correct hand. If both poles are the same, you can put either pole on either hand.

Adjust the strap so that you wear the pole instead of gripping it.

To put the strap on, turn the pole so that the strap comes out of the handle toward you, hanging in a loop. From underneath the loop, bring all of your fingers and your thumb up through the loop so that the strap runs across the back of your hand and around your wrist and then circles back up to the handle beneath your palm.

Open your hand so that your thumb is on the inside of the handle and your fingers can wrap around the outside of the handle. The strap will emerge from between your thumb and your fingers and be between the pole handle and your palm as you push down on the pole. The junction of your thumb and index finger should be slightly below where the straps come out of the handle. If it is higher or lower, tighten or loosen the strap. In essence, you want to wear the pole instead of holding it.

Some more complicated designs convert the pole strap into a harness for the hand. As with standard straps, the important thing is to adjust the harness so that the junction of your thumb and forefinger lies just below where the straps emerge from the pole handle.

DIAGONAL POLING

In the diagonal stride, you plant and push with only one pole at a time. Use the pole opposite to the foot you are on. This is what you naturally do when walking or running, so just do it instead of thinking about it.

As you push back on the pole, relax your hand and let the strap or the harness do the work of keeping your palm against the pole

Plant the pole with the basket near your front foot and the pole shaft angled to the rear.

shaft. At the end of the pole push, let your palm come off the shaft and continue to push on the strap with the crook of your hand. As you swing your arm forward to bring the pole back for the next push, guide it forward by squeezing the handle between your thumb and the first joint of your index finger.

POLING FOR PUSH

Keep the bottom of the pole (the pole basket) behind the handle.

To achieve the best push, plant the pole with the handle in front of the basket (the circle or teardrop located on the bottom of the pole). To discover the proper timing and angle to plant the pole, allow the basket to drag in the snow as your arm swings forward during a stride. When the basket is even with your opposite foot, plant the pole and push on it.

DOUBLE POLING

Poles alone can move you forward, especially if you use your back and

stomach muscles in addition to your arms.

You can move forward using just your poles, particularly if you use both of them at the same time, which is called double poling. Double poling is even more effective if you get some help from the bigger and stronger muscles of your back and abdomen. To see how this works, try double poling without relying on your arms. As you flex forward from your ankles, keep your elbows close to your body and your back rounded. Just after you plant your poles, contract your stomach muscles as you would if you were doing a "crunch" or as if you had just received a blow to your midsection and use that motion and your back muscles to push yourself forward.

Once you've discovered how to move forward in a double pole without relying on your arms, add them back. Extend your arms after the "crunch." As you stand back up, let your arms and poles swing forward. Bend at the elbows as your arms pass your hips to bring your hands up for the next pole plant.

PUTTING IT ALL TOGETHER

Balance, glide, grip, rhythm, and poling. The simple tips listed above introduce the basic elements of moving gracefully over the snow. To put it all together, go skiing. Don't focus on tips and drills all the time, just ski along and enjoy being out on the snow. When you're ready to concentrate on more details, take a look at Chapter 9.

Use your stomach and back muscles to pull and push yourself forward.

CLIMBING HILLS

To go up hills what you need is grip. Grip comes from staying over your feet and pushing your skis straight down into the snow.

GOING STRAIGHT UP
A light jog on your skis will usually do the trick if you raise your head and look at the top of the hill. Keep your strides short and use a light touch on your poles.

When you can no longer get the bases of your skis to grip the snow, it's time to use their edges. The two methods of climbing on your edges are called the herringbone and the side step.

HERRINGBONE
Keep the backs of your skis closer together than the front. Press the sides of the ski into the snow to avoid slipping back.

In a herringbone, your tracks look like the skeleton of a fish. To climb in a herringbone, place your skis so the tails form the point of a V as you spread your tips apart.

With your legs, not just your feet, turned out, walk up the hill by picking each ski up from the knee and setting it back on the snow with your ankle bent. Keep your knee over your toe. You should look like a cowboy fresh off the trail after a long ride. Collapsing your knees toward each other to dig in the edges does not work very well and looks bad (need a bathroom, pardner?).

Plant the pole opposite to the foot you're lifting, moving your arms as you do while walking or in the diagonal stride.

Keep your body over your feet by stepping onto a flexed ankle.

The airborne ski will pass over the tail of the stationary ski. This is OK—you do not need to swing your legs out and around. By the time you step onto the ski you are bringing forward, it will have cleared the tail of the rear ski.

If you find yourself struggling, be sure you are not squatting between your skis or stepping up the hill with just your foot instead of moving your body forward to be over each ski as you move onto it.

SIDE STEP
Keep your body over your feet, and place your skis side to side across the hill and level from tip to tail.

COMMON PROBLEMS

Uncoordinated arms and legs. Thinking too much can cause this problem as can fear of sliding.

Verbalize the movement from one stride to the next with phrases such as "one, two" or "hi, ho." Once you've established a rhythm, your arms and legs will fall into sync.

To make getting your arms and legs to work together less complicated, ski without your poles along the flats. Then pick up your poles and ski down a slight hill using only your poles but no leg motions. You can also try using just one pole and then the other, with or without leg motions.

If fear of sliding is the issue, find a slight uphill where you can work on grip and glide without going too fast. Slide back down by just standing on your skis and letting them run, while your arms and legs stay loose and relaxed.

No glide. A lack of glide between strides is often the result of being too tense. Flexing your ankles is one of the simplest ways to make it easier to balance and relax on your skis.

Gliding on two skis instead of one at a time may be another reason for limited glide. Take one ski off and glide on the other as if you're a kid pushing a scooter. Make sure to transfer all of your weight to the ski and glide forward on the "scooter" after each push. You can use your poles, set them aside, or hold them horizontally out in front as if they were the scooter's handlebars. Keep the pushes and the glides small and within your comfort zone. With both skis back on, extend your glide by reducing the number of strides it takes to cover a certain distance.

To generate more glide, ski without poles and sharply swing your opposite arm (as in walking) forward with each stride, driving your elbow forward and up. This gives a little extra oomph to each ski. Transfer this same forward motion to your poling once you pick up your poles again.

Skis slip backward. Slips usually result from a combination of gliding on two skis instead of one at a time and pushing back instead of down when you want the ski to grip the snow. See the suggestions just above to improve your ability to ski on one ski at a time. To get better at pushing down instead of back, exaggerate the push down into snow with a leap from ski to ski, like a lion pouncing on its prey.

To isolate what it takes to make a ski grip the snow, take one ski off. With all your weight on the ski that remains, push down over the ball of your foot to make it stick to the snow. Then leap forward and land in balance on the foot without a ski. It will take practice to "stick" your landing on just your boot. After each leap and landing, pause in balance over your ski-less foot with your other foot and ski extended to the rear. Then reach forward and set the foot with the ski back onto the snow, rock onto the ball of that foot, and push the ski into the snow again to make it grip. Then leap forward onto your ski-less foot. Once you start to have some success getting your ski to grip the snow to provide a platform to leap from, eliminate any exaggerated up-and-down movements. Leap forward and land softly and quietly on your boot.

Step onto a flexed ankle and keep your skis across the slope as if you were climbing a set of stairs.

When the hill gets too steep, the snow too deep, or the herringbone too tiring, use the side step. Keep your skis level and across the slope, as if you were climbing a stairway with your skis placed lengthwise on the treads. Keep your body upright and centered over your skis. Move your torso sideways and up the hill first, then bring your ski beneath you, digging its edge into the snow.

Keep your skis parallel as you step from "tread" to "tread." If you place your ski across the tread it will slip toward whichever end is pointed downhill. Don't let your uphill ski get too far above you. If you do,

the uphill edge will be unweighted and refuse to bite into the snow as you try to step up onto it.

If your tip catches in the snow as you step up the hill, lift your toes toward the top of your boot as you bring your knee toward your chest. If your tail catches, bring your heel toward your butt while keeping your knee low.

GOING DOWNHILL

Skiing downhill on any type of equipment is a lot like riding a bike—far more important than any specific technique is the balance acquired from spending time on skis. Practice on gentle hills so you can relax before attempting steeper hills and other maneuvers.

If you find yourself on top of a slope that is more than you can handle, don't be ashamed to take your skis off and walk down. Be careful, though, since many ski boots are more slippery than skis.

STRAIGHT RUNNING DOWNHILL
Skis will slide downhill all by themselves. Slouch and go along for the ride.

Choose short hills that flatten or go back up at the bottom to avoid any worry about stopping or turning. Get in the right position before you start. Stand normally on your skis, then flex your ankles, bend your knees, and bring your hands up as if you were preparing to catch a jug of water. This is your basic position on hills. As you slide down keep your ankles flexed and your hands forward. If you find yourself straightening up as you approach the bottom of the hill, bend your ankles more deeply to help push your knees and hands forward. Tightening your gut muscles as if you expected a punch in the stomach will also help you stay in this rough and ready stance.

As your ability to stay in this flexed position increases (and the knot of fear in your stomach disappears) gradually increase the pitch of the hill. Seek out dips, rolls, and uneven ground to learn how to absorb bumps and changes in terrain. Remember to keep your arms and legs soft and supple and your hands out in front.

STEPPING FROM SKI TO SKI
The first step to successful downhill turns is learning to step from ski to ski as you slide downhill.

Find a hill you would be willing to ski straight down without any hesitation. Place a line of pinecones, breadcrumbs, or what have you directly down the middle. Glide down the hill, stepping back and forth across the line as you go. If both skis feel glued to the snow, first shift your weight over one ski so you can pick up the other; then move your hips sideways across the markers, and finally bring your airborne ski across and underneath yourself. Leading with your hips is crucial. If you reach across the markers with just your foot as if testing the water in a swimming pool, you are likely to get hung up between your skis. I would not suggest this approach—doing the splits on skis is no fun.

Lead with your body as you step across the line.

STEP TURNS
If you want to go left, look left, turn your torso to the left, and then step your left ski in the new direction.

It is a good idea to practice your first step turns on flat ground. Get up some speed and then decide which direction you want to turn. To step turn to the left, first move your hips so they are slightly over your right ski, so you can pick up the left ski. As you shift your weight onto the right ski, face your hips, shoulders, and head to the left as you move your left ski tip in the same direction. Step forward onto your left ski and then bring the right ski alongside. Take small steps instead of big ones to avoid getting caught between your skis. Once you

Turn your hips and torso toward where you want to go, and then move your ski beneath your body.

have some success on the flats, try step turns on a hill. As your speed increases, your movements will need to be quick, accurate, and aggressive to keep up with rapid changes of direction. To step turn at speed, "frame" the turn between your outstretched hands as you step quickly and accurately through the turn.

Accelerating through the turn by pushing off on each ski in turn as you step from one to the other is called a skate turn.

SLOWING DOWN

Tipping a ski on its side (edging), while it sideslips (slides in any direction other than toward the tip or tail) slows the ski because the edge digs into the snow. Edging can be done with your skis in parallel position (side by side), but it is easier to balance if your skis are in the wedge position—tips together, tails spread apart, forming an A.

Mastering the wedge (sometimes called the snowplow) gives you a means of controlling your speed and develops the ankle strength needed for many other ski techniques. The wedge is also a stepping-stone to other ways to turn and stop.

The Half Wedge. *Brush one tail out to form half of a wedge. Move your weight over the angled ski to slow down.*

To help move one ski into a wedge position, mark a path with your pole tip for your heel to follow as your tail moves out. This path should start at your heel and arc forward and away from your ski in a quarter circle. Follow this line in the snow with your heel as you move one foot out and forward to form a half wedge. Let your leg turn in the hip socket and keep your tips together as the tails of your skis move apart.

Start out on a flat section and practice moving into the half wedge position without moving forward or down any hills. As your tail moves out drop your waist closer to the snow to maintain the flex in your ankles and knees.

As your tails spread apart, your legs will angle toward each other and your foot and ski will tilt on edge. If the ski that has been angled out does not tilt up onto its edge,

The wedge position—tips closer than the tails and outside edges off the snow

Trace a forward arc in the snow with your heel to move into the half wedge position.

press down on your big toe and the ball of your foot to bring your foot and ski back into natural alignment with your leg.

After you can brush either ski into the half wedge position, get up some speed on the flats and try it while moving. If you are on groomed tracks, leave the forward pointing ski in the track to guide you and help you balance. Be aware that the ski angled out into the half wedge is your brake. Place your weight onto it gently to avoid the same unwanted reaction that results from slamming on the brakes of a car.

After trying your half wedge on the flats, head down a slight hill and use the half wedge to slow and stop. Lift one ski

out of the tracks and brush the heel of the unweighted ski out into a half wedge. Gently weight this angled and edged ski to make it plow some snow. For more stopping power, place more weight on the angled ski by sliding farther sideways until the zipper of your jacket is between your feet. If you need even more stopping power, bring your zipper farther out over the angled ski.

What the angled ski really wants to do is to flatten out and go straight (from the bestseller *True Confessions of an Angled Ski*). To keep it angled and on edge, push out with your heel as you turn your toes inward.

On groomed trails, picking one ski up off the track and moving it into the half wedge will help you slow down while the other ski continues to guide you down the trail. This works best when you remember to get the ski out of the track before you pick up too much speed.

The Full Wedge. *Brush both tails out into a wedge for more stopping power. Flex your knees and bend your ankles to stay forward and between your feet.*

Practice making a full wedge on a slight hill with firm or packed snow and well away from any set track that could catch your skis. As you begin, push out on both heels to spread your tails while keeping your tips together. Sink quickly into a slight crouch to lighten your skis and make it easier to spread the tails apart. As your skis tilt on edge, keep a lot of spring in your legs and keep your hands out in front where you can see them.

Point your knees toward your ski tips and not each other. Your tips should be considerably closer together than your tails, but they needn't be touching. Somewhere between six inches and a foot is about right.

Sink between your feet as you press through your arches, plowing snow up in front of both skis. To speed up, rise and let your skis come together and flatten as they slip sideways instead of digging into the snow. To slow again, sink and brush out your tails. Press the entire inside edge of both feet into the snow to plow snow and decrease your speed.

Before you head out to any real hills, make sure you can stop on demand. Glide down a known slope with your skis together, then brush out into a wedge at a

Move the zipper of your coat over the angled ski to increase the stopping power of the half wedge.

designated spot. Mark how far it took you to stop. Make multiple runs and try to stop in a shorter distance after the designated spot each time. If your skis want to straighten as you apply pressure, push your heels out as you turn your toes inward. Keep your ankles deeply flexed, your knees over your toes, and your hands out in front to avoid being tossed on your rear end.

WEDGE TURNS

Turn your skis using your feet and legs, not your arms and shoulders.

Coming to a full stop with a single wedge is awkward and tiring—it is much easier to control your speed with a series of wedge turns. When you want to turn, stand a bit taller in your wedge. This will take some pressure off the inside edges of your skis and narrow your wedge into a shallower form called a *gliding wedge.*

To start a turn, move toward where you want to go with your hips and chest while in a gliding wedge. Moving your hips and chest to the left will press the inside edge of the right ski deeper into the snow while flattening your left ski. With the right ski up on edge, it will go where it is pointed, which is to the left. With the left ski relatively flat on the snow, it will be able to pivot beneath you and go along for the ride to the left.

To make quicker wedge turns, steer the tips of your skis through the turn. Turn your feet as you move toward where you wish to go just like you turn your hand with your arm when you wave to all your adoring fans along a parade route. Rising as you turn your feet will help move you into a gliding wedge and make the skis easier to steer.

If your skis don't turn, you are probably resting on your heels. Throwing your shoulders around won't help at this point. Stop, take a breath, and flex forward from your ankles to get back over your feet.

COMMON PROBLEMS ON DOWNHILLS

Most problems stem from anxiety caused by a practice hill that is too steep. If you find yourself holding your hands and poles stiffly out in front and your legs are rigid, move to a gentler hill.

To loosen up your legs and hips, try this. Ski down the hill while you flex to touch your knees and then your ankles. Then move your hands back up to your knees, touch your waist, and then reach for the sky. Repeat until too embarrassed to continue. Bounce as you ski down the hill, first on two legs, then on alternate legs.

To loosen up your arms, ski like an airplane, flap like an eagle, or do arm circles without your poles—anything to get your hands up and out away from your side.

A common cause of over-edged and uncooperative skis while trying to move into a wedge position is trying too hard to force your skis apart or allowing your knees to collapse inward. To spread the skis with a finer touch, push your heels apart as if you were icing a cake with both skis. Keep enough room between your knees that someone could toss a poodle between them when you are in wedge.

Keeping your focus on moving down the hill will also help. Ask a friend to stand at the bottom of the hill and "entertain you" as you make turns. Paying attention to their antics will prevent you from turning your head and chest uphill in search of safety and security.

On the Way to Parallel. Shift both your knees across your skis and toward where you want to go as you rise toward the next turn. Flex your knees and ankles more as you finish each turn. As your speed increases, you may find you can make turns with a small wedge, or no wedge at all. Hey! You're parallel skiing on skinny skis!

Now go ski!—Up, down, and around!

Move toward where you want to go with your chest and belly button to start a turn while in the wedge position.

Crossing Lake Bygdin on a hut-to-hut tour in the Jotunheim region of Norway

CHAPTER 3

Equipment

In an ideal world, a cross-country ski shop would be within driving distance of anyone interested in the sport. Each shop would stock a broad selection from all the different categories and makers of ski equipment as well as clothing in a wide variety of sizes to fit everyone. In this ideal shop, every salesperson would be a passionate skier, a real student of the sport, and a great listener.

If such a shop is not available, you have several options. If you expect to ski with friends, the simplest way to decide what to rent or buy is simply to choose the same type of gear that they have. With similar equipment, you will be ready to ski with them in the same terrain and at a similar pace. If something breaks, someone in the group is likely to have the experience or the spare part needed to fix it. As an added bonus, you may be able to swap skis with your friends to see how their brand or version performs.

Renting different types, sizes, and brands of equipment is another excellent way to decide what kind of ski gear you want to own. The best place to try before you buy is at a Nordic center with a well-stocked rental shop so you can try a variety of equipment in a short time. A day or even a season of rental fees is a small price to pay for the chance to discover what you like and do not like before purchasing. Ski shops away from the trails usually rent as well, and some will apply all or part of your rental fees toward purchase.

Another option is to attend so-called demo days at a local Nordic center. At these events, ski shops and manufacturers let you try their equipment for free or at a nominal charge. Call your local ski shop or search the Internet for an event near you. They are usually held in early December.

Demo days provide a chance to try different skis, but it is often hard to find a suitable pair of boots that fit. Bring your own if you have them or consider renting a pair in town before you go. Use the same pair of boots on all the skis you want to try, or at least on all of the skis within the same category. Be sure to compare the same types of skis with each other so that you do not end up comparing apples with oranges.

Each piece of cross-country ski equipment you choose is a compromise between competing features. Skis wide enough to float in most snows can be a burden to lug around. Skis soft enough to grip in all conditions will hardly glide in most situations. Nimble, lightweight boot and binding systems for packed trails are often useless off the trail. The rest of this chapter provides the information you will need to help you sort out all the options for yourself.

CATEGORIES OF SKI EQUIPMENT

The type of equipment you should choose depends on the kind of skiing you intend to be doing.

SKI TOURING

If you're interested in casual outings in the park, on the golf course, on snow-covered roads, on designated ski trails, or on machine-groomed trails you should look for touring equipment. Touring skis are medium-width and boots are similar to light hiking boots. Poles are sized for striding with average-sized baskets and durable, lightweight shafts.

Wider touring ski with sidecut, a waxless pattern base, and a heavy-duty manual BC system binding for striding and turning. Thinner, straight cut track ski with a smooth, waxable base with a manual system binding for striding.

TRACK SKIING

You'll need track equipment for performance skiing on machine-groomed trails. Track skis are narrow, and the boots resemble walking or running shoes. Poles are lightweight with small baskets. Poles for skating will be longer than those used for traditional striding. This category includes three types of equipment:

- Classic—equipment for the traditional diagonal stride.
- Skating—equipment for moving over the snow with a motion similar to ice or roller skating.

■ Combi—equipment that can be used for both.

BACKCOUNTRY SKIING

If you'll be skiing in deeper snows and on more varied terrain, including going up and coming down steeper slopes, you should consider backcountry equipment.

Very wide telemark ski with a smooth waxable base covered with a climbing skin and a cable binding for maximum turning power and floatation in deep snows. Backcountry ski with sidecut, a waxless pattern base, and a heavy-duty three-pin binding for turning power.

Backcountry skis are wider, boots are heavier, and poles are more durable (and some are adjustable). Metal edges are common and the equipment design gives as much importance to ease of turning as to grip and glide.

Telemark Skiing. Now often used at lift-served resorts, telemark skis are designed for turning. They were originally a subset of backcountry equipment and the line between the two is fuzzy. Vast distances can be traversed on telemark skis waxed for grip, while backcountry skis can be used to ski downhill at an alpine resort. Climbing skins are often used on both types. Try both types of equipment if you like—skiing is more fun when you have more things to do!

SKIS

There are a number of things you need to consider when choosing skis. Understanding a bit about these characteristics will help you make an informed decision.

CHARACTERISTICS OF SKIS

All skis share some basics. The front is called the tip, the back is the tail, and the middle is the waist. The underside of the ski is the ski base, or base, and the upper surface of the ski is the top, or topsheet. The sides of the skis are often called sidewalls. Where the sidewall meets the ski base is the edge. To bite into hard and icy snow, some skis have a thin strip of metal along both edges. Ski widths are measured in millimeters (25.4 mm = 1 inch), ski lengths in centimeters (2.54 cm = 1 inch).

Knowing something about how the characteristics of cross-country skis affect their performance can help you choose the best skis for you.

Camber. Set a ski on a flat surface and look at it from the side. The arch formed by the ski from tip to tail is called camber. Building camber into a ski allows it to be thinner and lighter. Without camber, a ski would have to be thicker and heavier to support the skier's weight. Think of an arched bridge versus a flat bridge. An arched bridge transfers weight and pressure from the middle of each span to the support piers. This has two results—the materials used to construct the bridge can be lighter and the area beneath the arch does not need to be supported. To carry the same amount of weight, a flat bridge must be made of much stronger materials and must be supported by piers along its entire length. Camber can be manipulated to control where and how much pressure is applied to the snow along the length of the ski, making it springy and responsive.

Width. The softer the snow, the wider the ski should be. If you expect to ski mostly on machine-groomed trails, choose narrow skis. If you plan on tromping through a lot of deep snow, go wide, although wide skis can be heavy and cumbersome when traveling long distances. A short, wide ski may float better than a long, skinny one with the same amount of surface area, since more of the support is concentrated directly beneath the skier.

Length. Skis for striding are the longest, while skis for skating and turning continue to shrink. Since they will be used on hard-packed groomed snow, skating skis do not have to be able to float up in deeper snows and thus can be shorter, which makes them more maneuverable. Skis for turning have become wider overall and shaped more like an hourglass. The wider width provides more surface area to help the ski to float, while the hourglass shape places more edge onto the snow in a shorter length.

Sidecut or Shape. Sidecut refers to the shape of the ski when looked at from above or below. Some skis are as straight-sided as a length of lumber, while others look like Dolly Parton.

Skis with minimal sidecut go straight better, and skis shaped like an hourglass turn better. For most skiers something between the two extremes will probably work best, with the amount of sidecut determined by what percentage of skiing time will be spent going straight versus turning.

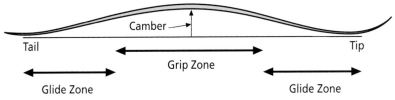

Fig. 3.1 – Camber, tip and tail, and grip and glide zones

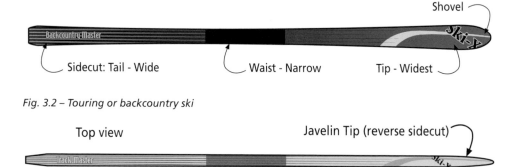

Fig. 3.2 – Touring or backcountry ski

Fig. 3.3 – Track ski with javelin tip

Some straight-sided classic track skis have a narrow, tapered tip, called a *javelin tip*. A ski with a javelin tip turns toward the middle of the ski when it is tipped on edge, helping the ski stay in the tracks, and reduces drag for added speed.

Some skating skis have a small amount of normal sidecut, which functions to move the ski back under the skier as it is edged at the end of the skate stroke.

Flex. Flex refers to how much force is needed to push out the camber of a ski. A ski with a stiff flex takes more force to flatten or bow into a reverse arc than a ski with a soft flex. A ski with the "right flex" for a particular skier and technique will flatten to grip the snow while striding or allow the entire edge to contact the snow to aid in turning or to provide a platform from which to push off from when skating.

Torsional Stiffness. Grab each end of a thin metal ruler and you will easily be able to twist it lengthwise—it has very little torsional stiffness. A thick and stout wooden ruler, on the other hand, would be very torsionally stiff.

Striding skis for track skiing and lightweight touring skis have torsionally soft tips that when edged flatten to follow tracks and terrain, providing a smooth ride.

Skate skis have torsionally stiff tips and tails so that the entire edge will bite into the snow when the skier tips one ski on edge to grip the snow and then move to the next ski.

Backcountry skis are also torsionally stiff, especially in the tip. Placed on edge, these skis will hold their line during a traverse or a turn. On smoother, packed trails, a torsionally stiff ski will be more nervous and may be hard to keep pointed straight ahead while skiing in the diagonal stride.

Metal Edges. Metal edges are one of the most visible and least understood features of a ski. A metal edge on a torsionally stiff ski with a shape and camber designed to turn will help that ski hold its line during the turn if the snow is hard or icy. A metal edge on a straight ski that is torsionally soft will do

THE SKI SWAP PRIMER

Ski swaps are excellent places to pick up inexpensive ski equipment, but you usually get what you pay for. Skis and boots have to fit, and the chances of finding what you really want in your size are pretty slim.

Boot and binding compatibility is another thorny problem. Most skis can be re-mounted at least once with a new binding, but this incurs additional costs that may make your purchase less attractive. Place the boot of your choice into the binding on the ski you are interested in and make sure the binding will close and hold the boot securely. If you have to force it, it does not fit.

The boot also needs to match the ski or the combination will not work very well. A wider ski will overpower a light boot, while a big, heavy boot will negate all the advantages of a lightweight ski.

The pattern on waxless skis can wear down, blunting the sharp edges that grip the snow. Inspect it carefully. Look over the bases of any skis before you buy them. Small scratches are no big deal, but large gouges are hard to fix.

Do not buy any ski with cracks across the topsheet or along the sidewalls. Reject any ski that shows any sign of delaminating at the tip or tail or where the base or topsheet meet the core. On metal-edged skis, make sure the edge is not pulling away from the base. Rusty edges can be filed back into functional use for the backcountry but may be hard to sharpen for performance skiing on ice.

Poles are often a great bargain at a swap. It is easy to tell if they fit, and a strong, light pole from a decade ago is not much different from a strong, light pole of today. Keep in mind, however, that carbon and other composite poles can fail suddenly from nicks and scratches inflicted long ago. Look at and feel the shaft, especially the lower half, and check for any cuts or marks. It is hard to find replacement parts for old straps and handles, but you can probably find a new handle and strap to fit onto a worthy shaft. Replacement baskets are available for most poles as well. This is when a well-stocked and knowledgeable local shop really comes in handy.

If the swap is held at a local shop, or the local retailer has a staff member on hand, take advantage of their knowledge. They will let you know if it is worth changing bindings on a ski to fit your boots or if the base can be fixed up. What they charge for tuning and repair work is usually a bargain.

Carefully check any gear before you buy—for a bit more money, you may be able to get something that fits you precisely and is exactly what you want. If you take something to sell at a swap, and you want it to sell, price it low.

nothing to help it turn, but it will help the middle of the ski bite into the snow while traversing, sidestepping, climbing in a herringbone, or slowing in a wedge.

Metal does not glide well and makes a ski slower, so increased edge grip comes at a noticeable cost in other areas of performance. Metal edges slow a ski too much to be useful on track skis. Partial metal edges can be useful on touring skis, since they help prevent them from skittering sideways while traversing, turning, or sidestepping on hard, icy snow without adding too much weight, drag, or stiffness.

Waxless versus Waxable. A ski that relies on the application of sticky wax for grip is called a waxable ski. A ski that relies on a pattern in the middle of the base for grip is called a waxless or no-wax ski. These terms create confusion since the need to wax or not to wax applies only to getting the ski to grip. Both waxable and waxless skis will glide better and last longer when the tips and tails are waxed for glide.

The changeable spring conditions of the Midwest that make waxing a nightmare are common all season long in the West, the Northwest, and parts of the East. In general, no-wax skis are common along the coasts where the weather is changeable and often wet, while waxable skis work better in interior climates where long periods of dry and cold weather are more the norm.

Waxless skis do not glide as well, they are noisy, and you can feel the pattern vibrate beneath your foot. A hidden disadvantage is that nothing can be done to make a waxless ski perform like a waxable ski in

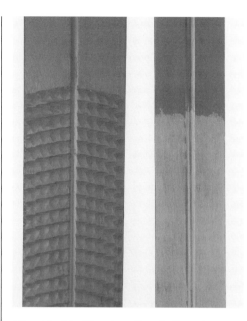

Waxable ski with grip pattern in the grip zone. Waxable ski with several layers of grip wax applied to the grip zone.

conditions such as colder, drier snows and hard, icy conditions. Skiing with a waxless base has been compared to playing a round of golf with one club.

In spite of their disadvantages, even veteran skiers who have mastered the art of waxing often have a pair of waxless skis in their quiver for changeable conditions. These come out when they want to avoid the time and hassle of waxing. Unless you live where it is almost always cold and dry, your first pair of touring or classic skis should be no-wax skis.

Compact or Traditional Sizing. When all skis were made of wood, making a ski

THE SHORT STORY ON NO-WAX SKIS

No-wax skis are convenient, reliable, and easy to use. They are consistent in nearly every condition. But what you gain in convenience you lose in performance, most notably glide.

Waxable skis will give solid grip and smooth glide. But they involve making a choice between multiple options of grip wax. Any time you need to make a choice you risk making the incorrect decision and ending up with skis that perform miserably. In the Midwest where snow is most often dry and cold, a waxable ski is a good choice for 90 percent of the season. It's the remaining 10 percent of the time that can drive a skier to distraction.

No-wax skis rule in deeper snow where glide is reduced by the resistance of pushing through the snow. No-wax skis are a great choice for the casual skier—the person who may ski a half dozen times a season and has no interest in learning to wax (and very little opportunity to acquire the skills to do it correctly). And no-wax skis are a great option for any skier during the great days of spring skiing, when changeable snow conditions can make waxing a nightmare.

Mitch Mode of Mel's Sports in Rhinelander, Wisconsin

longer was the only way to make it stronger and stiffer to support more weight. Skis were then matched with a skier's height—if you were taller, you skied on longer skis. This worked fine if the skier was of average build, but resulted in ill-fitting skis for tall thin folk or short rounder skiers.

Modern materials now allow designers to make skis of the same size in different flexes for skiers of different weights. As a result, skis now come in two sizing systems—compact and traditional.

Compact skis come in shorter lengths than traditionally sized skis for the same weight of skier. They are easier to ski on and to transport. To help them float over the snow they make up for their lack of length with extra width. Compact skis are less fussy skis for the less fussy skier.

Traditionally sized skis offer a more precise fit between ski and skier and more precise performance for the more precise skier. If the Odd Couple went skiing, compact skis would be for Oscar, while Felix would go for the precision and perfection of traditional sizing.

Compact skis for touring are easy to maneuver through the woods and in choppy terrain, and they turn well. They come with a high camber that works particularly well with a waxless pattern. Traditional skis for touring are smooth and silky, and usually glide better. So why not own a pair of each? Use the compact skis like a Jeep for off-trail adventures and keep a traditionally sized pair for cruising. The same boots, poles, and bindings will work for each pair, so the extra cost is not extravagant.

Easy-to-learn-on compact skis for skating are also available. These skis are fun and convenient, but most skiers quickly outgrow them. Your best bet is to rent some short skaters to learn on and then buy a more traditionally sized pair of your own.

Backcountry skis have also been affected by the down-sizing trend. Skis with larger sidecuts and compact-sizing for grip and glide are now available from most manufacturers and are quickly becoming the standard against which all backcountry skis are judged. One caveat: be careful not to buy a shapely ski that is too long or too stiff for you. If you do, the middle of the ski will never contact the snow during a turn and all the advantages of the extra sidecut will be lost.

Color and Graphics. If you cannot stomach the color scheme or the graphics of an item that is otherwise perfect, another manufacturer probably makes a comparable product in a color or with a graphic that you like.

Price. You probably do not need the most expensive skis but avoid the cheapest ones. The value of your vacation time and

NONE OF YOUR BUSINESS, SONNY!

When skis were made of wood, to find the right size skiers held their arms over their head and chose a pair that came to their wrist. This method only worked if the skier was neither unusually skinny nor unusually plump, but it let salespeople avoid the question "how much do you weigh?" The brave souls who did ask in an effort to provide a better fit between ski and skier often got more than they bargained for in reply.

By 1980, wood skis were pretty much a thing of the past, but skis for heavier skiers were still only found in longer sizes. In 1992, the folks at the Fischer Ski Company realized this was due to habit and tradition more than necessity. They introduced a one-size fits all line of skis called the Revolution that came in two models—one for classic skiing and one for skate skiing. The Revolutions were a hoot on hard-packed groomed trails, especially the skate version, but the short, 147cm length was impractical on softer snows. The true revolution started by these skis was the realization that camber could be independent of ski length and should be matched to the skier's height and weight instead of just his or her height.

Charts that match a skier's height and weight to a specific ski size for both compact and traditional skis soon replaced the old method of holding your arm above your head. Fortunately for today's salesperson, each size covers a range of weights. Finding your weight on the chart and then reporting the proper size is a lot like the financial disclosures we get from politicians these days—"last year the esteemed legislator reported holdings between $500,000 and $1,000,000 in stocks and bonds." You reveal a little about what you might prefer to keep private, but you get to keep the specifics to yourself.

Skier's Weight	Suggested Traditionally Sized Ski Length	Suggested Compact Ski Length
90-100 lbs	180	168
100-110 lbs	180	168
110-120 lbs	180, 185	168
120-130 lbs	185, 190, 195	168
130-140 lbs	190, 195	168, 178
140-150 lbs	195, 200	168, 178
150-160 lbs	195, 200, 205	178, 188
160-170 lbs	200, 205, 210	178, 188
170-180 lbs	205, 210	178, 188
180-190 lbs	210, 215	188
190-200 lbs	210, 215	188
200-220 lbs	210, 215	188
>220 lbs	215	188

Fig. 3.4 – Example of a sizing chart illustrates that compact skis are designed to fit a broad range of skiers with a shorter length than a traditionally sized ski. When buying a ski, refer to the current sizing chart of the ski's manufacturer.

the money spent on transportation, lodging, and food far outweigh the amount you might save by buying shoddy gear. Don't let cheap equipment ruin your ski days.

HOW TO CHOOSE YOUR SKIS— CONSIDER FLEX AND LENGTH

The guidelines that follow are intended to help you sort through the issues of flex and length to choose the correct size, depending on the type of skis you're considering.

Compact Skis. Match your weight and height to the ski size listed on the manufacturer's sizing chart (available from your dealer or on the ski maker's website). If you're considering choosing the next

longer size than recommended in hopes of getting more glide, keep in mind that a longer size will glide better, but the extra effort needed to make it grip and turn may not be worth it. Trust the sizing chart unless you can ski on the longer ski in a wide variety of conditions to see how it performs before you buy it.

Traditionally Sized Skis. For ski touring, backcountry skiing, and casual track skiing, select your size from the manufacturer's chart based on your height and weight.

High-Performance Track and Skate Skis. For these skis the fit between skier and ski needs to be more exact.

Performance classic skis are made with what is called a second camber, which makes them stiffer than touring skis. It takes considerably more force to flatten the middle of the ski (the second camber) onto the snow than to flatten the tip and tail (the first camber).

To unlock the magic of effortless grip, the second camber in a classic ski must "fit" the skier, meaning the skier must be able to flatten it against the snow. Conversely, the first camber must be stiff enough to support the weight of the skier on just the tip and tail. If it's too soft, the middle of the ski will drag as the skier attempts to glide.

To provide this precise fit between skier and skis, high-performance classic skis of a given length come in several flexes or cambers. To complicate matters, different pairs of skis of the same make and length will be marked by the manufacturer as having the same flex or camber but will vary enough to make a difference.

A USEFUL RITUAL

No matter where you shop for skis, you'll find that "checking the flex" has become an almost obligatory ritual. For this exercise to be useful, you need to know what you're looking for.

First, hold the ski eight to twelve inches back from the tip with the base facing down and push down in the middle. This gives you a feel for the overall flex and camber of the ski. Then hold the ski by the tip with one hand while you flex it with the other hand about a third of the way down—look for a smooth bend in the forebody of the ski without a hinge point. Now twist the tip against the midsection as if you were trying to wring water out of the ski. This gives you a feel for the torsional stiffness. A soft torsional flex in the tip makes for a supple ski that follows the tracks and the terrain while striding, while a stiffer torsional flex will be better for turning and holding an edge. Check tail flex by holding the ski with one hand palm up and one hand palm down on either side of the middle of the ski as you flex the tail against the floor. A soft tail allows the tip to lever the entire ski up toward the surface in deeper snow, while a stiffer tail stores energy that can be released into the next turn, stride, or skate. A stiffer tail can also serve as a rudder to keep your ski on track in loose, unconsolidated snow.

Skate skis. A skating ski should have a relatively stiff single or overall camber to evenly spread your weight over the length of the ski. If a skate ski is too stiff, you will ski mainly on the tip and tail and will find the skis to be wobbly in hard conditions and slow in soft conditions. If your skis are too soft, you will ski mainly on the middle of the ski. In this case, the ski will wander as you glide and fail to grip the snow well when on edge during your push-off from one ski to the next.

Testing for Fit. The best way to achieve the precise fit needed for high-performance skis is to find a ski shop with a test board or a flex tester and follow their recommendations about which ski is right for you. Make sure they consider your weight, your skiing style and skill level, and your fitness level as they help you select a pair of skis.

The equipment that a shop has to test skis is not as important as whether there is someone on staff who has the experience to use it. Mitch Mode explains his shop's approach to matching ski and skier:

We use a flex tester on higher-end recreational and race skis. The percent of body weight we use is determined by our familiarity with the ski; [for] some we go a touch higher, some a bit lower. Essentially we're looking to put half the skier's weight on a ski and to find an 18-to-24-inch section under the middle that is off the table. We'll then apply pressure to bring the base to the table; the pressure we apply is based on the skier, the ski, and our

cahl
kohl

experience. A bit vague perhaps, but that's what we do.

Success in selecting high-performance skis also requires a large selection of skis to choose from—shop early in the season and expect to pay full price. Waiting for skis to go on sale will put both you and the shop in a situation where fit may be compromised.

If your shop doesn't have test equipment, the simplest way to determine if a ski is worth further testing is to hold the skis in the middle with one hand, base to base, and try to squeeze them together. If you can get the bases to touch along their entire length, the skis are likely to be too soft for you. If you cannot squeeze the skis together in the

Testing a new pair of skis in the Minocqua Winter Park ski shop to check that they fit the customer. The ski tester shown in the photo uses a sliding plate of metal to replace the paper of a paper test. (Photo: Steve Hindman)

middle with two hands, then they are probably too stiff. If you can get the bases to touch in the middle using two hands, they should be about right.

If the skis pass this preliminary test, you can use the paper test to judge if the flex of the skis is suitable for your weight. Stand on both skis with your toes on the balance point or with your boots in the bindings on a very flat, firm, and smooth surface. Place a piece of paper between the flat surface and your skis, directly beneath your feet (you will need a friend to help). The paper should slide forward and back. If it doesn't the ski is too soft. For classic skiing, the ski is probably too stiff if it slides more than the length of your foot beyond your toes. A skating ski that fits will allow the paper to slide twice as far in front of the ball of your foot as behind.

Now balance with all of your weight on one ski. If you're testing classic skis the paper should now be trapped beneath the flat surface and the base of the ski. For skating skis the profile will be a bit different. There should still be a slight opening between the base of your ski and the surface you're standing on. That opening should fall two-thirds in front of the ball of your foot and one-third behind. A skating ski should close with the surface behind your heel but not under it. If it closes beneath your heel it is probably too soft; if it closes well behind your heel it is too stiff.

QUALITY CONTROL

Once you have decided on the type and length of ski you want, inspect the ski for quality. The base material should be free of gouges or irregularities. Check to be sure there are no gaps between the base and the edge and between the edge and the sidewall.

No twist or warping should be evident when you sight down the length of the ski. When you place the skis base to base, tips matching tips and tails matching tails, the tips and tails should meet evenly across the width of the ski (you shouldn't be able to rock one ski when it is sitting on the other). As you squeeze the skis together, they should close evenly from the ends to the middle. If either the tip or the tail lifts apart as the middle closes, the ski is defective. Now place the ski base to base and tip to tail and run through the same tests.

BINDINGS

Two types of bindings are common today: three-pin, or 75 mm, bindings and system bindings. Choose three-pin bindings when you want to maximize side-to-side control while maintaining reasonable forward flex. For maximum forward flex with reasonable side-to-side control choose system bindings (system boots and bindings are the only options available for performance classic and skate skiing).

THREE-PIN (75 MM) BINDINGS

Today's three-pin bindings, sometimes called toe-bail bindings, work only with boot soles shaped like a duckbill at the toe. Three-pin boots and bindings are not interchangeable with system boots and bindings.

The three pins at the front of the binding fit into three holes in the toe of the boot. A bar called a bail levers down from the upturned sides of the binding to clamp the toe of the boot sole to the ski and is held in place by a catch at the front.

The duckbill sole that mates with the binding is 75 mm wide. This is the industry standard, or "Nordic Norm," which gives these bindings their alternate name. At one time, toe-bail bindings were made in several different widths to fit lighter boots. Unless you buy a very old boot at a ski swap, you should not have to worry about matching the width of any duckbilled boot with any three-pin binding.

The thickness of the sole is another matter. Three-pin boots made for ski touring typically have soles that are thinner than those of more heavy-duty boots made for telemarking and adventurous backcountry outings. Thick-soled boots will not fit into bindings made for thinner soled boots, and the bindings made for thick-soled boots will not close down far enough to firmly clamp a thin-soled boot to the ski. It's best to buy your boots and bindings together, or have one in hand when shopping for the other.

Cable bindings are based on the three-pin binding norm of 75 mm but have an added feature—the duckbill of the three-pin sole is wedged into the toe piece with a cable that can be tightened by a tensioning mechanism. The cable adds side-to-side control by keeping the heel on or above the ski.

Cable bindings are used mostly by telemarkers and ski mountaineers, since the cable restricts the heel lift that provides freedom to cross-country skiers. An exception is a cable binding with a removable cable, which allows a skier to tour and climb with just the three-pin binding, adding the cable for downhills.

SYSTEM BINDINGS

The first widely used cross-country system binding, the Salomon Nordic System (SNS) was developed by Salomon, a French manufacturer of alpine ski bindings. Salomon's original goal was to offer a lightweight combination of boot and binding that increased the length of a racer's stride and freedom of motion.

The Norwegians at the Rottefella company, not wanting to be caught sleeping in the snow, developed their own system and named it New Nordic Norm (NNN). Both systems continue to be sold today. They are not compatible.

The current version of Salomon's system is called SNS Profil. Profil boots have a deep channel in the sole and a bar beneath the toe that clips into the binding. A wide ridge mounted on the ski extends to the rear from the point where the bar mates with the binding. This ridge fits into the channel in the boot to provide side-to-side control. The latest iterations of Rottefella's system are called NNN II, NNN R3 or just NNN (there are further model breakdowns within these categories). These bindings attach to and mate with the boot in a similar fashion.

NNN bindings are sold under either the Rottefella or the Rossignol brand name. SNS bindings are sold under either the Salomon

or the Fischer brand name. Both Salomon and Rottefella sell their boot soles to other manufacturers to use on boots sold under their own name. To determine what system a boot is built for check for the NNN or SNS acronym attached to the model name.

Backcountry Binding Systems (SNS BC, NNN BC). Both Salomon and Rottefella also offer a heavy-duty version of their soles and bindings for more rugged skiing. Boots compatible with these bindings have soft rubber lugs molded onto the plastic outsoles to increase traction. Only bindings with the BC designation will work with BC boots within each system.

Backcountry systems are lightweight, comfortable, and offer an exceptional blend of touring ease and downhill control. Since they rely on keeping the heel of the boot on the ski for maximum control, these boots and bindings are not the choice for more extreme telemark descents. Another consideration is that snow can pack between the boot and the binding and compromise control.

SNS or NNN? Choosing between the two systems is usually a matter of what your local retailer carries and which boots fit you. Find a boot you like and buy the binding to match.

Compatibility. As mentioned above, you cannot mix and match between Salomon and Rottefella boots and bindings. What complicates things is that over the years both manufacturers have released versions of their products that are incompatible with current boots or bindings from the same system.

For example, the latest version of SNS

Pilot *boots* work with both SNS Profil and SNS Pilot *bindings,* but SNS *Profil* boots work only with SNS *Profil* bindings. Older SNS boots are compatible only with older SNS bindings. All NNN II boots and NNN II and NNN R3 bindings are compatible with each other, regardless of whether they are designated for classic or skate skiing. Older NNN bindings are compatible only with older NNN boots although NNN II boots may fit older NNN bindings if the flexors in the bindings are changed.

BOOTS

If your budget is limited, spend most of your money on boots. Skis are guided and controlled through your boots, so fancy skis are close to worthless with cheap boots.

The materials used for boot uppers range from all leather to all fabric, and most are a mix of materials. On the lightest boots, outsoles are made of molded plastic, which makes them extremely slippery in icy parking lots. Heavier duty ski boots have lugged soles just like hiking boots. These are easy to walk in, but they attract snow and are too heavy for track skiing.

Selecting boots is more intuitive than choosing your skis or a binding system. Lighter boots provide more freedom but offer less support. Heavier boots provide more support but usually restrict movement and are harder to fit. Most skiers need something in-between. Once you decide what type of boot you want, fit should

trump all other considerations.

Ski boots should fit snugly, but tight boots will make your feet cold and your mood unpleasant. A good way to judge the fit of a boot is to slide your foot as far forward as you can while standing up. With your toes just touching the front of the boot, you should just be able to slide your forefinger behind your heel. To check fit on a plastic boot, remove the liner and follow the same guidelines.

Take the socks you want to ski in with you to the store. Socks made of very fine yarns have largely replaced the need for liner socks. Before you go boot shopping consider buying a pair. Cotton socks are a sure ticket to cold, wet feet that are prone to blisters.

FINDING A BOOT THAT FITS

When you find a pair of boots that feels like it fits walk around in it for as long as possible. Flex the boots across your toes, walk on your heels, walk on your toes, kick the toes against something solid, walk down an incline, and walk on the sides of your feet. Put them in a binding in the store to see how they feel as you stride forward. If you wear only sandals and low shoes in everyday life, ankle-high ski boots may feel uncomfortable even when they fit properly. Spend the time to get used to wearing something a little different.

Most boots will stretch a little in width but not in length. The one exception is plastic-shelled boots—the liners will pack down and get bigger in all directions, sometimes by as much as half a size or more. For the best

THREE-PIN VERSUS SYSTEM BOOTS AND BINDINGS

Three-pin bindings and boots offer these advantages:

- The boots are more like hiking boots, making it easier to walk on a trail or in the parking lot.
- Most three-pin boots are ankle high, providing support for rougher terrain and for turning.
- Since side-to-side control and resistance to twisting come from the sole of the boot, with some help from the wings on the sides of the binding, it is less affected by snow accumulating between the ski and the boot sole or by lifting the heel during a telemark turn.
- Most skiers on three-pin bindings can trade skis with other three-pin skiers, provided the soles of their boots are roughly the same thickness.
- Three-pin bindings are relatively inexpensive.
- While three-pin bindings are easily bent, creating a sloppy fit, they can be easily straightened.

System bindings and boots offer these advantages:

- Easier forward flex.
- Greater control than a three-pin boot and binding of comparable weight.
- More boot options are available.
- Boot and binding connection is positive (unlike three-pin bindings where the holes in the boots can be ruined by misalignment with the pins on the bindings).
- System bindings maintain the same fit with boots as they wear, but if they do break, they are hard to repair.
- Bindings and boot toes are narrow, eliminating drag against the side of the tracks.

performance while turning, you may want to start with plastic boots uncomfortably tight. This is only recommended if you are willing to sacrifice comfort, warm feet, and even a few toenails for improved turning power.

The very lightest boots are usually the easiest to fit, since, like running shoes, they are basically a strap system covered by a weatherproof sock that pulls your foot onto the sole.

It can be very difficult to know if heavier boots truly fit until you ski with them for a while. If you encounter fit problems after you have worn your boots, the services of an experienced boot fitter are invaluable. A small fit pad around the heel, perhaps a supportive or even a corrective insole, and a little stretching can do wonders. The money you spend will make every moment you spend in those boots more fun, and many adjustments will even improve your skiing. Good boot fitters are craftsmen and cultural treasures—appreciate and patronize them. Ask other skiers or at your local ski shop where to find one.

POLES

Knowing a bit about the anatomy of a pole will help you pick the right one.

POLE CHARACTERISTICS

Length. For striding, poles should push up into your armpit, although for general ski touring you may want them a little shorter. For skating, they should come to somewhere around your mouth. Check for length while standing upright, wearing either your shoes or your ski boots.

If you expect to spend your time climbing up to enjoy the ski back down, adjustable poles may be for you. These can be lengthened for the climb and shortened for the descent. The handles of adjustable poles can be awkward on long tours and their baskets tend to pry out of the snow while touring. However, the big bugaboo with adjustable poles is the internal mechanism that adjusts them. The most reliable ones at the present time are the FlickLock poles from Black Diamond.

Shaft Materials. Cheaper poles tend to be fiberglass or aluminum. For the very cheapest poles, fiberglass is the best choice since it will usually crush instead of breaking. With a few twigs and some duct tape, a crushed fiberglass pole can be splinted to get you back to the trailhead. Aluminum poles usually bend instead of breaking, but often break when you try to straighten them back out. Heating the area of the bend with a camp stove or some other heat source improves your chances of straightening a bent pole. If you do succeed in straightening an aluminum pole it will always be considerably weaker than it was before. Replace it as soon as possible.

In the mid-range, $30 to $60 will buy an aluminum pole that is less likely to bend and lighter than fiberglass. From $60 on up, a wide variety of composites, usually of fiberglass, carbon, and other aerospace materials, offer amazingly light and stiff poles that are reasonably durable.

Straps and Handles. So many straps, so many handles, so little time. A properly designed grip and strap will allow you to hold the pole lightly and release it at the end of the pole stroke without losing control. At a minimum, the handle should extend above where the strap emerges from it, and the strap should be easy to adjust.

Fancy straps are designed to hold your palm to the handle, making it easier to control the pole. Many do this well, but some do not, and the basic loop strap serves the same purposes and is much easier to use. If you go for a fancy strap, make sure you can adjust and use it easily with gloves on. If you ski with small children, dogs, or have any other need to frequently take your poles on and off, consider sticking with simple, standard pole straps.

Baskets and Tips. The deeper the snow, the bigger the basket needs to be. Really tiny baskets only work on hard-packed trails, and really big baskets get very heavy on longer tours. Big baskets also deflect off harder snows when you reach downhill for a pole plant on descents. Somewhere between really tiny and really big is usually the best choice. More expensive poles come with

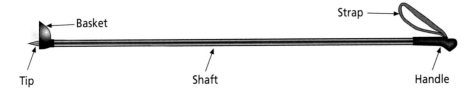

Basket

Strap

Tip

Shaft

Handle

Fig. 3.5 – Anatomy of a pole – tip, basket, shaft, handle, and strap

more durable tips made of carbide steel.

Baskets on adjustable poles are round and come in different sizes. These baskets are usually removable so you can change baskets to adjust to snow depths or to convert your ski poles into hiking poles. They can also come off when you do not want them to, so carry a spare.

CHOOSING A POLE

Pick up the pole and put it on to judge the strap and handle. Can you adjust the strap? Is the handle comfortable?

Swing it back and forth—how does it feel? Good poles concentrate the weight near the handle, making the pole a joy to use. Clunky poles feel like swinging an axe.

Plant the pole into the carpet in the store and pull down on it with your body weight—how much does it bend? As poles get longer, they need to be stronger to avoid bending when they should be helping you move forward. Be cautious of poles in the middle price range that seduce you with a

nice swing weight but lack stiffness, especially in the longer lengths used for skating.

Lower-priced poles are seldom stiff enough to transfer much force. The more you pay the stiffer and lighter the pole will be. If you have to choose one, opt for stiffness at the expense of lighter weight. Be aware that if you start out with stiff, light poles it will be hard to go back to a heavier stick.

Stiff and light poles are fragile, so if you buy them, take care of them. Nicks from banging around in the back of the car, hitting other skiers, and general wear and tear can cause weaknesses that lead to broken poles. Use more durable poles in mass start races (or make sure you're in front!), choose stout poles for off-track adventures, and use some sort of protective tube while transporting your poles. For plane travel, you can protect your poles in your ski bag by alternating the grips and baskets so that the shafts mate closely, then use duct tape to strap them together into one strong carbon rod.

QUICK TIPS FOR CHOOSING EQUIPMENT

LIGHT TOURING—equipment for casual outings in the park, on the golf course, on snow-covered roads, and on groomed trails

- Don't be oversold—skis between 50 mm and 70 mm wide at the tip and a system boot and binding will keep everything light and flexible so you can ski instead of plod. Avoid metal edges and adjustable poles.
- Choose widths in the middle of this spectrum for maximum versatility. If you expect to ski mostly at groomed areas, go narrower. If most of your days will be spent knocking around wherever you find snow, go wider.
- Plastic cuffs for ankle support are great, but backcountry system boots and bindings are unneeded and add unnecessary weight.
- A lightweight three-pin boot and binding will work, but system bindings excel in this category and offer step-in convenience. Find a boot that fits and buy a binding to match.
- Choose a pole that is comfortable and easy to use. Choose an elliptical basket sized for where you want to ski (bigger for more snow, smaller for less).

TRACK SKIING—when light is right. Equipment for skiing on machine-groomed trails.
CLASSIC EQUIPMENT

- Skis are narrow, with waists around 45 mm or less and minimal sidecut.
- Compact and traditionally sized gear is available.
- The lightest, narrowest skis in traditional sizing are called racing skis but are used by most skiers for fun and exercise.
- A lightweight track ski or a citizen-racing ski will be more durable, less expensive, a little easier to ski on, and offer almost as much glide as a high-end racing ski.
- Choose a system boot and binding.
- Manual or step-in bindings both work. Step-ins are convenient but manuals are lighter.
- Stiffer plastic soles are slippery. Wearing them in icy parking lots is dangerous. Wearing them in rocky parking lots scratches the soles, attracting ice and snow that sticks to the sole while skiing.
- Boots for high-performance skiing should be low cut with an unrestricted forward flex.
- Less expensive boots (combi, pursuit, performance, or sport boots) are a great choice for the majority of classic skiers.
- Avoid soft, squishy boots. They are heavy and lack control on the trail.
- Less expensive stiff poles tend to be heavy.
- Light, stiff poles are worth any extra spare change you can scrape together.
- Spend money on the pole shaft before paying for fancy handles and straps.

SKATING EQUIPMENT

- Skating skis are shorter than classic skis, with a low, rounded tip.
- Compact and traditionally sized gear is available. Compact skis are especially fun on snowmobile tracks and other "found" groomed trails.
- You do not need the most expensive racing ski, but the magic of skating is hard to feel on skis more than one or two notches below the best.
- Learning to wax for glide is a crucial component. Buy a basic waxing iron and a small selection of waxes. Wax your skis for glide every second or third day you skate ski.
- Only system boots and bindings are made for skating.

COMBI EQUIPMENT

- Skis made for both skating and classic are not worth buying.
- Combi bindings are classic bindings that are more resistant to forward flex.
- Combi boots are not bad—choose them for extra support while classic skiing.
- There is no such thing as a combi pole for track skiing.

BACKCOUNTRY EQUIPMENT—tools for cruising through the park or climbing a mountain. This is the broadest category of equipment. If you are new to skiing, be sure to rent before you buy to understand the wide variety of options available.

- Backcountry skis usually weigh less than 2500 grams (5.5 pounds) per pair.
- Choose full metal edges if you make turns on icy slopes. Choose partial metal edges if you want extra security touring in icy conditions but do not go around seeking slopes to make turns on.
- Match the boot to the ski. A wider ski requires a higher, stiffer boot.
- Choose boots that are at least ankle high but don't over do it. The heaviest boots are needed only for traveling in extreme terrain and carrying heavy loads.
- Backcountry system bindings are up to all backcountry tasks short of ski mountaineering and steep telemark descents.
- Choose plastic telemark boots and cable bindings for extreme terrain and ski mountaineering.
- Backcountry poles can be fixed length or adjustable. Choose baskets large enough for the snow you expect to ski in. Size fixed-length poles to fit easily beneath your armpit.

CHAPTER 4

Modern attire may work better, but vintage skiwear looks better. (Photo: Steve Hindman)

Accessories and Clothing

Choosing the right clothing and taking along a few, well-chosen accessories will make your time on skis more enjoyable.

PACKS

The lightest *waist packs* are simple holsters for a water bottle. Some have an extra pouch for a snack, a tin of wax, and a car key. This is the way to go if you are out for a quick workout and do not plan to stop.

Fanny packs offer more room without putting straps on your shoulders. Choose packs with several compartments to keep items from sloshing around while you ski.

Technical details are few on smaller waist packs—if you like it buy it. Larger fanny packs with straps and panels to control the bulk, and even little internal frames to carry the weight, are available.

Shoulder packs equipped with water bladders have become widely available due to the hydration craze that started in the 1990s. These packs consist of a sleeve to carry a water bladder and a hose routed through the pack and onto the shoulder straps so you can sip as you ski. Look for a durable bladder with a large opening (so you can add ice and clean the bladder more easily) and a bite valve tight enough not to leak but which will deliver all the water you want without having to suck so hard that you get dizzy. Camelbak popularized the hydration bladder and pack concept and still offers the best products on the market.

Different sizes of bladders and packs are available. A one hundred–ounce bladder provides enough water for a long day on skis but will still work with even a third of that volume in the bladder for shorter jaunts. A hydration pack with a volume between 600 and 1,300 cubic inches has room for some snacks, an extra shell, some wax, and other incidentals. Bungee straps and mesh pockets can be used to carry an extra layering piece or two on the occasional trip that requires them.

To prevent horrible things from growing in the water bladder, never put anything but water in it and store it in the freezer when you are not going to use it for awhile. When outdoor temperatures dip much below the very high 20s, water tends to freeze in the hose of a hydration system. To keep the water flowing, you can wear small, thin hydration packs made just for this use beneath an outer jacket. These come equipped with an insulated hose and are the best solution for colder weather. You can also add insulation to your bladder's hose, but if it gets cold enough any hose outside of your jacket will freeze. To help prevent freezing with either option, blow the water from the hose back into the bladder each time you finish drinking.

For information on backcountry and overnight packs, snow shovels, climbing skins, and snow camping equipment, see Chapter 13.

SKI AND BOOT BAGS

Skis can be thrown in the back of the rig, but a ski bag is more convenient and will also protect your skis. Models that hold more than one pair are available. Two pairs of cross-country skis will fit into a bag made for one pair of alpine skis. If you want to fly with skis, choose a bag with convenient carry straps that can be removed or tucked away when you check your bag. Swanky ski bags now come with rollers.

Early morning light, Canadian Ski Marathon. (Photo: xczone.tv)

Take the kid with you in a pulk. (Photo: Don Portman)

PULKS

Take your kids skiing with you (if you want to, that is) in a pulk, which is a plastic sled with runners made to fit into groomed cross-country tracks and straps on the inside to secure a child. Several companies sell these and many cross-country ski areas rent them. Clear plastic hoods keep out the elements and allow you to see in and junior to see out. Long, lightweight rigid arms attach the sled to a waist belt worn by mom or dad. Pulling your kid behind you is a great workout. Bundle the kid up and take the corners with caution lest you spill your precious cargo.

Accomplished skiers often prefer backpack kid-carriers because they interfere less with glide. They are awkward and the consequences of falling can be serious, so use them only if you have the confidence and the skills. Choose carriers with good restraints that will keep the kid in the carrier if you do fall.

RACKS AND CAR-TOP CARRIERS

If you have no room for skis in the back of your car, you will have to get a roof rack.

Inexpensive strap-on racks are fine for occasional use, but sturdier racks attached to the rain gutters or the doorjambs are worth the investment. On most cars, you can add different attachments to the roof rack to carry bikes, boats, a few pieces of lumber, and even the odd piece of furniture while moving.

Car-top carriers allow you to carry a collection of items, including your skis, in a weatherproof container on top of your car. This is where wet, dirty, or smelly gear goes after an outing. Remember to take all that stuff out and dry it when you get home. If you forget it "upstairs" in your car-top carrier you may have to call in a HAZMAT team to safely remove it when you find it later.

Naked skis on a ski rack are a bad idea. Road grime gets into your bindings and can ruin most of the work you've put into your ski base. Buy a light bag that you can cover your skis with before you clip them into the rack.

CLOTHING

Clothes prevent you from radiating all of your heat outward to all of creation, they block the wind, and they insulate you from cold objects. To keep you dry they have to repel moisture from without while allowing excess heat and perspiration to escape.

For skiing close to home or for your first short jaunts at a cross-country ski area, wear whatever is on hand that you think will work. If you get cold or wet, go inside.

This is a quick way to learn what works and what doesn't.

LAYERING

The concept of layering is simple—start with a thin layer that moves moisture away from the skin, then add layers as needed for warmth and weather protection that do not interfere with the eventual release of that moisture to the outside air.

Water moves away from humidity and heat. The entire modern layering system depends on this principle, so keep it in mind as we journey out through the layers. When the weather is warm or you have on too many layers, the middle layers get as hot as your inner layers, and moisture quits moving outward.

Stay away from cotton as part of your layering system. "Killer cotton," as some call it, is great at absorbing moisture and can quickly become saturated. Dousing your cotton T-shirt with water is a great way to cool off on a hot day, but it is not a great way to keep warm.

Highly specialized layers for each and every outdoor activity are available in a multitude of thicknesses, fabrics, and styles. These items look good and work great, but you can benefit from the layering concept with less specialized and less expensive items if you are just getting started.

If you get outside in the winter to do more than just walk to your car, you probably already have everything you need. If not, you can pick up inexpensive items at general clothing stores and thrift stores that will work until you want to commit to more specialized purchases.

Thin, nylon track suits and other synthetic tops and bottoms made of nylon and polyester can be used in place of specialized long underwear tops and bottoms. Buy these items closer fitting than fashion may dictate and choose thinner rather than thicker pieces. For mid-layer insulation, polyester fleece jackets and pants are widely available at very reasonable prices. Once again, choose close-fitting and lightweight articles.

For outer layers, unlined but coated lightweight nylon jackets and pants will work. These are usually sold as windbreakers in department and sporting goods stores. They won't breathe, so take them off when you do not need them.

The Next-to-the-Skin Layer

This is what most folks call long underwear. It removes moisture and helps to keep your skin at a more constant temperature by creating a layer of still air next to your skin.

Synthetics, especially nylon or polyester yarn or polypropylene filament, excel at helping moisture move away from your skin. Several companies offer thin long underwear made from wool that feels wonderful, although some people still find it itchy. This wool underwear is warm, good looking, comfortable in a wide range of temperatures, resists wind better than most synthetic fabrics, and allows air to circulate when you are hot. When wet it will smell a bit like a wet dog, but that is better than how many synthetics smell after use.

What wool does not do well is pass moisture on to the next layer. Wool is a great choice if you tend to be cold and do not sweat much, or for short jaunts. Otherwise, choose synthetics.

Choosing between the many types and brands of synthetic long underwear is a matter of personal preference. Things to consider are how it feels, how warm and dry it keeps you, how much it smells after use, and how it looks. Buy a few different types and decide for yourself.

For tops, thinner is better since you can always wear two if it is cold. A collar and a deep neck zipper will extend the comfort range on both ends of the temperature scale. Lighter colors are cooler on sunny days when you have to shed all your other layers. A snug but not skintight fit is best. A top that is big and baggy defeats the whole idea of a next-to-the-skin layer.

For bottoms, a close fit is important so they won't interfere with outer pants or bunch up in the wrong places and restrict movement. Choose the right thickness for the temperature you expect. Long underwear bottoms with smooth fronts can serve as tights when you strip down on hot days. Men should avoid front flaps that add useless bulk.

The Middle Layer

The middle layer provides insulation appropriate for the day. Synthetic fleece, wool, down, and puffy synthetics will all keep you warm, but only synthetic fleece will move moisture outward to the next layer.

Because cross-country skiing generates a lot of heat, if your middle layer is too thick you'll be too warm. For your upper body, an extra long underwear top or a lightweight synthetic fleece top should suffice. Carry a heavier coat in your pack. When you stop for lunch, get it out and snuggle in.

After stopping, I put a shell over my middle layer and then top that with my puffy synthetic jacket. This way, I can buy a shell that fits closer and the shell will stop all the sweat I have accumulated from moving into my puffy jacket. Any accumulated moisture is pushed out of the shell after I take off the jacket and start moving again.

Avoid mid-layers with abrasion patches, wind- or water-resistant membranes, nylon pockets, or anything else that will trap moisture. Underarm zips for venting belong in the outer shell, not in this layer. If you find you are too hot, take off your mid-layer.

Your "lunch" jacket can be almost anything you choose, but down or synthetic down is lighter and packs smaller. Nothing surpasses down for warmth until it gets wet, and then it is absolutely, utterly useless. Polarguard 3D is currently the most respected of the down imitators, but Primaloft and Qualofill work just fine. Add an extra warm hat and a dry pair of warm gloves to your lunch outfit and you will be set.

Legs do not radiate as much heat and they sweat less than your torso. Loose tights or snug pants (depending on how you want to look at it) should keep them comfortable. Pants made from dense polypropylene, marketed as 3SP fabric, can usually be worn without a separate next-to-the-skin layer. Tightly woven knit pants from Shoeller and other manufacturers are also great for cross-country skiing. Both types shed snow and drizzle, resist the wind, breathe well when you overheat, insulate when it's cold, move with you as you ski, and wear like iron. Until it dips well below freezing, they may be the only layer you need.

When temperatures drop into the twenties, men need to add wind protection inside the front of any lightweight pants that are not absolutely windproof. Buy wind briefs with a nylon front panel (in a pinch you can use a plastic bag). You will ignore this advice only once.

The Outer Layer

This is what most people call a shell. It keeps rain and snow out while allowing moisture from the inside to escape. It should keep the wind from chilling you and snow from sticking to you. At least one pocket for your car keys is nice, a few more can be very useful. On longer trips, it's nice to have a hood.

Waterproof-Breathable Shells. When you are working hard and perspiring, moisture will build up inside any garment. The great advantage of quality waterproof-breathable garments (Gore-Tex is the most famous maker) is that they don't trap this moisture, but allow it to evaporate, so you stay dry. A lightweight waterproof-breathable shell (also called a hard shell) is nice to have for longer day trips and overnights. Buy one with a hood that sheds drips and cuffs large enough to go over your gloves (otherwise the water running off your sleeves will fill up your gloves). The lightest, simplest waterproof-breathable shells breathe best and cost less.

Soft Shells. In dry, cold climates, moisture can freeze to the inside of your outer jacket, even if it is a waterproof or waterproof-breathable shell. Soft shells, which are made of tightly woven nylon, polyester, or a combination of the two, allow moisture to escape to the outside more quickly, helping you stay dry and warm over a wide temperature range. Another advantage is that they are quiet, unlike stiff and noisy hard shells.

Wind Shells. Wind shells will keep you from losing heat in any climate, as long as they don't get soaked by rain or snow. For exercise skiing, they are the only choice, since anything more waterproof will quickly get soaked from the inside. Shells made from microfiber breathe very well and block the wind. Some are so light you can hide them in your fist. Be cautious of inexpensive wind shells—to qualify for a cheaper import duty they often have a light waterproof coating applied to the inside of the fabric. These shells do not breathe as well, although repeated washings can remove the coating.

Bottoms. If you are wearing a waterproof or waterproof-breathable top, you need waterproof bottoms. Otherwise, all the wetness that your top shell sheds will roll down and soak your legs.

Breathability on the bottom is helpful but not as important as on top. In wetter climates, you may need a pair of heavier waterproof-breathable pants and a lighter pair of wind pants if you ski both on tracks and in the backcountry. In dryer and colder

climates, a light- to medium-weight soft-shell pant will be adequate for most conditions throughout the entire season if you vary what you wear beneath it.

FEET AND HANDS

Clothing for your legs and torso attracts most of the attention, but when it comes to staying warm, dry, and comfortable, gloves and footwear may be the most important items.

Cold hands and feet have shortened many ski days. Keep your hands and feet happy and everyone will be happy.

Socks. Anything but cotton is the rule here, with the nod going to wool socks knit from fine, soft yarns. Avoid ragg wool socks as their coarse knit causes blisters; they also stretch and sag, bunching up in all the wrong places in your boot.

The best wool socks on the market are designed to vary in thickness to cushion the different parts of the foot and to pull moisture up the ankle and away from the foot. They do not itch, can be machine-washed and machine-dried, and last for years. They seldom cost more than fifteen dollars per pair. If you do not own a pair, go buy some.

Some people still swear by wearing a very thin synthetic liner sock beneath an outer sock, but newer socks eliminate the need for this extra cost and complication.

Boot covers. Insulated boot covers work very well. These are made to work with specific boot and binding systems, including three-pin bindings. If you struggle to keep your feet warm, these are a good option.

More help for your feet. Insoles

with slots for chemical heat packets work for some but can be problematic (placed beneath your foot they can lump up and some boots don't have enough room to put them over your toes). A better option may be to slip one or two heat packets in around your ankle between your sock and the boot. These packets can get quite hot, especially when they hit the air after being starved for oxygen inside your boot. Be careful.

Keeping the ankle area warm is crucial. Make sure your pants are long enough to stay below your boot top. Gaiters bridge this gap and keep snow out of your boots if you are in deeper snows, but long pants that do not ride up as you ski are usually sufficient.

Gloves. Bulky gloves made for general wear or downhill skiing generally do not work well with cross-country pole straps. The one all-purpose glove you might consider are those made with Windstopper, a light synthetic fleece bonded to a windproof membrane. Choose a pair that fit well and have grippy, tough synthetic patches on the palm and fingers. These resist wear, are comfortable in a surprising range of conditions, are somewhat water resistant, and dry quickly when they get wet. They are not inexpensive, but you will find yourself wearing them all the time once you own a pair. You will also be surprised at how long they last.

Gloves made for cross-country skiing are your best bet. They have a cuff to cover your wrist and extra reinforcement along the inside of the forefinger and between the thumb and forefinger; most have a strap that cinches above your wrist

to prevent the glove from being worked off by the pole strap. Gloves made for springtime alpine skiing also work well and share many of the same features, as do "park and pipe" gloves made for freestyle skiers and snowboarders.

Synthetic leather is the most common covering for cross-country specific gloves. It is extremely durable and can be machine-washed and machine-dried. Since gloves get pretty sweaty, this is a huge advantage. Real leather gloves have a tacky grip and look and feel great, but they are not washable. If you buy leather gloves, waterproof them after four or five days of use with a treatment such as Nikwax, Biwell, or SnoSeal.

The weight you choose is strictly personal preference. Ski gloves are insulated with a variety of materials. Look for linings that make it easy to get the glove off and on. For thicker gloves, choose those with removable liners that allow the glove to dry out more easily. As an added bonus, you can use them without the liners when it is warmer.

If you have really cold hands, or ski in really cold places, use mittens. Mittens made for cross-country skiing are called lobster claws. They have a split between the second and third fingers and are made to work with pole straps. A regular mitten can work if it is covered with a tough shell material and fits snuggly. Bulky mittens and large overmitts are hard to ski with.

If your hands get cold while skiing, increased activity will usually bring them back, but it can take a long time. When my hands start to feel like wood I ski far enough to get a little torso warmth going, then stop, take off my gloves, and shove my bare hands under my armpits (inside my jacket and under all my layers). This skin-to-skin contact is a little shocking, but my hands warm up quickly this way.

More help for your hands. Chemical hand-warmers can be useful inside a pocket or in the backs of gloves. Again, be careful as these packets can get quite hot. Rechargeable hand-warmers are nice for the environment, but they do not stay warm very long.

HATS

If it seems that all outdoor books are required by law to advise you to wear a hat, there is a good reason for it. Your head is like a steam radiator that is first in line as the hot water comes out of the boiler in an apartment building. Keep it covered and you keep the circulating water warmer so it can heat the rest of the building. Uncover it to shed excess heat by cooling your circulating blood.

A fairly light knitted wool hat is a required piece of cross-country equipment. Unless you live in Florida, I'm sure you have one somewhere. To complete your cross-country haberdashery, all you need is a heavier wool or synthetic fleece hat and perhaps a rain hat if you ski near either coast. Hats are available in the same Windstopper fabric that works so well in gloves, but I don't recommend these because when you pull them down over your ears you can hear absolutely nothing.

THE REAL WORLD

Each type of skiing requires some adaptations of the layering approach to clothing. Here are a few suggestions.

Day Touring. Your basic outfit should consist of a medium-weight next-to-the-skin layer, a wind shirt, a pair of loose tights (or snug pants), a light wool hat, and a pair of gloves. A heavier shell and a warmer mid-layer such as a light fleece jacket or pullover should be in your pack along with some sort of warmer coat for lunch stops. A small closed-cell foam pad to sit on is a delightful luxury. Buy a chunk and size it to fit your butt with a pair of scissors. Use the extra to set your stove on when you go snow camping or when you brew up something for lunch.

A pair of simple coated nylon pants will work well in case of a snowstorm or colder weather. Fancy pants are not really needed since breathability is not as important for your legs on short trips. Ankle zips in shell pants make it much easier to get them on and off over your boots.

In really cold weather, a windproof vest (or a wind shirt over your first layer but beneath your middle layer) will add a lot of warmth. Vapor barrier socks and gloves, available at mountaineering stores, will do the same for your hands and feet. Plastic bread sacks will also work for your feet.

Track Skiing. You will be amazed how little you need to wear when you ski at a jogging pace or faster. Start with the same items listed under Day Touring above (you might want to wear a lighter next-to-the-skin layer). Stuff a medium-weight under-wear top in your hydration pack, or a puffy vest, if you think you might chill down during the ski. A bicycle wind-vest (solid in front, mesh in back) is small enough to put in your pants pocket for those times when you want to carry nothing extra but still have some protection if the wind comes up or you hit a long downhill.

As long as you keep moving, you don't need to worry about getting wet. Your next-to-the-skin layer and wind shirt will keep you from chilling down. Wearing something to keep the water out will just keep all of your water in. Have dry clothes to change into when you're finished.

When it is so cold that you cannot start out dressed as you need to be once you warm up, figuring out how to carry all the clothes you're going to shed can be hard. One option is not to bundle up at all; climb into a hot tub to superheat your body before you start. Jump out, jump into your ski clothes, and hit the trail before you cool off. Be sure to head back at the first sign of any chills if you have left most of your extra clothes behind.

Use caution when it is cold out. Strenuous exercise in below zero Fahrenheit temperatures can be hard on the lungs, especially for those with asthma. Frostbite on toes, fingers, and exposed parts of your face becomes a real danger.

Overnight Tours. On overnight tours, anything you get wet you will have to somehow get dry again. Choose clothing that absorbs little moisture and is compressible. Stop and take off a layer before you get too hot. Stay warm in the evening in your tent and sleeping bag—you do not need to take a lot more clothes than what you need when you stop for lunch on a day trip. More information about heading out into the snow on overnight trips can be found in Chapter 13.

Racing. Lycra is still the king on the racecourse. It does not bind and it does not flap in the wind. One-piece Lycra suits prevent icy gaps from forming, but two-piece suits are more convenient. Layer underneath for conditions with next-to-the-skin synthetics, be sure to protect your privates, and wear insulating and shell layers over your Lycra while warming up. Pants with full-length side zippers, which can be removed without taking off your boots when you are ready to race are especially handy.

If you are uncomfortable wearing Lycra, or do not want to buy specialized clothing to race, then you can join the majority of casual racers who wear loose tights and the type of top that works as a next-to-the-skin layer. The one fashion requirement of the racing world is that your hat should be thin and worn so that it comes just over the top of your ears and above your eyebrows. If you ears get cold, you are supposed to wear earmuffs instead of pulling down your hat.

CHAPTER 5

Skiing with Kids

If you live in snow country, placing skis alongside the sleds and saucers in the garage will probably be all you need to do to get your kids hooked on cross-country skiing. If snow is something you drive to, you will have to work a little harder, but you can still set up situations that will entice them into playing with cross-country skis.

Skiing as a family can be as much fun as going to the beach, walking in the park, or riding bikes together. When it snows, cross-country skis can transform your backyard into a playground right outside your door. Turning your kids on to cross-country skiing may even lead the whole family into longer outings, far-flung adventures, or competitions.

Helping kids discover the magic of winter can be deeply rewarding, but also deeply challenging. Knowing what to expect and how to arrange and organize your outings will make it easier on you and more fun for the kids.

The biggest obstacles to overcome are your own expectations and desires. Try to let go of how they should ski, where they should ski, and how long they should ski, and just let them play as long as they are intrigued. Your patience will pay off later.

Being outside in the cold and the snow and in a strange new place is often more than enough for kids. Try to relax if they do not even put their skis on for the first few trips.

A few cagey moves on your part may help spark their interest in skiing. If it does snow in the backyard, be sure to ski there yourself so they can see you enjoying it. Making a big deal about how much fun you have when you go skiing on your own is another sly way to pique their interest in wanting to go along the next time you pack up your gear.

Once they do get on skis, try not to worry about whether they're doing it the right or the wrong way. They learned to walk without you telling them how. The same will work for skiing. Choose a safe learning area, keep it interesting, and lead them into activities that develop their balance on skis. Like learning to ride a bike, they will figure it out mostly on their own.

EQUIPMENT AND CLOTHING

The basic guidelines for choosing ski equipment are outlined in Chapter 3. The most important consideration when choosing equipment for kids is fit. Purchasing equipment that children can grow into is a false economy since it is unlikely they will ever be interested in skiing if they start out with sloppy boots and skis that are too long. Skis should be no more than head high for younger skiers (up to about third grade), and only two to four inches longer than the child is tall for older kids. Poles can come up as high as the armpit for older kids, but mid-chest is better.

Try on boots with the socks you expect your child to wear when they go skiing. Avoid cotton socks completely, as they suck up water, are cold, and often lead to blisters. Determining if a boot fits is tough. There should be no more than a forefinger of room between the heel and the back of the boot when the toes are touching the front. Shop personnel should be able to help out here—do not take your child's word for it.

It is sometimes possible to get a few seasons out of boots by adding an extra pair of socks, maybe two. Poles that were originally chest high for younger skiers can be used until a child's growth shrinks them down to tummy ticklers. It's OK to look for ways to stretch your purchase over several seasons, but always choose fit over economy.

For their first season or two, choose sturdy ski touring equipment with waxless bases when you rent or purchase. This go-anywhere, do-anything gear will let your kids discover and explore all the different facets that cross-country skiing has to offer. Outfitting them with equipment specific to skiing on groomed trails or in the backcountry will limit their fun.

If you can, try several different sets of rental gear before buying. Be aware that there are bindings that work only with boots made specifically for that binding. Rent everything from the same shop and make sure that you put the boot in the binding at the shop or at home (if you are borrowing equipment from a friend) to check that it works before hitting the snow.

Many shops offer trade-in programs that allow you to keep your children in properly fitted equipment as they grow. Typically, you begin by purchasing new equipment at full price. As your kid gets bigger, you use this original equipment as a first trade-in for the shop's rental equipment. Successive trade-ins are allowed until a child quits growing. Then the deal is over, and they ski off with the first pair of skis and boots they can truly call their own.

Again, clothing is covered in Chapter 3, but there are some specific considerations for kids that you should keep in mind. They will be playing in the snow while they ski—touching, scooping, rolling, and tumbling in it far more than any adult does. Outer layers that shed snow and a lot of extra hats, gloves, and mittens are essential. Although it may be tempting to use some of the cotton sweatshirts and pants that you have at home, don't do it. Two or three pairs of synthetic warm-up suits from the thrift store under an inexpensive set of nylon wind jacket and pants will work fine. Outdoor clothes with fancy labels are not needed.

A lot of light layers work best, so take a pack to carry the extras and to store the discards. Water and some favorite foods also belong in that pack. A towel and a change of clothes should be in the car.

Kids get both hot and cold faster than adults, so help them learn how to add and subtract layers before they need to. Chemical hand- and foot-warmers, and a thermos of hot cocoa, will salvage many a ski day when kids are along.

HOW KIDS LEARN

Kids learn how the world operates and how to operate in the world by playing. Rather than trying to *teach* them to ski, your goal should be helping them *learn* to ski by playing on skis.

Preschool children live in a purely physical world, immersed in the sensations of feelings and touch. They usually lack the ability to understand lengthy instructions or to translate spoken directions into actions. They may not be able to reverse the movements you demonstrate if you are facing them. Their attention span is short, and they are not interested in drills or explanations. They want to play.

Most school-age children can follow a series of instructions, are more interactive, and can benefit from the use of images such as "ski like a cat," but they often won't understand explanations of cause and effect.

Games, activities, and images can help kids learn to ski. Telling them what to do, or explaining how to ski, does not work as well. Showing them how is better, but the best approach is to get them to learn something by actually doing it. Kids learn to ski by skiing.

The best book ever written on teaching kids *or* adults how to ski was written by two Norwegians, Asbjörn Flemmen and Olav Grosvold. Translated by Michael Brady, *Teaching Children to Ski* was published in the United States in 1983. This chapter, and ski instruction in general, owes much to their work. They offer these reminders about teaching children to ski:

- Children can learn to ski before they can comprehend what they are doing.
- Learning is more important than teaching.
- Rhythm is more important than technical finesse.
- Terrain teaches better than most people do.
- Balance is vital; it is learned through a lot of skiing.
- Ski gear does not produce skiing proficiency.
- Children are not small-sized adults; their world is different.

PHYSICAL DEVELOPMENT

Strength and coordination develop from the head and torso outward to the limbs. Younger kids find it easier to bend at the waist than at the knees or ankles because they have more strength in their torso. They have trouble controlling their poles, and fine movements of their feet or hands are often replaced with large movements of their hips and torso. Kid's heads are bigger in proportion to their bodies than those of adults, which means their center of gravity is higher.

Kids do the best they can with what they have. If they will not do something on skis that you ask them to, they may simply not be able to. What they can do is find their own way to ski in the different situations that you create for them.

For example, kids tend to bend at the waist without bending their legs, creating forward imbalance. To compensate, they shove their butt out. Rather than telling them to bend their knees, try leading them through undulating terrain. They will soon discover that if they bend their knees and ankles like a caveman walking through the woods they can stay upright and have fun.

START AT HOME

Introduce your kids to skis at home. Set skis and boots out where they can be seen, and your child will soon be playing with them, even in the summer. Putting on the boots, attaching boots to skis, walking, changing directions, and getting up can all be figured out while they are in a familiar environment. They can do this in the yard or even indoors, although it's a good idea to move the breakables out of the room!

Shop the spring closeout sales, and get them started skiing at home in June. General-purpose skis that will stand up to snow play will survive playing around on grass and carpet.

If you start in the summer, your kids will be bursting with excitement to get on skis when the snow flies. Make your first outing in the snow a short one, have fun together, then stop before fatigue and boredom set in. Do not expect to get any skiing done yourself. These early trips are an investment in the future.

THE LEARNING AREA

The ideal learning area is relatively flat, with a gentle hill on the side. Packed snow is better than deep snow or ice, but it does not have to be a machine-groomed area. Food, shelter, and bathrooms should be close by.

Such friendly terrain is crucial as kids experience trying to deal with gloves, hats, poles, and skis for the first time in the cold and snow. Most kids adapt quickly and will want to venture off as soon as they can ski twenty feet without falling down. Following the Teaching Basic Skills section are some tips for taking advantage of this enthusiasm.

TEACHING BASIC SKILLS

Although the elements of skiing described in Chapters 2, 9, 10, 11 and 14 apply equally to kids, if you want to help them learn it is important to understand those elements from

Help kids uphill to conserve energy on their first days.

a child's perspective. It is also important to remember that because kids' bodies are different from those of adults, they won't do things in the same way and won't look like the examples pictured in those chapters.

Keep in mind that kids are not interested in learning techniques and maneuvers; they just want to have fun. As Flemmen and Grosvold say, "need produces technique." Your job is to create learning situations. Let the kids produce technique on their own.

Once you help your kids get their skis on, lead them in creating snowflakes, stars, letters, and other designs in the snow to help them learn how to manipulate these new long, strange feet.

As they begin to walk around on skis, the skis will start to slide, giving them a new thrill. No doubt they will fall down a few times. That's OK, since trial and error will teach them to keep their legs bent and their hands forward. Don't worry if at first they hold their poles out in front of them

for stability or if they don't even want to use their poles. You should let them do whatever works for them.

If they are struggling to climb a hill or get up after a fall, it's OK to help them since this will conserve their energy for sliding on skis, which is how they will learn. Once they start to have fun, back off and let them get up after they fall and climb back up the hill by themselves. If they are having fun, it should not take long until they figure it out. If they continue to need your help, look for a flatter place to play.

Be sure to provide plenty of breaks for food, water, bathrooms, or for just sitting in the snow. To get them energized and moving again, organize a game of tag, a relay, or a line or circle game.

FALLING DOWN AND GETTING UP

Kids may prefer to get up from a face down, spread-eagle position rather than using the technique described in Chapter 2. Show

Push up from between spread skis with tails pointed down the hill.

them how to untangle their skis by rolling onto their back in the "dead bug" position. Then have them flop over on their bellies with their head uphill and the tails of their skis in a spread-eagled V below them and use their arms to push up.

THE BASIC STRIDE

Kids will figure out how to balance on skis if you keep them moving. Ways to do this include games, adventures, and leading them over modified terrain (see Creating a Training Course later in this chapter). Over time, they will discover how to move faster on skis, shifting from a walk to a jog or even a running stride. As they learn to move their body farther forward on their skis, they will glide more and be able to get the skis to grip the snow better.

Practice. Place two ski poles upright in the snow. Suspend a third pole, held in place by the straps of the first two, between them. Be sure to attach the horizontal pole on the back or downhill side of the upright poles so the straps will be lifted off the vertical poles and the horizontal pole will fall free if a skier hits it (hula hoops cut in half are another easy way to create arches). Have kids ski through the arch, clearing it by crouching forward or doing the limbo to learn to flex for balance.

Skating on Skis. Skating on skis often feels more natural to kids than trying to keep their skis parallel, especially those with some experience in ice skating or street skating. You can introduce the technique by having them spread their tips apart, then push off the edge of one angled ski as they glide onto the other (see Chapter 11 for more about the basics of skate skiing).

CLIMBING HILLS

Once kids have gained some control of their skis, you can introduce the two moves they need to be able to climb a hill: the herringbone and the side step. Climbing a hill with ski tips spread apart in a V position while pressing the inside edges of the skis into the snow is called the herringbone.

Climbing a hill with skis positioned horizontally across the hill using the edge of the uphill ski for traction is called sidestepping (for a further description of these techniques, see Chapter 2).

Practice. To show kids how to place their skis on the snow for either sidestepping or the herringbone, lay poles on the snow where their skis should go or mark the snow with food coloring (diluted in a spray bottle).

Set up a corridor of poles or markers that are wide enough in places to herringbone through but narrower in others, forcing kids to sidestep as well.

Skating on skis is fun and natural.

The herringbone is a walking skate used to climb hills.

If kids have trouble keeping the ski perpendicular to the slope while sidestepping, have them bring their knee to their chest to get their tip out of the snow. Bringing their heel to their butt will bring their tails out of the snow.

DOWNHILL FUN

Once kids figure out how to get up a hill, getting them to slide back down is usually not a problem. Choose a gentle hill to lessen any fear or apprehension. Their speed on the first downhill you choose should be about walking pace. A flat or slight uphill at the bottom will provide a natural stop.

Terrain is the best teacher. Let kids try hills of different lengths and gradients for variety and challenge. Waves, bicycle dips, and jumps (described below under *Creating a Training Course*) will provide hours of entertainment and let them learn by doing.

Kids over the age of three should be able to ski downhill. If they cannot, the hill is either too steep (clues: their legs are rigid and they are holding their poles stiffly out in front), or they are tired and should come back another day.

Practice. Use markers such as poles or food coloring to create narrow lanes running directly downhill. First have kids try to stay within a lane while sliding downhill. Once they get bored with this, have them

Schussing the hill in fine form

try changing lanes by hopping sideways from ski to ski, across the lane markers.

Use ski poles or other markers to set up a figure-eight course that goes downhill and then back up again. Have kids ski between, through, and around the markers. Construct arches made from two upright ski poles supporting a horizontal ski pole (see above under *The Basic Stride*). Offset the arches so they have to turn across the hill to get to them as they ski downhill and have them duck as they go through each one.

At the bottom of the hill mark out a curve (using poles or other markers) to guide skiers into gentle turns that will bring them to a stop.

SLOWING, TURNING, AND STOPPING

As they learn to move down gentle hills using the practice drills outlined above, most kids will naturally do step turns. In order to tackle steeper hills, they will need to master the wedge, or snowplow (see Chapter 2). For most kids pushing a ski out and across the hill to slow down is a natural reaction to too much speed, so they will often create a wedge position on their own.

Usually all that is needed to start kids turning in the wedge position is to place markers down the slope and ask them to ski around them. As they see and move naturally toward the next marker, the angled and edged ski of the wedge that is "in the way" will flatten, allowing the other ski, which remains on edge, to take them to their goal.

If kids are resting back on their heels, work on getting them to spread their skis apart using images—asking them to imagine they are spreading peanut butter on toast or squishing a bug beneath their foot as they push the tails apart can help. Keeping their knees apart can also help kids spread their heels. Make a game of tossing something soft but wide through their knees as they wedge down the hill.

Practice. Find a gentle hill and help kids learn to spread their tails into a wedge and then back together again (or vice versa) by imagining a piece of pizza and then two hot dogs, a caterpillar turning into a butterfly (tails spread into the wedge as wings unfold from the caterpillar), or a fighter jet followed by two rockets. You can mark these shapes on the snow with food coloring, create a song, or place sets of poles or markers (one set narrow, the next wide enough for a wedge) in a line down the slope to signal the changes.

Have kids say "small" as they sink into a wedge and "tall" as they rise while bringing their skis together. Pretending to be balloons that inflate and deflate will also get this up-and-down motion going. Use poles to create a series of arches and then have them spread their skis into a wedge while going under each arch, bringing their skis together as they rise on the other side.

As their speed increases, some kids will continue to use a very wide wedge, while others will start to narrow their wedge. Some will even reverse the angle of the inside ski and sideslip on the uphill edge as they turn. That is great—they are on their way to parallel skiing.

COMMON PROBLEMS

Uncoordinated arms and legs. Have kids verbalize the movement from one stride to the next with phrases such as "one, two" or "hi, ho." To make it less complicated have them try to ski without their poles or ski down a slight hill using only their poles and no leg motions.

No glide. Ask kids to see how few strides they can take to cover a certain distance, which will help overcome their tendency to "churn" quickly from ski to ski without pausing. Play "sneaking behind enemy lines" to encourage kids to crouch low, which will cause them to flex from their ankles and improve their balance so they can balance longer on their front ski.

Skis slip backward. This is usually caused by kids pushing back on their skis instead of down. Have them focus on this down motion by leaping from ski to ski like a lion pouncing on its prey (have them imagine digging their "claws" into the snow) or throw out a series of snowballs and ask the kids to squash them like bugs.

As speed increases and skills develop, leaning into the hill may become a problem. Marker poles that lean to the outside of the turn will keep kids' upper bodies over their feet as they turn around the pole. Set up a challenge to see how close they can get their skis to the bottom of the leaning pole.

See the sidebar in Chapter 2 for more tips on how to address common problems on downhills.

ORGANIZED SKI PROGRAMS

Clubs, racing teams, and other ski programs have a lot to offer both you and your kids. Kids motivate each other to chase, wrestle, and explore both on and off their skis. Groups of children, and the parent volunteers who come with them, make creating terrain features, adventure trails, and other learning areas both easier and more worthwhile. With a larger number of kids it becomes possible to play group games, and more parents means a bigger knowledge base—different parents will know how to lead different games.

Local civic groups, nonprofit foundations, park districts, and Nordic centers all sponsor youth ski programs. Many are members of the Bill Koch Youth Ski League, named for America's first Olympic medalist in cross-country skiing, which offers programs for both girls and boys age thirteen and younger in all the Nordic sports except the biathlon.

Some communities offer their own programs, usually as a branch of a strong local ski club or foundation. Ask at your local ski shop, or search the Internet for the Nordic ski club nearest you.

Youth ski programs rely on parental participation, but adults without kids enrolled

Maine Bill Koch Youth Ski League. (Photo: Phil Savignano)

in the program are needed as well. Learning side by side with your children and with others is a great experience. You will meet other parents and families who like to go outside and play together. In fact, you may discover a community that you did not know existed. Do not worry if you lack ski experience—training in skiing, teaching, and leading kids is usually provided.

GAMES

Games are a part of play, and a great way to keep kids moving. Children under three

are typically too young for any game. With pre-school kids, play and invent games that keep everyone involved but avoid definite rules or competition. Make sure no one has to wait his or her turn to participate. Kids seven and older begin to enjoy competition, but it's best to choose games that reward improved personal performance—games with just one or only a few winners may discourage the losers from skiing.

Have a purpose in mind for every game you play. Your purpose may be to get kids moving because they are cold, to rekindle their excitement for moving on skis, or something as specific as developing one-footed balance. Given kids' psychology, it's probably better not to tell them what your ulterior motive is but just to focus on having fun.

John Mohan directs a ski school based in Seattle, Washington. He offers these tips for organizing games:

- Teach one rule at a time.
- Give clear directions.
- Play a practice game to make sure everyone knows the rules.
- Use a whistle to stop all activity.
- Feel free to change the rules to improve the game.
- Stop games when kids reach a high level of excitement so they will want to do it again.
- If you try a game and it is not working, try something else.

Mohan's favorite teaching aids include:

- Food coloring diluted with water to mark paths, directions, ski positions, or whatever in the snow. Put it in a pump sprayer with a hand-held wand for easy application.
- Colored foam pipe insulation cut into ten-foot lengths. These have a wide variety of uses but are particularly good for making quick arches (see Teaching Basic Skills above).
- Plastic sleds—great for hauling all your stuff out to the learning area.
- Plastic grain scoops. You can purchase these in a variety of scoop sizes from large to huge. Snow does not stick to plastic, making these the tool of choice for creating terrain features (see *Creating a Training Course* below), but keep in mind that they will not stand up to chopping ice.

Some of Mohan's favorite games are:

Whistle Means Stop. Have kids race to a certain spot. When you blow the whistle, they must stop by a count of three. If they don't stop in time they must move back ten ski lengths.

Balloon Stomp. Tie a lot of balloons to a long string attached to your waist and weave over the snow while the kids chase you and try to break the balloons by stomping on them with their skis.

Scooter Races. Have the kids take one ski off and race using the remaining ski, as if they are riding a scooter.

CREATING A TRAINING COURSE

Not only is terrain the best teacher, but transforming your learning area into an adventurous challenge course with waves, bicycle dips, and jumps will help keep kids interested in learning. A small snow shovel (or plastic scoop) and ten to twenty minutes of your time is all it should take to create some basic terrain features—less if you get your kids to help, too.

Terrain features give kids something fun to play on and keeps them on skis long after they would have quit skiing if you just took them on a tour or played games.

Waves in the snow are just that. Make small, smooth waves relatively close together on a slight hill so kids have enough speed to get over the crests. Test the form and placement of your waves with a child,

MORE GAMES AND ACTIVITIES

Washington's Methow Valley is known for its trail network, which totals some 200 kilometers. A founder of the community association that created and maintains these trails, Don Portman also directs the premier cross-country ski school in the Pacific Northwest. Here are a few of his favorite kids' activities.

- Do the Cha-cha, 1-2, 1-2-3. Glide on the three. Do it as a group. Do it up hill, do it downhill, do it all around. Get rhythm!
- Ski like a cat. Curl the claws on all four paws (poles and skis) to grip the snow and spring forward.
- On the flats, have kids put their skis in the A (wedge) position and use their poles to push themselves around. Have them go right, then left, then straight. Do the same in a train of kids (skis of the child in back placed inside the wedge formed by the skis of the child in front). Make train sounds. Expect a crash.
- With their skis in the V (herringbone) position and edges tipped inward, tell kids to walk and quack like a duck. Start on the flats, then waddle up a gentle hill.
- Downhill drill: Start out with knees on skis, hands on tips for the first run. Do the next run upright with hands on knees. On the final run have kids try to bite their pole handles as they slide downhill.
- Red light, green light. Same as the game on foot. Leader holds poles baskets up for go, poles crossed means stop.

not an adult. Kids seldom glide as fast as adults do since they weigh less and their skis are usually slower to start with. Skiing downhill over the waves will teach kids how to absorb changes in terrain by flexing and extending. They will also discover how to adjust their stance to avoid falling forward or backward. When kids have acquired some ability to go uphill, lead them up through the waves to further develop their climbing skills.

Bicycle dips are essentially two side-by-side sets of out-of-phase waves that push one ski up as the other goes down. Setting these up so there is twelve feet between crests is about right. Bicycle dips force kids to develop independent leg action and to further refine their balance on skis. Make sure the size of the dips matches the size of the kids' legs—keep the difference between the bottom of one trough and the top of the adjacent wave to slightly less than the length of the smallest child's lower leg (knee to foot).

Jumps send skiers airborne. To build a jump, look for terrain that drops away after a flatter pitch, followed by a stopping area large enough to avoid collisions. The approach to the takeoff area should be smooth and consistent, with enough pitch to give

Going for a grab on skinny skis. (Photo: Tor Brown)

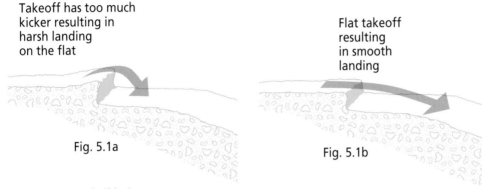

Takeoff has too much kicker resulting in harsh landing on the flat

Fig. 5.1a

Flat takeoff resulting in smooth landing

Fig. 5.1b

Fig. 5.1 – How to build a jump

the skier sufficient speed to reach the landing slope but not so much that they fly over it to the flats. The takeoff itself should be relatively flat without an upturned lip, or "kicker." The landing area should be concave, with the hill dropping away to match the arc of the airborne skier. The run-out at the foot of the slope should be flat or sloped gently back uphill so that kids will coast to a stop. Jumps motivate kids to cycle up and down, and to forget any fear they might have of speed. Kids will usually attempt a jump before they have the skills to avoid a fall upon landing. That's OK. Keep the jump small to avoid injury, and kids will try again, learning how to fall and get back up in the process. With practice, they will learn how to stay forward on the takeoff and to absorb the force of the landing with their ankles, knees, and hips.

Following a trend that began at alpine resorts, terrain parks have begun to appear at Nordic centers and club facilities. These playgrounds offer a ready-made learning area. Take the kids there and set them loose. *One caution:* to avoid broken equipment and the possibility of injuries, some monitoring may be necessary to keep kids from attempting fancy tricks before they have developed the required skills.

CHAPTER 6

Hot waxing increases glide, decreases effort, and protects the ski.

Waxing for Grip and Glide

Observe the mad scientist at work over his waxing bench. Acrid smoke rises as he heats magic potions, while reciting secret incantations barely heard above his raspy breath. Beady eyes dart from tip to tail. He grabs one arcane device after the other, madly stroking from tip to tail. His skis will be the fastest! His skis will dominate! He is the wizard of wax.

You, too, can be a wizened wizard of wax if you want to be, although you don't have to be. If you're one of those skiers who would rather spend their time skiing than bent over a hot iron, you can keep your skis sliding by taking them to your local cross-country shop to have them hot waxed at the beginning of each season. When the weather takes a radical change or you notice a whitish cast on your base, take them in again.

If you are interested in waxing your own skis, this chapter tells you what you need to know to reap 90 percent of the benefits of the wizard's work with only one tenth of the time and effort and none of the obsession.

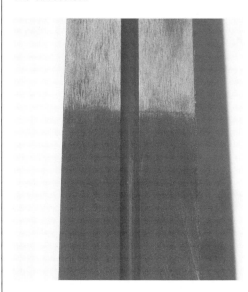

White fuzzy base needing wax and base after hot waxing

WHY WAX?

Periodic waxing lets both waxable and waxless skis glide as they were intended to do and makes the base last longer because it prevents oxidation (rust never sleeps). Not bad for thirty minutes of your time or about $10 at a shop. Waxable skis must also be waxed for grip (more on that later).

If you get serious about ski performance, hot waxing your own skis is the way to go. For skating, it really is the only way to go, because without good glide, skating is no fun at all. You may not need to reapply glide wax every day if you skate, but the more you glide wax your skis, the faster they will become. Waxing your own skis also allows you to easily adjust the glide wax to match conditions when they change.

The fraternity of wizened waxing wizards is constantly inventing new waxes and new ways to combine and apply wax. If you want to see what they are up to, the most up-to-date and useful book currently available is Nat Brown's *The Complete Guide to Cross-Country Ski Preparation* (Seattle: The Mountaineers Books, 1999).

WAXING FOR GLIDE

To hot wax your skis yourself, you need four things: a selection of glide wax, an electric iron, a ski scraper, and a place to work. You can get by with any old iron, but it is best to avoid those with steam holes in the bottom as these are a fire hazard. Never walk away from any iron without unplugging it.

Irons made for clothes fluctuate widely in temperature, and smaller, lighter irons are the worst. For casual hot waxing, this is not a huge problem, but overheating the wax causes it to smoke and changes the chemical properties of the formulation, and overheating the base can damage the ski. Irons made specifically for ski waxing are available at various prices. The most expensive models have digital thermostats, and soon will undoubtedly be able to send a report to your PC on their temperature profile during use. Less expensive waxing irons work just as well for general use, and some of the most affordable are found at snowboard shops. Choose one that fits your budget.

Ski scrapers are sharp pieces of Plexiglas available from your ski shop. Ski scrapers are cheap. Buy a stout one.

Some sort of bench is handy, but in a pinch you can pull two chairs together back-to-back and set your skis across them. Ski vices are the best, but here we are veering off into wax wizard territory. Do your waxing in a garage or utility room where drips do not matter or place several layers of newspaper or a plastic tarp beneath your work area.

To choose a selection of wax, ask your friends or the local shop what the favorite brand of wax is in your area. Buy wax for three or four different temperature ranges from the least expensive line of glide wax offered by that manufacturer. Get to know these waxes before branching out into more expensive waxes or trying a different manufacturer.

HOT WAXING

Ready? Let's wax. Read the labels on your waxes and choose one that comes closest to matching the temperature you expect to ski in. Close is close enough. A choice on the colder side is usually safer if you are between two waxes.

Plug the iron in and turn the thermostat about a third of the way up. Once it has warmed up, adjust the temperature so that the wax will melt when you touch it to the base but does not smoke.

Clean Your Base. Turn your skis base up and wipe off any dirt and grime. If you cannot clean your skis with just a cloth, a small amount of citrus-based solvent, made for cleaning skis, can be used. Avoid petroleum-based products or other cleaners, which may be flammable. Wax accumulates over time, making your skis glide better with each waxing. For this reason, you should minimize the use of base cleaners since they not only remove grime but also the wax.

The best way to clean the glide areas of your base is called a hot scrape. Follow the directions below for hot waxing and scraping and use a generous amount of an inexpensive, soft wax. As soon as the hot wax solidifies, scrape your skis, lifting off the dirt before it settles back to the surface.

What to Wax. If you have skating skis, hot wax the entire base with glide wax, but do not apply glide wax in the grip zone of a waxable striding ski—keep glide wax out of an area equal to the length of your ski boot both in front and in back of the toe piece of your binding. If you have waxless skis for striding, hot wax only the smooth portions of the base, that is, the tips and tails. If you need help determining which type of skis you own, flip back to Chapter 3.

Using the Iron. Hold the edge of a piece of wax against the iron and drip wax down each side of the groove in the area of the base where you want to apply glide wax. A pea-sized drop every inch should be adequate. You can also use the point of the iron to just touch the ski as you run a continuous bead of wax down each side of the groove. Apply enough wax so that when you spread it out it completely covers the ski to prevent the iron from coming into contact with the base. But don't apply too much—any wax that runs down the sides of the ski is wasted.

Holding the iron flat spread the wax evenly across the base. Once the entire

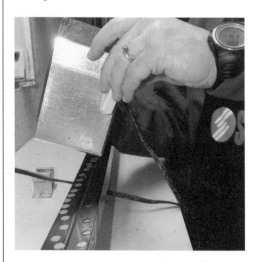

Drip wax onto the base on each side of the groove.

surface is covered, make one or two passes from tip to tail to melt the wax into the base, spending about 20 seconds to move from tip to tail. Keep the iron moving at all times. Don't madly move the iron back and forth since with this method it is hard to judge how much heat you have applied in any one spot. If the iron smokes it is too hot. If the topsheet of the ski gets hot to the touch you are ironing the ski too slowly or for too long. Skis can come apart when the glues that hold them together are overheated, and base material can melt. Err on the side of too little instead of too much heat.

Scraping. Use the rounded corner of your scraper, or a specialized groove scraper, to remove the wax from the groove just after it solidifies. Then put the skis aside for at least a half an hour or longer to let the bases cool. Keeping the skis and the ski bases warm will allow more wax to penetrate, so do not set them outside. Now, put the skis back on your bench and scrape all the wax off that has not been captured by the base. Start at the tip of the area you waxed, angle the top of the scraper away from you, and peel the wax from the base. Hold a finger along one or both sides of the ski as you scrape to prevent a sideways slip that could gouge the base. If your ski has metal edges, be careful with your finger.

The surface should be shiny when you are through. You can buff the base with Fiber-Tex (sold in ski shops) or with medium to fine Scotchbrite pads. You can also use a soft nylon brush if you like.

Scrape off any excess wax not absorbed by the base.

Brush to remove any remaining excess wax to reveal the base structure.

Clean up the drips from the sides and top, and you are ready to go. A pair of ski ties that separates the bases while holding the skis together will prevent wear on your wax job during storage and transport. For more protection while traveling, apply a thick coat of wax and do not scrape until you arrive at your destination.

Summer Waxing. When you are done skiing for the season, clean any wax or grime from your skis and apply a thick coat of warm wax. Do not scrape them and store them in a cool dry place. The thick coat protects your skis from dirt, scratches, and the ravages of oxidation, while you are out playing in the sun. In the fall, you can scrape and go skiing, or scrape and apply new wax.

GETTING SKIS TO GRIP

If waxless skis fail to grip, there is little you can do about it except use climbing skins or, in desperation, apply a thick coat of grip wax or klister. The latter is problematic because removing wax from the pattern in the base is tedious work, and any remnant left after cleaning will interfere with grip in the future.

Sometimes waxless bases can grip too well. This happens around freezing when water penetrates the base and then freezes. To prevent this from occurring, get in the habit of applying some sort of rub-on wax to the pattern base before starting your ski day. Over time the wax will build up and make your base more resistant to icing. Once your base has begun to ice you will need to thaw it out and let it dry before any wax or other treatment will have much of an effect.

Liquid preparations like MaxiGlide work well in warm, wet weather but tend to drag in colder weather. Swix F4 and Toko flouro

paste wax are slightly more expensive but work in all conditions that favor waxless skis. Do not apply the paste waxes over MaxiGlide as the combination turns to bubble gum.

HOW GRIP WAX WORKS

Grip waxes come in two forms, hard wax and klister, and which you choose depends on the snow conditions. Hard wax for grip comes in a range of hardnesses to match the sharpness of the snow crystals. The pointed arms of a snow crystal are sharpest when the temperature is cold, humidity is low, and the wind is not blowing. As snow temperatures warm and humidity increases, the crystals become rounder. Wind, skiers, and grooming machines can also round off the sharp edges.

If snow temperatures go above freezing, the crystal structure is destroyed. Now you are skiing on little balls of ice, and there are no sharp protuberances to reach up and poke into your hard wax. If you want to wax for these conditions, you will need klister—a sticky grip wax that comes in a squeeze tube. Klister has the consistency of very thick jam or even silicone caulk and comes in a range of hardnesses to match the temperature and water content of the ice balls masquerading as snow.

CHOOSING GRIP WAX

As with glide wax, the best way to acquire your first selection of grip wax is to ask your friends and the local shop what the favorite brand is in the region. If that is not an option, match where you ski with where the wax is made. Waxes from manufacturers located in coastal areas work well in wet and warm conditions. Waxes from manufacturers in interior areas seem to work best in interior climates.

Once you settle on a brand, buy enough different categories of hard wax to cover temperatures and snow conditions from 10 degrees above zero Fahrenheit up to the freezing point. Klister is also sold for various temperature ranges. Start out with the same brand you choose for hard wax. Pick up one for below freezing, a universal type, which sort of bridges the gap, and one for above freezing. Many skiers, ski shops, and wax containers use the Celsius scale more often than Fahrenheit. After using waxes marked in both for a while, you will soon become "bilingual."

Get to know one brand of grip wax before branching out into others unless a friend or acquaintance you trust advises you to start with a different mix. You will also need a cork to smooth out the wax. Synthetic corks work the best. If you want to be fancy, buy one cork for warmer, softer waxes and one for colder, harder waxes.

If you are driving somewhere to ski, wait until you arrive at your destination to choose your grip wax for the day. Find a thermometer or make a good guess at the outside temperature after actually being outside. What matters is the temperature of the snow (not the air) and how beat up the snow has become since it has fallen. If you cannot tell by looking, ask around to see when the last snowfall occurred.

Most hard waxes will have different temperature ranges for old snow and new snow listed on the container. Find the wax that matches the temperature and snow condition of the day.

APPLYING GRIP WAX

If you have any doubt, start with a wax that may be too cold for the conditions. Colder waxes are harder. If they are not right, the only penalty is that your ski will slip. Warmer waxes are softer. If you choose a wax that is too warm, snow may become imbedded in the wax. This is a problem.

Softer warm wax can be applied over harder cold wax, but the opposite does not work well. The common analogy is that the peanut butter goes on the bottom and the jelly on top.

Wax is applied to the grip zone of your ski, or roughly from your heel to about the same distance in front of the toe piece of your binding. Expose the end of your chosen wax tube and crayon on a thin layer from the tip toward the tail. Start with a short layer that does not reach the ends of your grip zone. Several thin layers are more durable and easier to apply smoothly than one thick layer.

Smooth this layer with your cork and then add more layers on top, smoothed again with the cork. Do the other ski and then set both outside for a few minutes to cool. Do not set the skis on the snow. A warm ski straight from the inside will sometimes melt snow and cause icing problems.

Put on your skis and ski for at least a few minutes to decide if the wax is working. Go for a secure grip in spite of what your racer friends might say. Worrying too much about losing glide to grip has turned more people off to grip waxing than anything else. Wax for grip so you can relax and learn to trust the ski. After a while, your technique will improve to the point where you can begin to adjust your wax for better glide.

A tried and true piece of waxing advice is "thinner, thicker, longer; then warmer." If several thin, short layers are not working, add one or two more short layers. If that does not work, lengthen your grip wax. If that does not work, then move to the next warmer wax or to a wax for older or wetter snow in the same temperature range and go through the same process.

This is a cautious approach, and with a little experience, you will know more about what works and be able to come very close on your first attempt. Minor corrections and additions are common on the trail for anyone, so carry an extra tin or two of wax and a cork in your pocket when you head out.

In colder conditions with consistent temperatures, one good multilayer wax job can work perfectly and last for a week or more with only the occasional addition of another layer.

WHEN TO CHOOSE WAXLESS SKIS

The crystal structure of snow rapidly deteriorates when temperatures range from the high twenties on the Fahrenheit scale to the freezing point. This makes it hard to get grip wax to work. Going up or down in elevation or skiing through areas where the wind or sun has affected the snow can also make successful grip waxing elusive.

When it is warm and wet or when your ski route includes widely varied conditions and terrain, you'll be better off with high quality waxless skis. Another option is to skate when grip waxing is tough.

At temperatures colder than the mid-twenties, the crystal structure of the snow is more stable and waxing is easy. These conditions are commonly found away from the coasts or during fine cold winter weather in any locale. Waxless skis are horribly slow and unnecessary at such times.

KLISTER

Because it is very sticky, klister is tricky to use, but sometimes there is simply no choice. When waxless skis struggle to grip in icy conditions, a waxable ski with the correct klister applied may be the only thing that will work.

Once you master a few tricks, you may become one of the many skiers who secretly look forward to klister conditions. When klister is needed, glide is fantastic since the snow is either wet or icy and a short layer of klister underfoot often provides bomber grip with seemingly no effect on glide. Another attraction to klister conditions is that the grip from klister is more of an on-and-off feeling. Those of us with less subtle technique are on more of even footing on klister days than on some hard-wax days when the wily masters with their subtle tricks and mysterious "feel" for the snow can make skis grip and we cannot.

Applying Klister. If it is cold, warm up

the klister indoors or in your pocket so it will come out of the tube and spread easier. If the tube has already been opened put it into a plastic bag before putting it into your pocket.

Start a bit back from the front of your grip zone and spread a thin layer of klister in chevrons on either side of the groove, working your way back to just in front of the heelpiece of your binding. The little plastic scraper that comes in the box can be used to spread the chevrons, but the extra pressure and heat from the heel of your hand works best. Wipe the excess klister off your hand on the inside of your boots or on a rag if you have one. Do not use paper towels.

Be sure to cool your ski before skiing to prevent icing. Klister will be catchy and jerky at first, so ski cautiously for the first one hundred feet or so and it will smooth out. If it does not grip, go thicker, then a bit longer. Be sure to err on the cold side and the thin side when choosing and applying klister. Once snow starts to stick to klister, you will need to go inside, clean your ski, and start over. If the trail you are skiing on climbs at first, or the weather looks like it may change, tolerate some slip until you get into colder conditions. If you are still slipping, then add more or move to a warmer, stickier klister.

Keep klister away from the extremities of your grip zone to avoid spreading it to the glide zones. Klister often sticks when you stand around on your skis, so either keep skiing or shuffle your feet back and forth as you stand around and gab.

Avoiding the Mess. The aftermath

of klister is what turns people against it, so manage the carnage. Be sure to put the cap back on securely when you are done. Keep your klister in a Ziploc bag, with no more than two to a bag so that one sticky tube does not make them all sticky. In the winter, keep all your klister in an unheated garage or outbuilding. Keep it in the freezer during hot weather. Never keep klister in a drawer over the summer where leaks can ruin other items.

When handling skis with klister on the bottom, pick them up by the tip or tails or by the bindings. Clean them at the trailhead after skiing if possible. If not, take them home in a dedicated klister ski bag, or cover the middle of your skis with a thick garbage bag after strapping them together (this will prevent thin bags getting stuck in the klister and pulling apart into pieces when you try to remove them). Klister will stain anything it touches like the upholstery of your car or your clothing.

Klister left on skis over the summer

Apply klister in chevrons on either side of the groove in the grip zone.

sometimes needs to be chipped off with a metal scraper or putty knife. Clean your skis as soon as you get home. Scrape as much off as you can with a plastic scraper. Then use some citrus-based solvent to remove the rest, being careful not to let it run into the glide zones. Paper made from spun fibers that does not pull apart when used to wipe klister from scrapers and skis is available at most ski shops. It is pricey, but a roll lasts a long time.

GRIP ZONE PREPARATION

Hard wax and klister will stay on your skis longer if you lightly sand the grip zone with 100-grit wet/dry sandpaper. Binder waxes or a very thin layer of very cold klister can be ironed into the grip zone to help wax and klister last longer and to protect the base from oxidation. Rub the binder or klister on the ski and then iron it in. Apply just enough so that all of it is absorbed into the base.

Irons used for applying binders should not be used for applying glide wax. Use a discarded one from the house, pick one up at a used clothing store, or buy a cheap travel model. The quality of the iron and any steam holes are not as much of an issue with this iron, since klisters or binders are unlikely to flow into the iron and the base in the grip zone does not see the iron very often.

AN ART NOT A SCIENCE?

Grip waxing is always called an art, to contrast it with a science or a paint-by-numbers project. Actually, it is a combination of all three. If you read the directions on the wax containers, you can figure out which wax to try when. The art and science part comes from what you learn when you follow the directions.

The truth of the matter is that waxing your own skis is not required. You can have years of fun skiing on waxless skis if all you do is take them to be hot-waxed by a shop now and then. If you want to get more involved with skiing and learn how to wax, hot waxing your waxless skis for better glide is a place to start. Then the next step is to acquire a pair of waxable striding or skating skis and start concocting your own secret potions to make them grip and glide.

It's all part of the fun.

CHAPTER 7

Skating in Gatineau Park, Ontario, Canada. (Photo: National Capital Commission of Canada)

Practical Tips

The more you do something, the better you get at doing it. Here is a collection of simple lessons learned by other skiers, which, I hope, will prevent you from having to learn everything the hard way.

IN YOUR PACK

What you carry with you depends on where you are going. If you are skiing on the groomed trails at a Nordic center, all you need is a credit card for your trail fees and your lunch, and perhaps a small waist pack with water, a snack, and an extra layer. At smaller club trails you may want some paper money to drop in the contribution box or to pay your trail fee since many of these low-key operations do not take credit cards.

For trips farther afield, your pack should include some extra essentials in addition to food, water, and extra clothing. Carrying a small first-aid kit (including a

blister kit), sunscreen, and sunglasses, lip balm, a small knife or multitool, a bit of duct tape (to cover blisters, to splint poles, to tape a blown-out boot back together or a binding onto the ski), several butane lighters, matches in a waterproof container, some toilet paper, and a space blanket or emergency tube tent will give you the tools to deal with most of the unforeseen emergencies that might arise.

FINDING YOUR WAY

Ski tracks have a way of disappearing, so do not rely on retracing your steps to return to your car. A map and a compass can help you stay out of trouble provided you know how to use them, know where you are going, and can keep track of where you are as the day progresses. If you are unfamiliar with "staying found," stick to marked trails and guided trips to avoid getting lost.

More information on winter navigation is included in Chapter 13.

For any trip on trails in the backcountry, someone should know where you are going, when to expect you back, and whom they should call if you do not return on time. If you've forgotten to do that, at least leave a note on your dashboard to give searchers a clue if you do get lost.

ELECTRONICS

A GPS (Global Positioning System) receiver will work on most ski trails, but you still need a map, must understand how to use the GPS, and be able to interpret latitude and longitude to find your location on the map. Cell phones may or may not work, depending on your locale, so do not rely on them unless you know they work where you will be skiing. Inexpensive radios, such as the Motorola Talkabout, are a great way to keep in touch when two parties are out of sight of each other but not too far apart. These so-called FSR radios have a typical range of a few miles, but their signal will not curve over hilltops into the next valley so do not expect too much of them.

SUN PROTECTION

In the gray of winter, it is easy to neglect shade hats and sunscreen, but unfortunately the sun has a way of sneaking up on you. Even if the sun stays hidden behind clouds, it can still cause damage, and wind and cold alone can chap your face until it feels raw. Err on the safe side and take care of your face and any other exposed skin with a sun and wind protection cream whenever you go skiing.

When the sun is blazing, its brilliant reflection off the snow makes the need for sunglasses obvious, but the reflection can be almost as strong under high overcast conditions. If you have any doubt about the sun's strength and the amount of glare, wear sunglasses—snow-blindness can be damaging and painful.

Higher elevations means there is less air between you and the sun to block the rays that burn your skin and your eyes. Be especially vigilant with your sunscreen and use darker sunglasses with quality lenses when you ski at elevation.

Sunscreen lotions with a SPF (sun protection factor) of at least 25 are needed to protect you from the intensity of the sun, both from above and as it is reflected from the snow. Choose a waterproof product and make sure to apply it to the bottom of your nose, chin, and ears. To keep sunscreen from running into your eyes wear your hat pulled low and you won't have to apply it to your forehead.

Once springtime hits at any elevation, the increased potency of the sun turns any ski day into an extended tanning-booth session. Expose any winter-white flesh with extreme caution! If you choose to ski without gloves, apply sunscreen to the backs of your hands and, if you roll up your sleeves, to the tops and bottoms of your forearms. SPF 40 creams applied in the morning and then again at lunch are needed in these conditions.

MY FAVORITE TIME TO SKI

Perhaps there truly is a veil between the worlds that thins at dawn and dusk. I am a little thin myself at dawn, but dusk often finds me out on the ski trails. _

In the evening, work is over and the pressures and priorities of the day fall from me like a salmon releasing her eggs. I burst onto the trail, lightened and full of pent-up energy. As the light fades, my internal spring winds down as the deep peace and contentment of rhythmic movement carries me onward into a half-seen world. I carry a headlamp on my evening flights, because I do not like to interrupt this state of body and mind with worries of having to return before dark.

I know I am only a visitor in this world between the worlds, and as darkness falls, my own world always calls me back. When I snap on my headlamp, the small pool of light shining from my brow brings me quickly to thoughts of dinner, chores to do before bed, and the next day as I slide back to the trailhead. But that brief pause between heading out and turning back, that time between the worlds, stays with me. It helps me remember that I am more than what I do and have to do. I am also that visitor who stood silently, surrounded by the velvety world of dusk, a small piece of a much bigger and unknowable other.

Sunset skiing. (Photo: National Capital Commission of Canada)

When it gets really hot, light and loose cotton or synthetic pants and long-sleeved shirts will keep you cool while protecting you from the sun. If your skin is particularly sensitive, clothing with SPF ratings is available.

GETTING READY

Feet sweat constantly. Keep your socks and boots dry until you get to the trailhead by not putting on even your ski socks at home. People with extra sweaty feet (you know who you are) should try using an antiperspirant before donning their socks.

Keep your boots inside the car on the way there, but don't put them beneath the heater vent. If they are hot when you put them on, not only will your feet immediately get sweaty, but snow will melt on the outside as soon as you step out of the car, wetting your boots from both directions.

If your drive to the ski trails is short, dress in your ski clothes at home, except for socks and boots. On longer trips, you may want to wait until arriving at the trailhead before changing into synthetics. Be sure to have dry clothes in the car to change into after skiing. Extra food and water left in the car are always welcome when you return, and another thermos can keep your cup full for the trip home.

One handy item to have is a small rubber mat to stand on while changing your clothes and stepping into your boots. In nice weather, bring a lawn chair and sit down like a civilized person. When you return, relax in your chair for a spell and socialize with other skiers before driving home.

Before you head out on the trail, check that you have locked your car (unless you are afraid the locks will freeze), that your headlights are off, and that your keys are in a secure place.

If your boots are plastic-soled wait to change into them until you're next to the snow, or consider being a Nordic geek and wear slip-on rubbers over your boots until you get there.

Put your skis on before standing around and kibitzing with friends on the side of the trail. Ski boots are not made to keep your feet warm while standing on the snow.

COMPANIONS

Adjust your expectations to suit the company you have chosen. If you are out for wild adventure or a hard workout and have invited your inexperienced friends from work, everyone is in for a miserable day.

A Nordic center is the best place for mixed groups since trails suited to different skill levels and temperaments are available, and less enthusiastic skiers can wait and socialize in the warming hut while the driven put in the kilometers. Groups of skiers should also be using similar equipment so they can move at a similar pace and be equipped to enjoy the same terrain.

Ski companions. (Photo: Fischer Skis)

LUNCH STOPS

Once you are out on the trail, the group should move at the pace of the slowest member, especially if it is a cold day. If the gazelles sprint ahead and then have to wait until the slow and steady crowd arrives, they will be cold and impatient and unwilling to wait longer as everyone rests. Move as a group to have more fun.

Take along a thermos full of tea, coffee, or hot cocoa for a morning break or for lunch. A small backpack stove will enable you to make soup or another hot drink at your lunch stop. Stop before anyone gets cranky and find a sheltered spot to rest, take a break, or wait for slower members of your party.

The top of the climb or the pass may be the most scenic spot but it is also likely to be the windiest. It's usually possible to find a more pleasant spot in the lee of the wind where most of the view is still available. Ten or twenty yards can make the difference between a pleasant lunch and a hurried refueling stop.

At times, it will simply be too cold to stop for long. Grab a snack, drink some water, and keep moving at a comfortable pace to keep warm.

If you can stop and rest a spell, make yourself comfortable. Put on an extra layer or two right away. Unless it is raining or snowing very hard, you can put your insulating layer right on top of a shell to conserve heat and hassle. A fresh hat and a warmer pair of gloves will also feel great. Put the gloves you were wearing inside your top so they will stay warm while you rest.

Many skiers carry an extra closed-cell foam pad to keep their backside warm and dry during lunch. If you sit on your pack instead, you may crush the items inside. Doing this over time may even bend or break the frame. Another trick is to find a slight slope and dig a platform across the hill with a trench in front of it. Place your skis lengthwise across your snow bench with the bases up. Have a seat on just your skis, or place your pad or pack on top for more comfort. The trench provides room for your legs so you can sit upright.

Energy bars and dense cookies such as Fig Newtons, dried or fresh fruit, and trail mix are good snacks for short rest stops. Sandwiches, cheese, dried sausage, baked and smoked tofu, nut butters, and durable crackers provide the calories needed to keep you fueled up for a whole day, but eating too much at one time can actually slow you down. Fat helps you keep warm, so this is not the time to start a diet. Include a treat or two in your lunch bag.

Pick a comfortable rest stop. (Photo: Steve Barnett)

Sweets provide quick energy at the cost of a quick decline when the boost runs out. Eat your chocolate with your lunch so that you have some backup fuel to kick in when the sugar buzz wears off. A packet or two of energy gel stuffed into your first-aid kit will come in handy when you run out of juice late in the day. One packet will keep you going for about an hour. After that, your burst of energy will be gone and you will be more worn out than before you ate it, so plan on being at your destination within that timeframe. If you're more than an hour from "home," don't start with the gel packets unless you have enough to be able to consume one per hour until you get to where you need to go.

Alcohol dilates your blood, causing you to lose heat faster. Save the libations for when you get to the lodge or return home.

PARKING IN SNOW COUNTRY

Parking in snow country is always a problem. Many states have sno-park programs, which use a permit system that allows access to plowed parking. Day and annual passes are usually available, but generally must be purchased in advance since few facilities have attendants. Ignorance of the system is no excuse. If you park without a pass, you will probably get a ticket equal to the price of an annual pass. A local outdoor or sporting goods store will often know if parking permits are required and may also be a vendor. In popular ski areas, wayside gas stations or grocery stores on the way to the trailhead also may sell parking passes.

If you are skiing on federal or state land, you may or may not need a pass to park in the winter. Check before you go. Free, plowed parking is one of the great amenities of a commercial Nordic center. It also represents one of the major expenses for these businesses, so do not park in their lot unless you pay to use their trails.

Parking along the roadside is not recommended. Snowplows and other motorists sliding into you are hazards not to be taken lightly. Wherever you park, it's a good idea to back in so that you can pull forward when leaving. Whether you park in a plowed parking lot or alongside a plowed road, don't get too close to the edge. Snowplow blades can create a flat area that masks a drop-off or ditch.

If you drove from rain into snow, it is best not to lock your doors. Weigh the risks of a break-in with the risk of having your locks freeze shut. Leave your emergency brake off when you park in the snow because it is likely to freeze in the on position. If it is snowing and your windshield is warm and wet when you arrive, pull the arms of your wipers away from the windshield and leave them in the upright position to prevent them from freezing in place.

Isolated trailheads are a favorite target of vandals and thieves. Leave valuables at home and carry your money, identification, and credit cards with you. Place whatever would attract a thief's attention in the trunk or cover it with a blanket. A locked car will deter the casual thief, but an unlocked car may save your windows and door locks from damage by a determined thief. You decide.

Part II: Skiing for Fun and Fitness

CHAPTER 8

Under the spell. (Photo: Tom Stillo Photography)

The Magic of Speed and Grace

For centuries, skiers have skied in the tracks left by others in order to go faster and farther with less effort. When snowmobiles first began to leave their marks in snow country, skiers jumped into those tracks, too. Soon, grooming attachments pulled behind a snowmobile were being used to create tracks specifically for skiing. Today, large over-the-snow track vehicles called snow cats use a host of specialized attachments to produce the wide, smooth, and firmly packed ski trails found at most Nordic centers. These attachments press grooves into the snow along the edges of the trails to guide the skis of those who choose to diagonal stride, while the snow in the middle is ground up and then packed smooth for skating. Modern grooming even goes so far as to texture the snow in the middle with a very wide-wale corduroy pattern to improve glide and edge grip for skate skiing.

As a result of all this mechanized effort, skiers can float and fly over the snow instead of wading through it. Very light equipment can be used since skis do not need to survive irregularities in the snow and boots do not have to wrestle skis from the grip of deep snows.

WHICH TO CHOOSE: CLASSIC SKIING OR SKATING?

Grooming makes skiing easier, grooming makes skiing fun, and grooming makes skiing fast. The only thing left to decide is how you want to take advantage of the speed and grace of groomed trails—do you want to skate on your skis or use the classic diagonal stride to float over the trails?

Don Portman of the Sun Mountain Ski School in Washington's Methow Valley offers this comparison to help you decide when to do which.

Classic: Easy to Begin

If you are a beginner, start with classic skiing. Even if you have never done any downhill skiing, ice skating, or other gliding sport, it is easy to learn to shuffle around on skis and even glide.

Skating: Hard to Start

People with no experience in gliding sports find skating hard to learn, since from the very beginning they must be able to balance on a single gliding ski.

Classic: Difficult to Master

Very few people actually stride with grace and efficiency; it usually takes years to develop the balance and timing needed.

Skating: Easier with Experience

Experienced striders, downhill skiers, inline skaters, and ice skaters all find skating easy to learn and master (however, a lesson or two will speed the process).

Classic: Stop and Go

In the diagonal stride, each ski has to come to a complete stop to get a grip on the snow. The skis themselves must be waxed for grip (or have a no-wax pattern that serves the same function), which further offsets the glide. No matter how fluidly a classic skier appears to be moving down the track, her or his movement is still essentially glide, stop, glide, stop, so classic

The diagonal stride, also called striding, classic skiing, traditional skiing, and the kick and glide
(Photo: Fischer Skis)

Skating, also called skate skiing, free technique, and freestyle skiing

skiing tends to be slower than skating.

Skating: Glide and More Glide

Skating skis are waxed to glide fast—no grip wax and certainly no fish scales or other patterns on the base. The skate skier moves sideways and forward from one gliding ski to another. Glide-glide-glide with no stops means more speed.

Classic: Fast in Slow Snow

On those beautiful, cold crisp winter days when the snow crunches underfoot and the temperature is in the single digits or colder all skis glide less. But classic waxed skis grip so well that this makes up for the diminished glide. Kicking and

gliding feels fast and effortless. Skate skis just feel slow in cold, powdery snow.

Skating: Ice Is Nice

Springtime or any time there's a melt/freeze cycle is great for skating. The same icy surface that makes classic skis slip backward makes skating almost too effortless. The uphills seem flat; the flats seem like downhills and the downhills—wow! These are some of the best skating conditions so long as the snow has a bit of texture for balance.

Classic: Slower and Gentler

Experiencing the magical winter wonderland, observing wildlife, or just chatting with a friend as you ski is more in keeping with striding. Striding can be like a walk in the woods or a run that is gentle on your body.

Skating: More Intense Speed

Skating is really all about going fast. Downhill skiers tend to favor skating—it has a lot of the same movements and some of the speed. It is very difficult to carry on a conversation while skating.

Classic: A Controlled Workout

It is easy to stride slowly and easy to maintain an even heart rate. The difference in heart rate on hills and on the flats is not necessarily great. Most world-class racers use diagonal striding in at least 60 percent of their training, even if most of their races are skating, since it gives them a better and more controlled aerobic workout.

Skating: A Varying Heart Rate

Skating typically involves more variation in heart rate. When skating uphill the heart rate soars, then can drop almost to a resting level while cruising the flats.

Classic: Can Go Off-Track

Nicely groomed tracks make classic skiing much easier, but it is often fun to stride out into unbroken snow. Striders can travel through deep soft snow that skaters couldn't even move in.

Skating: Grooming Is Critical

Skating needs a wide platform of firmly packed snow that is textured like corduroy, which can only be achieved with the use of high-tech grooming machines.

If you already are a devotee of one style, try the other. As longtime skier and instructor Todd Eastman says, "Skiing is more interesting when you have more things to do."

A NORDIC CENTER NEAR YOU

According to Chris Frado, president of the Cross Country Ski Area Association, "There are cross-country ski areas to fit your every mood in the United States and Canada—from bustling alpine areas with Nordic centers to romantic country inns with trail systems. Remote western ranches with panoramic high mountain views contrast with Minnesota's ski lodges connected along a forested cross-country ski trail." New England boasts the highest concentration of Nordic centers on the continent, while California's Royal Gorge lays claim to being the largest cross-country center in the world.

Commercial operations offer the most reliable grooming and snow conditions. They have to get it right because the livelihoods of the owners depend on it. If it is snowing on Friday night, then they are out in the storm grooming on Friday night and on into Saturday morning. Trail fees run in the range of $10 to $20 per day. For a current list of Nordic centers and trail conditions, visit *www.xcski.org*. For news, tips, and other information to help you plan your cross-country ski vacation, visit *www.xcskiresorts.com*.

Hundreds if not thousands of kilometers of groomed trails are maintained by community groups, ski clubs, and government agencies. In the last decade modern

UNDER PRESSURE

In the late 1970s, all Bertel Kleerup wanted was a little Nordic center in the woods. The problem was his customers would try this new sport once or twice and then not come back. So he asked them why.

Turns out they thought it was too much work and not enough fun. After asking a few more questions, Bert discovered that the problem was that most skiers had skis that did not "work." Either they could not climb the hills or they could hardly slide back down. Some could do neither. Well, no wonder they did not like cross-country skiing! Bert knew that for skis to function properly they had to fit the skier.

A mathematician by training, he set out to find a way to quantify what mattered when it came to matching a ski with a skier. He discovered that as for grip what matters is how much of the force applied to the ski is transferred to the wax pocket beneath the foot and not out along the base toward the tip and tail.

The secret to good glide turned out to be a little more complicated since it depends not only on how much the skier weighs but also on how he or she skis and in what type of snow. Since building his first testing machine, Bert has collected data on the pressure profiles of 40,000 pairs of skis—information he uses to help him fit skiers at his Eagle River Nordic Center.

When you buy clothes, you avoid any that are too tight or too loose. You want them to fit just right. To get the same fit with your skis, check out what Bert is up to at www.ernordic.com.

grooming equipment has greatly improved the quality of these trails, but few get the same prompt attention as their commercial counterparts. This is largely because most noncommercial trail networks rely on volunteers or forty-hour-a-week employees to do the grooming. For that reason trails are groomed according to a schedule based on the availability of the groomers instead of on the condition of the trail and current weather conditions.

Regardless of where you find a groomed trail, be sure to appreciate it. Pay your trail fee or stuff what you can into the donation box. Season passes are usually available to reduce your cost per visit.

If you enjoy groomed trails, check out the available volunteer opportunities. You may be able to earn a discounted season pass for your efforts, and you will definitely meet a community of skiers full of potential new friends. Most areas need volunteer help to maintain the trails in the off-season. During the season, there may be opportunities to help as a part of the Nordic ski patrol or even as a host for the area.

THE BIRTH OF SKATING

Before taking his current job as Nordic Product Manager for Fischer Skis, Peter Ashley was a coach with the U.S. Cross-Country National Team. He tells this story about the birth of skating:

Skating, also called the free technique, made its first appearance in international competition in the 1970s. The Nordic countries, led by Norway, saw this renegade technique as a threat and wanted to eliminate it from competition. They argued that it destroyed the set tracks, it required trails to be widened, and it ruined an athlete's body. It was not traditional! It was not skiing!

Race officials in countries that objected to skating placed flags to keep skiers in the tracks and even built mounds between the tracks to keep upstart skiers in their place. But course designs did little to stop determined free racers—they skated through the flags and on the mounds, using skating to get to the finish line in the fastest way possible.

By the time of the 1985 World Championships in Seefield, Austria, a protocol had evolved to manage the situation. At the start of each race, all the coaches would gather and vote. Declaring a race to be a classic contest (no skating allowed) required a unanimous result. Anything less than unanimity, and the race became a "freestyle" contest in which the fastest skier to cover the course by any means would win. Technique in these freestyle races consisted of a combination of the marathon skate (one ski always in the track), which was used on the faster and flatter sections of the course, and the diagonal stride, which racers would switch to when the snow was slow or the hill too steep.

On the day of the vote in Seefield, the snow was warm and wet and everybody realized that using grip wax (necessary for the diagonal stride) would make their skis horribly slow. Once the vote came in for a freestyle contest, decisions had to be made. Racers lined up at the Swix and Exel booths looking for longer skating poles, and skis were stripped of grip wax and then re-waxed with glide wax from tip to tail.

The first race was the men's 30 km. Modern technique was born when the racers reached the first hill that was too steep for the marathon skate. As they broke out of the tracks into a herringbone, they realized that a little glide with each herringbone step was faster. Racers watched each other, learning as they raced. Need produced technique. By the end of the world championships, a rudimentary form of today's V-1 skate technique had developed.

For the next few years, Ashley and the other coaches found themselves coaching athletes in how to do what had never been done. They figured it out together. As racers began to train and race over longer distances with skis waxed just for glide, the V-2 and faster techniques began to develop. Skiing has never been the same, and the evolution of ski skating technique continues to this day.

CHOOSING YOUR TRAIL

Some trails are lighted for night skiing, some are marked but not groomed, and some are reserved for teaching or for skiing with dogs. Some trails are designated as one way. Occasionally trails will be closed for short periods for a race. The trail map available at the trailhead, ticket booth, or the day lodge should fill you in on all these details. Ask the staff and other skiers for current updates on snow and trail conditions, and what trails they would recommend.

Cross-country ski trails are rated Easier, More Difficult, and Most Difficult. The common symbols associated with these designations are a green circle, a blue square, and a black diamond. These ratings are always relative to other trails in that one area, so do not make the mistake of thinking all green circle trails are alike.

TRAIL ETIQUETTE

Groomed trail etiquette includes stopping where you can be seen, not blocking the trail, checking for others on the trail before starting out yourself, yielding to skiers going downhill, and being considerate when passing other skiers. A common courtesy is to say something like "on your left" a few seconds before going around them on that side. Most trails flow like a highway—stay to the right and pass slower traffic by moving into the middle.

SNOWMOBILE TRAILS

Groomed snowmobile trails stretch for miles in many places, usually on snow-covered roads. What they lack in interest they make up for in width, length, and frequent grooming. Touring and classic skiing are fun on snowmobile trails, but skate skiing on perfectly groomed trails that may be thirty or even forty feet wide is especially exciting.

Many snowmobile trails are groomed three or four times a week. Check with the local club or governmental agency for locations and grooming schedule. Early on weekday mornings is usually the best time to find fresh grooming and a lack of snowmobilers.

Keep in mind that snowmobile trails have been created for, yes, you guessed it, snowmobilers. Very few of them care if you use the trails, but it is bad form to scowl and turn up your nose at their smelly machines as they roar past. Many trail networks are the result of the hard work of active snowmobile clubs. If you ski on such trails often, find out what you can do to help out. If a trail or parking fee is assessed, be sure to pay it. Skiers are guests on these trails. Be courteous to any riders you meet.

Getting hit by a speeding snowmobile is a real concern. Wind and exertion can easily muffle the noise of a rapidly approaching machine. Be extra cautious near corners and do not even think about skiing at dusk.

In a report on conflicts on multiple-use trails, including those between skiers and snowmobilers, for the Federal Highway Authority, Roger Lohr recommends that when they hear a snowmobile approach cross-country skiers should get off the trail in a place where they can be easily seen. Skiers should give the snowmobilers room to pass, making sure their poles are out of the track, and be especially wary if either group is large. Although trail signage may indicate that the machine operator is the one who should yield, refusing to step off the trail because you have the right of way is not only very bad form, it may get you run over.

When there's ice and no snow, clip on Nordic Skates and go! (Photo: xczone.tv)

OTHER ALTERNATIVES

Grassy fields, parks, and golf courses covered with thin, wind-packed snow offer other options to stride and skate on. If you want to ski on a golf course, check first with the groundskeepers or risk their wrath.

In the spring, the freeze-and-thaw cycle tends to build an early-morning crust on the snow, which disappears as the temperature rises. As long as the crust holds, skiers can glide through woods, meadows, valleys, and even across mountainsides before the sun turns the snow to deep corn or slush. Skaters are especially fond of springtime "crust cruising." A word of caution, even though you may be skiing on thin, skinny skis using techniques usually reserved for groomed trails, this is backcountry skiing. Take extra clothes and provisions and be aware that the slog back to the trailhead may take hours if the snow suddenly softens or if a skinny ski or light pole not made to withstand backcountry conditions breaks.

LAKE AND RIVERS

Cold climates that produce little snow do provide safe, thick ice on lakes and rivers, creating ribbons and plateaus of pleasure for the skier who likes to float and fly over the snow instead of having to wade through it. Make sure the ice is safe and ski with a partner if you venture onto a frozen body of water. If the ice is safe but the snow is too thin to ski on, long speed-skating blades topped with a platform are available. You simply mount a cross-country ski skate binding on the platform, click in with your skating boots, grab your poles (or not), and go.

CHAPTER 9

Track Skiing Basics

This chapter builds on the descriptions of the basics of cross-country skiing found in Chapter 2, so beginners are encouraged to review those discussions before continuing here.

BALANCE IN MOTION

To succeed in either ski skating or the diagonal stride of classic skiing, you must

Balance in motion

be able to glide on one ski at a time while poling and moving toward the next ski. This is balance in motion.

Being able to balance on a moving ski starts (but does not end) with a good stance. Jump up and land as softly as you can. When you can land quietly without wobbling, you have discovered a good basic stance.

USING YOUR CORE MUSCLES

In order to keep your balance while moving you need to have strong core muscles. Your core muscles support and stabilize your trunk, and locating them is easy—just cough and you'll feel them contract. You can improve your awareness of these muscles and strengthen them through a variety of "functional exercise programs" (Pilates, stability ball exercises, mat exercises). One of the easiest ways to firm up your core muscles is to suck a point about an inch below your navel toward your spine while you run, jog, walk, or do any other exercise.

Strong and active core muscles limit how far you can be pushed out of balance and they can snap you back into balance as you ski. They take over balance duties so you can relax your arms and legs, allowing them to flex and extend to absorb bumps and dips in terrain. Unfortunately, many skiers have this backward. They hold their arms and legs rigid in search of stability and balance, while the core muscles of their stomach and back are flaccid and forgotten.

MOVING FORWARD

In skiing parlance, the word "core" refers not just to your core muscles but also to your center of gravity—think of the latter as being located somewhere near your belly button. No matter what you are doing, your center of gravity, or core, has to be balanced against your base of support (your feet if you are skiing, your hands if you are doing a handstand, the contact between your tires and the ground if you are on a bike) or you will fall over. As you glide forward or make a turn on skis, keeping your core balanced over your feet is more complex than simply standing still.

To stay in balance over a moving base of support such as a gliding ski, tip forward from your ankles. The idea is to move your core forward and toward where you are going. The faster you ski, the farther you will have to tilt forward to keep your core balanced against your moving base of support.

PLAYING WITH BALANCE

To find your own balance while you are in motion, put your skis on and play around with the following movements. As you glide over the snow, first reach for the sky, then pat your stomach, and finish by touching the snow. Then reverse the order. Repeat this sequence several times while sliding down a comfortable hill. For more balance challenges, hold your arms out to the side, then to the front, and then to the back as you slide. Make poling motions without your poles. Do a disco dance. Try skiing backwards.

Ski over little jumps (or big ones if you are bold). Lacking a jump in the terrain, start sliding and then jump up in the air off one foot, then off the other, then off both. Jump sideways. Jump forward. Jump back. Jump off one ski and land on that same ski in the middle of a skate or in the middle of a stride. Then jump from ski to ski while skating or striding (which is easier to do?). In all cases, land as softly as possible, setting your ski gently back onto the snow.

Put your poles aside and slide down a hill holding hands with a partner, clasping each other's shoulders or waists, or however else you can connect. Balance together on four skis, then on two skis. Grab a longer, larger pole, such as a piece of bamboo. Ski side by side with a partner with the pole held in front of you both. Ski on one foot as you lean away from one another. Then switch which foot you are on. Try it leaning in. Try to push each other over (be nice!) with or without holding the pole between you as you slide side by side.

As you play around with these and other activities that challenge your balance, remember to push your knees forward and over your toes to maintain ankle flex and the forward-falling position that keeps your core over a moving base of support (your feet and skis). To keep your ankles flexed, contract your core muscles by sucking that spot below your belly button toward your spine which keeps your pelvis neutral and should drive your knees toward your toes. Maintain a position and an attitude of relaxed tension, playful readiness, fierce suppleness, or whatever metaphor works for you as you play.

EFFECTIVE AND VERSATILE DOUBLE POLING

Mastering the technique of double poling will enhance your enjoyment of both classic and skate skiing.

Start by flexing forward from your ankles to move your torso over your poles. As you plant your poles, keep your hands up, as if you were "putting up your dukes" for a fight. This bent-elbow move will transfer more of the power from your trunk to your poles than will a straight-arm plant.

Apply pressure against your poles by flexing at the waist—contracting your stomach muscles rather than folding like a hinge and "falling through your poles." Then drive your elbows down using your upper back muscles (don't bend too deeply at the knees). Extend your arms to drive your hands toward the pole baskets, then finish with a push on the straps as you open your hands and fingers.

Flex forward from your ankles to move your torso over your poles.

Use your stomach and back muscles to double pole before extending your arms.

FINDING MORE POWER IN DOUBLE POLING

Simply falling forward (to start the double pole described above) creates a slight pause while your body weight shifts. This slight pause can cause your skis to move in a slow, fast, slow rhythm that is more tiring than if you maintain a more consistent ski speed.

To avoid this pause, start your double poling motion before your baskets ever touch the snow. Coil prior to planting your poles and then begin to push back against your poles right before they are planted, much as paddlers start their power stroke just before the blade touches the water. Catch your weight as it drops back against your poles on the coiled springs of your stomach, back, and arm muscles.

As your weight comes onto your poles your core muscles should be firm, your back rounded, and your ankles bent, creating a C shape. To tighten the C bring your shoulders toward your knees using your sit-up muscles. Drive your pole shafts back, keeping your elbows as high as possible and driving them up toward the sky as you follow through. This opens your chest and keeps your hips forward for the next catch and pole stroke. Note that compared to a more passive double pole, there is more bend at the knees which must be matched with an equal bend at your ankles to avoid falling too far behind your feet.

The instant power and quick recovery of this double pole technique makes it ideal for skating. When you have less glide, or want faster acceleration, end your pole stroke when your hands reach your thighs.

Coil as if preparing to jump forward just before your pole baskets hit the snow.

"Hang" your body weight on your poles and then drive your shoulders to your knees.

Drive your elbows toward the sky as you finish your double pole stroke.

From this position, bend your elbows to lift your hands as you bring your hips up and over your feet to be ready almost instantly for another cycle. This is especially useful in higher tempo skating, when passing other skiers, and during mass starts and other sprints.

GLIDING

Standard double poling technique calls for finishing on your heels. This may help your skis glide better, but it can also disrupt your balance. Rocking too far back can actually disrupt your glide, if it causes you to press your wax pocket into the snow when you rock forward for the next double pole. Maintain some forward flex in your ankle throughout the double-pole cycle to improve your balance and to ride a quieter ski. When your command of this is solid, experiment with moving back on your heels to discover how and when you can maximize the glide in specific conditions.

POLING PRINCIPLES

Let your arms swing back and forth from your shoulders—Imagine you have a weight in each of your hands as you let your arms pendulum back and forth.

Push on your poles with the handles in front of the baskets—Poles can't push you forward unless they are angled to the rear.

Push on your poles with your elbows bent—You'll get a stronger push with your arms bent than if you keep them straight.

Push toward the basket—Pushing "back" rather than "down" converts more of your effort into forward motion at the end of each stroke.

Use your body weight to help move you forward—Flex at the ankles to move your core over your poles.

Fall onto your poles, not through them—Avoid hinging at the waist and collapsing your body between your poles.

Drive your torso forward after the push—Avoid arching your back by keeping your core muscles firm (pull your belly button against your spine).

Recover your poles quickly—Concentrate on taking more time to push on your poles than on bringing them forward.

POLE PLAY

The two versions of double poling detailed above are not the only ways to double pole. Experiment with different ways to use your body weight and your strength to maintain a consistent speed that takes less effort. Plant your poles with your baskets farther behind the handles when digging for power on hills or in slow conditions. As glide increases with speed and conditions, you will need less power at the beginning of your stroke. Reach farther forward from your ankles at the start, flex less at the knees, and rely more on your body weight falling onto your poles to save energy in these situations.

DOWNHILL MANEUVERS

Many competent and downright excellent classic and skate skiers who have mastered the basics still struggle on the downhills, especially with turns. At first glance, this makes no sense. They are comfortable with speed, have excellent balance, and know how to move from ski to ski. So what's missing? They don't know how to balance on a ski that is sideslipping (sliding in a direction other than toward the tip of the ski).

LIFT THE FORWARD EDGE

One basic thing to remember when making a wedge turn or any other sideslipping maneuver is that you need to keep the forward edges of both skis raised to prevent them from catching in the snow and sending you sprawling.

Basic stance: ankles flexed, knees over toes, rounded back, hands up

STANCE

The same flexed and relaxed stance used while gliding on the flats is essential on hills. To maintain ankle, knee, and waist flex as gravity pulls you onward drive your knees toward your ski tips and keep your hands low and in front of you. Your ankles should flex enough so that if you looked down your knees would cover your toes. Don't stare—looking down for too long will cause you to straighten your legs.

TURN WITH YOUR FEET AND LEGS

As you turn and sideslip, make sure you turn your hips and torso less than you do your feet and skis.

In other words, as your skis turn across the hill, your hips and torso will face more toward the bottom of the hill than your tips will. This feels counterintuitive to your reptilian brain, which wants to turn up into the hill and hold onto the ground for dear life. Tame your inner reptile by doing this exercise: place your poles across your shoulders with your knuckles forward. With your tips facing straight downhill your poles will form one axis of a plus sign (+) with the other axis being your skis. As you turn across the hill, hold your hips and shoulders stable so that your poles turn less than your skis. This will bring your skis more in line with your poles and the plus sign will begin to merge into a single line.

Use the twist created by this maneuver to link one turn with the next. At the end of each turn you'll feel this twist build up as if you were a wound spring. To start a new turn, push the poles down the hill and across your feet. As you do, your legs, feet, and skis will unwind (and the plus sign will reappear), automatically starting the next turn.

BEND TO BALANCE

To sideslip, turn, and stop you need to edge your skis. Although you can do this by tipping the ski on edge with only your ankle, tilting your entire leg is more powerful and effective. That's the good news. The bad news is that tilting your leg pushes the rest of your body away from your feet, making it hard to avoid sliding out and falling. To avoid this, bend sideways at the waist to bring your torso, shoulders, and head back over your feet. During turns, your natural tendency is to bank with the turn like an

Bend sideways at the waist to stay over your feet as you edge your skis.

airplane or bicycle; this will cause you to fall into the hill. With your poles still across your shoulders, edge and turn while bending sideways at the waist to avoid banking. Keep the ends of both poles the same distance above the snow—the downhill hand should be lower than the uphill hand.

DOWNHILL TACTICS

To carry the most speed possible through the corners, step or skate turn. When things get too fast for that, keep your legs loose and bent, turn your skis more than your chest, and keep your shoulders level to the slope as you skid and sideslip to turn through the corners. Once stepping and skidding turns

Face the outside track with your chest as you point both knees around the corner.

are mastered, all that is left is learning how and when to step, skid, or both.

RIDING THE RAILS

Even on downhills with good tracks you will sometimes feel like your skis are going to stray out of the tracks when you attempt to stay in the grooves. To stay in control as you "ride the rails," envision where you would go if you did blow out. Turn at the waist and face your hips, chest, arms, and head in that direction as you roll your skis onto their edges, riding against the sides of the track. This will balance your weight over the outside ski and make it far more likely that you will stay in the tracks. If you do come out, you will be balanced over the outside ski as it skids forward and sideways

on edge. Step off its outside edge and continue to step turn through the corner to complete the turn.

ON FRESH, FIRM SNOW

Fresh, firm snow is ideal for wedge turns, parallel turns, or a combination of the two. When edged, narrow skis that lack sidecut may resist sideslipping and want to go straight. To avoid this problem, move into a sideslip before you start to turn. Lighten your skis by making a distinct upward movement (extend at the ankles, knees, and waist). Then roll your knees into the hill or the inside of the turn to lift the downhill edges slightly as you twist your feet to turn the skis sideways. Be sure to turn your skis with your feet and not with your torso (keep your eyes and your chest pointed down the trail or to the outside of the turn).

With your skis slightly edged and sliding sideways as you enter the turn, you'll be able to guide your skis by turning your feet and tipping or flattening your skis as needed. Balance over your outside ski by bending sideways at the waist. Flex your outside leg to avoid shying away from the turn or the bottom of the hill and falling backward.

As you become more confident and skilled you will be able to start some turns without this preparatory sideslip and to follow a more precisely skidded arc through the corner.

ON ICE

Skiers commonly try to edge more to get a grip on ice. This works about as well as slamming on the brakes while driving on ice. A better approach is to keep your speed

Drive both hands downhill and across your skis to stay over your feet.

low and make small and rapid step turns. Avoid any move that forces you to rely on one ski or one edge. If you need to bring your skis sideways for additional speed control, use more of a sideslip than a turn, with your skis turned well across the trail but delicately tipped on edge. If you have to edge more, drive both hands downhill and across your skis on either side of your feet, with your chest facing directly downhill as much as possible as you bend both sideways and forward at the waist.

If you slide out from this position, it is not so far to fall and you will land on your hip instead of your face. Once you are down, stay collected over your feet with your skis below you. Press the sides of your feet and skis into the snow to stop. Unfolding your body and flopping onto your belly to claw at the snow behind you with your hands won't work.

If you are more concerned about breaking your equipment than about coming to a stop, roll over onto your back and slide with your feet and hands in the air until you come to a stop.

Practice falling and stopping on icy trails before you face an urgent need to do so or stay off hills when it is icy.

ON REFREEZING SNOW

At the end of a warm day as the snow sets up, grabby and icy conditions prevail. This is tricky stuff. Use many small step turns to negotiate the corners and move quickly from foot to foot as if running in place even while going straight. Constantly lifting your skis prevents them from getting stuck in the slushy, freezing soup. Small, frequent steps also force you to keep moving your core forward to stay over your feet, which is what keeps you in the game in these tricky conditions.

ON GRABBY SNOW

When the snow is grabby and you attempt to push out into a wedge or make a parallel turn at high speed, the pressure of the thick snow against the boot as it turns sideways with the ski is often great enough to stop you in your tracks and send you headfirst off the trail. If you want to make parallel or wedge turns on lightweight gear in such conditions, start your turn before you pick up too much speed.

Step and skate turns are better when the snow is grabby, but they are still tricky. Since the ski will not slide sideways, you will not be able to adjust it after you set it

Step quickly and with commitment onto each new ski when making step turns at speed.

back in the snow, so your moves must be very accurate. As your speed increases, your steps need to be quick and aggressive.

You come quickly to a stop when you fall in thick snow. This can be joint wrenching and can break equipment if you are going fast. Step and skate turns do not dissipate speed, so keep your speed down or know when and where to bail out. Sit down sooner rather than later.

To prepare for making step turns in challenging conditions, practice in advance.

Make hundreds of tiny, frenetic step turns back and forth as you go down a groomed trail in decent snow conditions.

TELEMARK CONDITIONS

If you have some experience with it, the telemark turn may be a successful choice in grabby snow, including deeper powder conditions. On classic and skating gear, this is the time to bring out the old-school version—rear tip against the front ski or foot with the skis angled to each other. Ride that big curve and then move out of the turn, forward and down the trail, to avoid falling inside as the turn finishes. Read more about the telemark turn in Chapter 14.

Turn two straight skis into one long curved ski with a telemark turn.

CHAPTER 10

The grace of striding. (Photo: Don Portman)

Classic Skiing

The central technique of classic skiing is the diagonal stride. Striding is how people have moved on skis since skis were invented. It started as an adaptation of walking and running when skis were being used as basic transportation in unpacked snow. The diagonal refers to the cross-lateral movement of the skier's arms and legs—left arm and right leg forward, right arm and left leg back. With modern track equipment and a firmly packed trail, the diagonal stride transcends its utilitarian roots to become a continuous motion of power and grace. The pleasures of the diagonal stride are elusive but addictive. Many who fall prey to its allure are seduced into a life-long pursuit of the perfect kick and glide.

THE DIAGONAL STRIDE

A powerful and efficient diagonal stride combines a forward-falling stance, a long push with the gripping leg, a quick and deliberate forward swing of the rear leg, a quiet glide, and effective poling. The exercises and drills in this chapter separate and exaggerate the movements of the diagonal stride to make it easier to learn. Play with the drills and exercises to get a feel for the movements, but don't mistake the parts for the whole. Avoid paralysis by analysis. Stay relaxed and have fun—the rest will come.

A gradual uphill on a groomed trail is the best place to put these ideas and suggestions into practice—modern skis and grooming create so much glide that you can quickly get going fast enough on the flats to make it difficult to maintain the rhythm of the diagonal stride.

USING YOUR POLES WHILE LEARNING

Many books and instructors recommend putting your poles aside and learning how to ski without them at first. This is good advice, since trying too hard with your poles tends to mess up what you are doing with your feet. The problem is that poling is part of skiing, so why not learn how to ski with your poles from the very start. You may need to set your poles aside when you work on some specific leg motions of the diagonal stride, but keep them with you as long as they do not get in the way. To avoid most problems caused by poles as you learn, keep your arms bent and your poles angled back.

Lead with your thigh and knee as you move from ski to ski.

STAY FORWARD

The natural tendency when bringing the rear leg forward as you move from ski to ski is to lead with the foot. This puts your core behind your front foot, forcing you to lift yourself up and onto that foot every time you want to glide.

Flex your front ankle to avoid leading with your foot as you swing your rear leg forward. Bring the rest of you along for the ride by thinking of your pelvis as a bowl full of water with the rim running from your spine around your hipbones to your belly. Deepen your front ankle flex as your rear leg swings forward and prevent spilling any water from the front or back of the "bowl." This will bring your core and torso forward with your new ski.

Some practice at home in the yard without skis will help you hone this crucial move. Facing up a slight hill, stand in a relaxed and ready stance. Bend your ankle to move onto the balls of your feet. Press your pelvis, hips, and thigh forward until you have to shuffle a foot forward to keep

Shuffle forward onto a bent ankle.

from falling face first onto the grass. Do not step—stepping puts your foot in front of your knee and blocks continued forward movement.

To avoid the urge to move too fast with strides that are too big, shuffle onto a bent ankle. The length of each shuffle should be dictated by how far your core is pressed forward. Try this same drill once you are back on skis.

RIDE THE RAILS

Another key to unlocking the power and grace of the diagonal stride is skiing on one ski at a time. To help develop this skill, imagine that the parallel grooves of the set tracks are the two steel rails of a narrow gauge railway. Guide each ski onto the snow by pressing your thigh and knee forward and down each separate track. Shift slightly sideways to move over each foot as you glide. Your right eye will move toward your right foot, then your left eye will move toward your left foot as you shuffle from ski to ski. Pause to glide on each ski while you are over there.

SKIM THE GROUND AND LAND ON THE RUNWAY

The best airline pilots bring a jetliner down so smoothly that it is hard to tell when the plane quits flying and the wheels touch the runway. The transition between air and earth is seamless. Your ski should follow a similar "glide path" as it approaches a landing onto the track.

As your leg starts to swing forward, adjust the approach angle of your ski by using your ankle to lift the rear tip. Close the gap

Shift sideways over each ski so that your right eye moves toward your right foot, and your left eye moves toward your left foot.

between your heel and the ski and bring the ski parallel to the snow. As you bend your rear ankle, your front ankle will bend too, accelerating your core forward and increasing your forward fall.

After what was your rear ski passes in front of the foot that is pressed into the snow, shift your weight onto that ski and keep it gliding forward by continuing to press your thigh and knee forward. As you transfer your weight to the forward ski, you should be on your whole foot. If you land on your toes the ski has been brought down too soon or you are not bending your ankle enough to lift the tip and close the gap beneath your heel as you bring the ski through.

This may be easier to understand back on your grassy hill at home without skis on. Three- or four-inch-tall grass works best. Stand in a ready stance and then move forward onto the balls of your feet by flexing your ankles. Swing your leg through as described above. If you bring your foot down too soon it will be obvious because you will hit the grass with your toes and abruptly halt the forward swing of your leg. To swing through without hitting your toes, flex your ankle to brush the grass with the sole of your foot for as long as possible before shifting onto that foot. The longer you can brush the grass with your foot, the farther forward you can stride.

Back on snow, a distinct slap as you swing your rear ski through and onto the snow will tell you if you are bringing your foot down too soon. Skiing with your core centered front-to-back between your feet instead of over your front foot may be the cause. This is easy to check. Glance down after you move onto the next ski and see if your front knee is blocking your view of your front foot. If you can see your foot, you are skiing with your core between your feet instead of over your front foot. If that is the case, go back to shuffling from ski to ski and focus on keeping your front ankle well flexed at all times. Build from there, always moving

Bend the ankle of your rear foot to lift your toe and bring the ski parallel to the snow as it swings forward.

Brush the grass with the sole of your shoe.

onto the forward ski with a flexed ankle.

So what's the point of all this? In the diagonal stride increased glide comes from increased speed, and speed comes from increased stride length and tempo. Stride length can be increased when you are able to move farther forward before your new lead foot is weighted. Learning to make a smooth landing maximizes the length of each stride.

LEG SWING

Powering your rear leg through into the next stride as if you were kicking a ball as far as possible adds tremendous momentum to your foot and ski. A quick, explosive motion translates into more speed and more glide.

Keep in mind that you want your ski to fly forward along the ground instead of arcing into the air as a ball would do, so concentrate on driving your hips and thigh forward and down the track instead of following through into an upward arc. Keep your knee over your foot as you move onto the next ski.

TIMING AND RELAXATION

Skiing takes effort; save energy by relaxing any unneeded muscles as you ski. Relax the muscles you do use as soon as you are no longer using them. When they are needed, they will be rested and ready for a concentrated effort. Relax more than you work while skiing, and the timing will come.

LEG PUSH

Leg push is what produces the power that creates speed. An effective leg push begins as your feet pass each other with both legs coiled beneath you and all of your weight on what was your front leg.

The push-off onto the next ski is powered by an extension of your leg as well as your ankle. You can add speed and pop to your push-off by deepening the flex of your ankle, knee, and hip through the quick down-and-up used in any jumping motion. This motion comes right before your leg

extension begins and is often so quick that it is hard to see.

As your rear leg moves forward of the standing leg, extend your weighted leg but keep your heel down as long as possible so that the ski continues to grip the snow. Then open your ankle and push off through the ball of your foot, directing the force both down and back, while moving your core forward and up in an arc that resembles the upward and flat part of a basketball's trajectory during a free throw.

As you get moving and stretch out into the stride, your rear leg will naturally extend backward in line with your spine. Swinging it back intentionally tends to pull your core backward and will impede your forward motion.

Legs coiled as feet pass. Right leg is swinging forward in this photo.

Continue to rise up and forward from push-off. Glide and begin to pole as your leg straightens.

RIDE THE GLIDE

You can extend the glide a bit as your front leg straightens after the push-off. Slide your foot forward to reduce some of the pressure on the wax pocket by shifting your weight toward your heel. This move takes advantage of your core's up and forward trajectory from the last push-off.

Don't slide your core backward when riding the glide—slide your foot forward by extending your ankle. Rising onto a straightening leg also puts you into a strong poling position.

EFFECTIVE POLING

Effective poling mimics the action of the legs to a degree. Relax your arm at the end of your pole push and then let gravity begin to swing it forward. As your hand nears your thigh, concentrate your efforts into a quick and forceful forward swing of your elbow as you raise your hand into position. Plant your poles by or in front of your toes—the faster you are going, the farther forward they will be planted.

The pole plant should be precise and deliberate—stop the forward swing of your pole with your fingers and guide your pole tip into the snow. This abrupt stop of your forward arm swing adds momentum to your glide.

You can reach farther and apply more power when your shoulder moves forward with your arm. Imagine that your shoulder is hinged at your sternum and reach with your shoulder blade rather than rotating your trunk around your spine.

To practice diagonal poling, single stick around on the flats (use alternate poles one after the other) without using your legs. Pull yourself past your pole with your abdominal and back muscles, then complete the pole stroke by pushing with your back, arm, and hand muscles (see *Effective and Versatile Double Poling* in Chapter 9).

Effective poling helps keep your skis moving. To maintain a consistent speed, begin your pole stroke as soon as you move onto the next ski and before the next leg push or kick begins. The exact timing will depend on how well your ski is gliding. In any case, the pole stroke should start before the forceful forward swing of your rear leg. This is a syncopated rhythm which may take some practice. To develop the rhythm, focus on recovering your poles quickly and planting them as soon as the basket swings forward and into position. In some conditions this may be a little soon, but that is better than the more common mistake of poling too late.

GET A GRIP

A quick and forceful leg swing combined with effective poling is all you need to glide and have fun on the flats. The secret to climbing hills, however, is getting your skis to consistently and reliably grip with a minimum of effort.

The concentrated camber underfoot in a classic ski is like having springs beneath your feet. While you are gliding, the camber

Glide position with weight spread over the whole foot.

Flex your ankle to move over the front half of your foot.

spreads your weight across the entire ski, keeping the middle unweighted. To grip the snow, you have to compress the camber, or spring, which is constructed so that it is easier to compress near the front of the bindings. When you want your skis to grip, move forward and place all of your weight over the front half of your foot. The simplest way to move from glide to grip is to flex your ankle.

To ensure grip on a hill, move onto the ski and keep your ankle flexed and your weight over the front half of your foot. Sliding onto your heel for glide is dangerous, since most slips occur while moving back from the heel to the ball of the foot. After you discover how to keep your weight over your forefoot for reliable grip, work on adding glide whenever you can.

The secret to both uphill grip and glide is learning to feel the ski and the snow though the sole of your foot to sense when it will glide, when it will slip, and when it will grip. To move your weight forward to grip, increase the flex of your ankle. To move the ski forward and your weight back to extend your glide, straighten your ankle.

ADJUST TO THE HILL

Skiers often have trouble climbing hills because they fail to adjust their degree of forward lean to the slope of the hill. As you ski up the incline of the hill, straighten your stance to maintain the same angle between your body and your skis as you would use on the flats. A simple way to adjust your body position relative to the slope

Match the flex of your waist and ankle.

Lift your body up the hill with a smooth and powerful leg and arm push. Keep your movements short and snappy to keep your core over a flexed ankle.

is to raise your gaze to the crest of the hill and match the flex of your waist to the flex of your ankle. If you over-flex at the waist with your chest out in front and your butt behind, it will be impossible to press the ski into the hill.

Jogging up the hill will help keep you moving if you tend to stall, but then you are running instead of skiing. To ski uphill instead of jogging, eliminate the up-and-down bobbing but keep the quick and light motions. Ski columnist Biff America, aka Jeffrey Bergeron, describes this smooth forward motion as rolling a marble up the hill beneath your lead foot.

TAKE YOUR TIME

If you spend any time at all skiing at a Nordic center, it will not be long until some old Scandinavian floats by going twice as fast and working half as hard. The good news is that the more you ski, the better you get. The bad news is that it takes time to get good at the diagonal stride. You can pick up where you left off with skating after a few strokes. For diagonal stride, each time you go out it seems to take three or four kilometers just to remember how to do it.

Ski as fast as you can and as slow as you can as you feel your way into the diagonal stride. Somewhere in the middle is where you will find the best combination for you of tempo, quiet glide, and a long push. Regardless of your tempo, always maintain a crisp weight transfer from ski to ski.

Ski as low as you can and ski as erect as you can. Once again somewhere in the middle will usually be the most efficient blend for you of deeply flexing for power and riding on your bones for increased endurance.

WHAT IT LOOKS LIKE

There is more to the diagonal stride than meets the eye. Here's what to look for behind the dash and flash.

Skier moves onto a flexed ankle. The knee and waist are also flexed and the spine is parallel to the shin of the front leg. The front knee leads the foot as weight is transferred to the lead ski, which glides smoothly forward. Extension of the rear ankle signals the end of the leg push and complete weight transfer to the next ski. The rear arm fully extends and the fingers release the handle of the rear pole.

Rear leg is relaxed as it swings back. Core is behind the front foot. The torso provides a counterbalance to the core and rear leg.

The core rises as a result of the last push-off. With weight transfer completed, the front leg straightens as the hips and torso move forward and the knee and waist open. Opening of the front ankle occurs from sliding the front foot forward and not from dropping the core back.

Arm is bent at the elbow as the pole push begins. Pole angle to the snow varies with speed, but the hand is high and the elbow is forward of the torso and outside of the shaft. Core continues to rise and move forward.

The core anticipates and leads the movement toward the next leading ski. Front ankle flexes to start movement onto the next ski with a forward fall. Rear leg is pulled forward by gravity. The upper leg swings forward from the hip like a pendulum. The skier flexes at the waist and the knee to keep the

Stride onto a flexed ankle.

Rear leg swings back as the core rises.
Photo: Fischer Skis

Body moves forward toward the next ski as the front ankle flexes and the rear leg swings forward.

spine parallel to the front shin as ankle flex increases.

Front ankle is deeply flexed as feet pass each other. Core is forward of the foot and the ski grips the snow and stops before the feet pass. Ankle and knee of the rear leg are also flexed as the ski swings beneath the hip. Poling hand is near the thigh; recovering hand is driven forward and is in front of the body.

Heel stays on the ski as the leg is being extended. Simultaneously, the next leading foot moves in front of the

push-off foot before weight is transferred. Heel lifts off the ski after the feet pass, then the ankle opens.

The next lead ski is set in motion before moving onto it. The knee, thigh, hips, and torso continue forward after the foot stops, moving the core well in front of the foot and driving the ski forward. Before weight is transferred to the next lead ski, it is up to speed, skimming the snow like a hovercraft.

Drive your entire body forward to stay over your foot and ski as it moves forward. Note that the left ski is still unweighted in this photo.

Timing of the kick: ski stops, feet pass. Right leg is swinging forward in this photo.

TRANSITIONS

Transitions help you conserve energy and cover ground with the most efficient combination of techniques. These benefits really became apparent to me on an April day in Norway while skiing from hut to hut on a very long lake. We'd been at it for some time, and all I wanted to do was get to the end of this seemingly endless journey. At one point, I found myself out in front,

rhythmically skiing along in a hypnotic trance. Slowly, I realized that the dot I had been watching grow in size was the much-longed-for hut. That is when I came out of my trance and noticed that I was no longer skiing with distinct and separate techniques. My body had taken over from my mind and was mixing and matching to keep moving forward with the least effort. Two double poles and one kick. Two kicks and one double pole. One single arm pole with two

MORE TIPS AND SUGGESTED LEARNING ACTIVITIES

Body Position

- Cup your body as if you were hugging a very large beach ball. This is the basic stance from which you flex and extend while skiing.
- Experiment with flexing only at the hip, or only the knees, or only at the ankles while striding. Then try flexing equally at the hip, knee, and ankle. Experiment with a tall stance (not much flex) and with a deeply flexed ankle, knee, and hip. Discover what works best for you.
- Keep arms and shoulders moving in your direction of travel, down the track. Avoid any excess rotation of the upper body.

Grip, Timing, and Push-off

- Concentrate on foot positioning and feel. Discover what grip feels like through the soles of your feet and what you have to do to create that feeling.
- Leg timing is ski stops, feet pass, and then weight is transferred to the next ski.
- Quickly increase the flex in your knee and ankle a split second before you begin to extend your leg for the kick. Mimic the down–up motion you would use to spike the needle on a bathroom scale. This increases the pressure on your wax pocket, helps your ski to grip, and powers your forward extension. This all happens quicker than you can blink your eye.
- *Leap* from ski to ski. Then back off and move from ski to ski with the same quick and concentrated effort but eliminate any unneeded up motion. Land each ski on the snow as if you were stroking the fur of a large cat with your foot.

Poling

- Swing your arm forward to eliminate excess shoulder movement. Point your thumb down the track as your arm swings forward.
- Poling should start before the kick. To help syncopate your arm and leg, wait until your poling hand brushes the thigh of your weighted leg before swinging your other leg forward and beginning your kick. This exaggeration of the delay between the start of the pole stoke and the kick will give you a feel for the timing.
- Use sound to help with pole timing. Listen for the pole basket to hit first, then for the ski to hit—click (pole plant)...plop (ski onto track)...click...plop. See how long a delay you can create, then find the amount of delay that is the most effective.

Relaxation

- Spend more time relaxed than you do applying power. Concentrate your exertions so you can snap and pop from ski to ski, then relax and glide when you arrive on each ski. Allow gravity and momentum to help maintain your forward motion and to start the movement toward your next ski as you briefly relax and glide.
- After completing your poling, relax your arms and upper body to let gravity begin to swing

your pole forward. To check if you are truly relaxed, PSIA Demo Team member Dan Clausen suggests that you have a friend hold your arms behind you as if you had just completed a double pole. Totally relax your arms, back, and shoulders so that your arms swing forward on their own whenever your friend releases them. Take this relaxation back into your double and single poling. Once your poles start forward from the pull of gravity, snap them forward with concentrated effort to recover your poles quickly.

Remember when doing any drill that accentuates or demonstrates an extreme position to return to the unexaggerated position or maneuver and integrate what you have learned.

kicks. Whatever it took to maintain the flow. This was skiing in the zone, far beyond any thoughts or concerns about technique.

To experience your own zone, try some of the transitions listed below, then make up some of your own. Practicing in the spaces between the designated techniques is fun and will teach you a lot about efficient movement on skis.

Kick-double pole. To reach even farther forward when double poling power your extension with a kick, or extension, of the push-off leg. For maximum power, complete the kick before planting your poles. The timing is kick, extend, double pole, glide. Let your arms relax and fall forward on the glide, then kick again as you bring them forward for the next pole plant.

It is easy to look like you are kicking between double poles when all you are doing is reaching a little farther forward by using your rear leg as a counterbalance for your arms and torso. To make sure you are actually kicking, drop your poles for a while and ski around without them, while practicing the timing and leg and arm motions of the kick-double pole.

Feet together is an awkward place to start a kick, so most skiers slide one foot in front of the other at the end of the double pole stroke to prepare for the next kick. Flex the ankle of the foot in front as you drive that knee forward and over the foot to start the next kick. Sliding the rear foot in front after each kick keeps you kicking with the same foot. Sliding the standing foot in front each time sets you up to alternate the foot you kick with.

From stride to double pole. Skip a pole plant during one stride, letting the pole basket swing forward as you wait for the other arm to recover, then plant both poles and begin to double pole; or you can leave one hand back at the end of a pole stroke and wait for the other to join it there, and then start your double pole by swinging both arms forward.

From double pole to stride. Move onto one ski as you swing both hands up for the next double pole but only plant one pole to start the diagonal pole motion. Stall the other pole out in front by letting the basket swing forward as you wait for the rhythm of your feet to catch up with that pole.

CHAPTER 11

The excitement of skating

Skate Skiing

Although skiers for centuries have spread their tips to fly over the snow whenever they found fast and firm conditions, skating as a distinct technique is a relatively recent phenomenon. It was made possible by a revolution in cross-country ski technology in the late 1970s that gave rise to lighter skis made with fiberglass and synthetic bases, which offered more glide and higher speeds. Skating is constantly evolving as specialized equipment, specialized trail design and grooming, and new skate techniques are developed to take advantage of specific conditions.

Skating is faster than diagonal striding for two main reasons. The simplest is that no grip wax is used, so skating skis glide better. The second reason is more complex—unlike the classic skier whose foot motion consists of glide, stop, glide, stop, a skate skier moves forward on skis that never come to a complete stop and can even accelerate during the push-off onto the next ski. This allows a skate skier to maintain speed and momentum more consistently than a classic skier.

BASIC LEG SKATING

Ski skating looks and feels pretty much as you would imagine. Skate skiers angle the skis and move from one to the other. If you have skated on ice, in-line, or roller skates you already know the basic motion.

The best place to give skating a try is at a Nordic center. Choose lightweight skis (no wider than 50mm and no heavier than 1500 grams) and wax them from tip to tail for glide. Find a flat, groomed trail to get the basics down. Put your poles aside and concentrate on your leg and foot motions when you start. Save yourself time and aggravation by staying on the flats until you have the balance and experience you need to relax and glide up the hills. If you need to climb a hill to a better practice place, herringbone up on your edges.

THE CHARLIE CHAPLIN DRILL

Skating is all about moving forward. To get started, stand on your skis in a relaxed position facing a very slight uphill on a firmly packed trail. Open the tips of your skis so that there is about a foot and a half of space between them. Edge your skis slightly to the inside and push both skis forward. To avoid doing the splits bring first one and then the other back in beneath you with a motion similar to Charlie Chaplin's trademark shuffle. Rock back and forth from ski to ski as you glide forward a short way on each ski.

As you get going, it will seem like both skis are determined to squirt out from underneath you. Keep things under control by not opening the tips of your skis too far and staying light on your feet. Avoid straightening your ankles and pulling up in a stiff scarecrow stance, which will make it hard to move forward at all. Guard against dropping back and squatting between your feet in the outhouse stance, which will keep you planted between your feet and prevent you from experiencing the glide that only comes from moving completely from ski to ski. A strong and stable core is needed to keep your hips over your feet and your ankles bent, so remember to suck your belly button toward your spine (see *Using Your Core Muscles* in Chapter 9).

This toes-out, falling-forward rocking

QUICK TIPS FOR CROSSOVERS

Street and ice skaters—Finish your skate stroke by immediately bringing your foot forward, beneath your body. If you let it fall behind you as you would on ice or in-line skates, you'll drive the tip of the ski into the snow. Don't worry about crossing your tails behind you, they will clear each other by the time you skate onto the forward ski.

Skateboarders, snowboarders, and other board and scooter riders—The major difference, of course, is that instead of pushing with one foot and gliding on the other, you need to glide from foot to foot, balancing strongly on the front ski after each skate. Concentrate on pushing forward onto the next ski instead of pushing back.

Alpine skiers—With less supportive boots and narrower skis, you'll have to use finesse to balance over your feet instead of leaning against your boots to stay upright. Don't let the lack of metal edges intimidate you. It's easy to get them to grip the snow if you remember to move forward off the edge instead of pushing back against it. Gravity is no longer the primary motive force—you are. Focus on moving forward.

Adding Poles. Skating poles are longer than the poles used for striding or alpine skiing, so bend your elbows and bring your hands up to chest level when you plant them. A host of poling problems can be avoided simply by not putting much power into your poles at first.

shuffle is the essence of skating—gliding on one ski at a time while continually moving toward the next ski. There are two common mistakes that new skaters make at this point: pushing back and trying to step forward.

Pushing back creates a lot of fuss but very little glide or power. It is like spinning your tires—most of the power is wasted behind you. As you move from ski to ski, apply just enough pressure to get your "tires" (the inside edges of your skis) to grip and use the rest of your horsepower to accelerate smoothly forward.

Trying to step forward as if you were walking or striding does not work. Stepping forward off the ball of your foot will send a skating ski scooting backward since there is nothing on the bottom to make it grip the snow. Instead, let the gliding ski take you forward while your other foot and leg swing back in beneath you. Then rock over onto the next ski and repeat.

Spend some time skiing like Charlie Chaplin with these tips in mind. When you are ready, risk a little more and lean farther forward from your ankles until you feel as if you are falling between your skis. You will be surprised how fast you can go as long as your legs and feet can keep up!

THE SKATE POSITION

To achieve the proper V position with your feet, turn your toes out by rotating your thigh bones in your hip sockets. Keep your knees aligned with your toes (as you bend your knee it should move toward your ski tip).

Explore this position without your skis on. Stand in one place and shift sideways from one turned-out foot to the other, while keeping your upper body and your pelvis facing straight ahead. From this position, increase the flex of your ankles until you start to fall forward. To catch your falling body, bring one turned-out leg forward, skimming the ground with the side and the sole of your shoe. Shift sideways onto your turned-out foot and keep falling forward. It is crucial that you skim the ground with your foot as it comes forward. If you step forward you are likely to end up with your foot too far in front, which will halt your forward fall. If you were on a lawn, both your big toe and the inside of your heel would brush

Shuffle forward from one turned-out foot onto the next.

the grass as each foot shuffled forward.

It may help to place your hands on your hips to press your core forward. Wait until you feel like you are about to fall on your face before you set your forward skimming foot on the ground and move onto it for support. This is the basic movement used to move from foot to foot in all the various skate techniques, regardless of the poling rhythm.

COWBOY BALANCE

Once you can move forward from ski to ski without pushing back or stepping forward, the next task is to become comfortable gliding on only one ski. An unexpected icon can help here. Imagine John Wayne with chaps

Glide and balance on one ski as the other ski and foot slowly shuffles forward.

on and a six-gun at his side, riding into Dodge City just after a blizzard has covered the streets with snow. He swings down off his horse, pulls a pair of skating skis out of his rifle scabbard, and clips into them. After the long cold ride, his stiff and saddle-sore legs stay bowed as he skates up the street, rocking from ski to ski as if he was still on his horse.

Imitate the Duke headed to the saloon for a hot toddy as you skate slowly up a very slight hill, balancing on each ski in turn as you hold the other ski out to the side. Cowboy balance helps you develop a long glide and a long push-off by forcing you to stay supported on one ski as you move slowly toward the next.

Notice that if you balance on one ski for too long you will "stall out." To avoid this, let your airborne ski slowly fall back in place. It should touch the snow just in time to let you slowly rock onto it. Think of this as slowly losing your balance as you move from ski to ski, which is a good description of the dynamic balance required for skating.

Slowing things down will help you discover the precise timing of when to transfer your weight from ski to ski. As you become more adept at skating, come back to this drill (do it both with and without poles). Slowing down will reveal the glitches in balance and rhythm that speed and a high tempo can hide.

A THOUSAND STEPS

This drill helps you develop the habit of continuously moving your core forward as you move from foot to foot. To review the basic step turn before trying to a make a thousand of them, refer to Chapter 2.

Start on a gentle downhill trail that you would be comfortable navigating without making any turns or braking maneuvers. After you start to glide downhill, make as many very small step turns in one direction as you can before you reach the side of the trail, then switch directions and do the same. When this is easy, move on to a steeper trail.

Align your core with where the new ski will be.

See how steep you can go while controlling your speed with just step turns.

BALANCE INTO THE FUTURE

Coaches and instructors insist that you must be able to balance on one ski if you want to skate. This is only a partial truth. The complete truth is that you need to balance on one ski but continue to move forward.

An example will help. If your ski wants to squirt forward when you step onto it while taking one of your thousand steps, then you are balancing either in the present or the past. Balancing into the future means directing your core toward where you will soon be. Otherwise, your core will fall behind your feet and you will fall on what is behind your core, otherwise known as your butt.

To experience balancing into the future, find a section of trail that contains a sweeping corner, either on a flat or after a downhill run. Get up some speed and step turn around the corner while imagining you have two headlights mounted on your pelvic bones and pointing forward. Move so that the headlights continually light up the middle of the trail as it bends around the corner. Another approach is to keep the trail framed between your hands as you negotiate the turn. Either of these techniques will serve to align your core and torso with your future position (where you soon will be).

As speed increases, you may find it hard to stay forward, which is a crucial part of moving into the future. To avoid sitting back as your speed increases, flex forward at the ankles even more than usual.

TIPPING IS NOT A CITY IN CHINA

When you first move onto a ski, it will be relatively flat to the snow. As your ski glides forward and toward the side of the trail, it will tip on edge provided your core continues moving forward and up the trail. The highest angle between the snow and the base of your ski is reached as you push-off onto the next ski.

If your ski does not roll from flat to edge during each skate, then you are either aligned with your ski as it glides off toward the bushes or your ankle is rolling outward as your leg tips. If your ankle is rolling out, press down on your big toe and the ball of your foot to bring your foot back into normal alignment with your leg as your ski moves out from underneath your core.

THE PUSH-OFF

The push-off is the last thing to add to your skate, but it makes the difference between a skater who struggles around the trails and one who glides and flies over the snow regardless of terrain.

The push-off is powered by an extension of your leg as well as your ankle. You can add speed and pop to your push-off by deepening the flex of your ankle, knee, and hip through the quick down-and-up used in any jumping motion. This motion comes right before your leg extension begins and is often so quick that it is hard to see. Keep your heel on the ski until your leg is fully extended, then extend your ankle and finish off on the ball of your foot. To avoid pushing back, drive your toes up and forward as you move

Moving forward and onto the next ski rolls the weighted ski up on edge.

off the ski. This helps to bring your leg and foot forward and back beneath your body in preparation for the next skate.

To get the most bang for your buck maintain your toes-turned-out-from-the-hip-socket skate position during your push-off. To get a feel for how this works, try the following exercises, by playing around either on or off the snow.

Start on one foot with your toes turned out from the hip as described above, and choose a direction to represent straight ahead in relation to the angle of your foot. Keep your pelvis and shoulders stable and facing your straight-ahead reference as you push sideways off your foot with equal pressure on your toes, arch, and heel. This should move you sideways and forward at a 90-degree angle from where the toes of your push-off foot were pointed.

Now try this again, but this time twist your pelvis toward your lifted foot as you extend your push-off leg. Did you go as far or feel as strong? Twisting to align with the lifted foot sucks up power into the soft tissue around your joints and causes you to lift the heel on your push-off leg prematurely, shortening your push-off.

Effective and efficient skate technique is more than a step-by-step assemblage of each element. Combining the two elements of balance into the future and push-off is a case in point: some movement of your core to anticipate the upcoming change in direction will be required to maintain your balance into the future. To avoid losing any of the power that each push-off generates, complete any movements to anticipate the future before the push-off begins, and limit your movement to just what is needed to align with where your core will soon be and not where the next ski tip will point.

Make sure your push-off is angled directly sideways, that is, perpendicular to your ski, by adjusting your alignment and stance so that you feel equal pressure from your toes to your heel as you extend your leg. It should feel like the entire sole of your boot is welded to the ski from the moment you start to push until your heel lifts and your ankle opens to complete the push-off on the ball of your foot.

Speed skaters practice this same push by standing next to a wall. They coil over

In fast conditions in a narrower V, push sideways off one ski and let the next ski carry you forward.

In slower conditions in a wider V, leg extension during push-off contributes more to moving you forward and up the trail.

their outside foot and initiate the push-off by picking up their inside foot and falling toward the wall. As they tilt sideways, they explode directly sideways off the weighted outside foot, pushing their hip and shoulder into the wall. Do not start this drill too far away from the wall unless you want to hurt yourself.

With your skis in a narrow V on flat and fast trails, pushing directly sideways will create the ski speed needed to keep your skis gliding forward—all you need to do is go along for the ride on each new ski before pushing off onto the next. In steeper terrain and slower snow, your skis will be angled more to the trail in a wider V. In these situations, a powerful sideways push-off will contribute more to moving your body forward as well as creating ski speed.

When you push off sideways against your ski, it is caught between the force of your push-off and the resistance of the snow against the edge. Unless you have totally missed the glide wax for the day, your ski will squirt forward from between these two opposing forces like a watermelon seed from between your fingers.

To maximize the amount of squirt, or acceleration, from each push-off, keep your weight against the ski until you complete the move. In other words, to be able to push off of your foot you must be supported by it. Time your movements so that you push off from ski to ski instead of falling from ski to ski. You have moved off the ski too soon if you feel little pressure along the inside of your foot as you push off or if the edge slides out.

GRADUATION—PUTTING IT ALL TOGETHER

The final step in your skating education is to integrate all these basics into a powerful and comfortable skate using just your legs. After that, you can begin the graduate course work of complementing and extending each glide with your poles. Take your skate out for a spin in rolling terrain to study for your final exam, but stay off the larger hills and continue to skate without your poles for just a bit longer. As you skate around, play with these extremes:

Skate with very straight legs, and then skate in a crouch. Move from ski to ski by falling from ski to ski, then contrast that with coiling over one foot and exploding sideways. Edge slowly from the moment you move onto the ski until you push off, then glide on a flat ski and edge all at once just before you push off. Skate at speed on the flats with a wide V and then skate up hills with a narrow V. Somewhere in the middle of all these extremes is the technique that will work best for you, but you need to find out exactly where your sweet spots are in the spectrum.

Play with your foot and leg recovery. Relax and let your unweighted leg fall in with no effort on your part, then see what it is like to bring your foot and leg as far forward as you can before you move onto it. Between each skate try bringing your heels in and clicking them together like Dorothy wishing to go back to Kansas. See if you can swing your leg way back after you push off and then power it forward as if you were

WHAT IT LOOKS LIKE

Here's what good skating should look like:

A

B

C

D

A. Heel stays on the ski as the leg is extended. The heel lifts off the ski only after the leg has been fully extended and the ankle opens, to complete the push-off through the ball of the foot. The ski continues to move forward after push-off as it lifts off the snow as shown in photos D and E.

B. The next lead ski is set in motion before moving onto it. As the leg swings in beneath the body, the pelvis, thigh, and knee move toward the ski tip, setting the ski in motion. As weight is transferred to the new lead ski, it is up to speed, skimming the snow like a hovercraft.

C. Skier moves onto a flexed ankle. The knee and waist are also flexed and the spine is parallel to the shin of the front leg. The front knee leads the foot as weight is transferred to the new lead ski, which glides smoothly forward. Complete extension of the rear leg and foot signals the end of the push-off.

D. The ski swings out to the side after push-off and then back in. Skier relaxes the leg after push-off; gravity starts it back toward the body.

E. Pelvis is driven quickly up and over the skating foot. After weight transfer is competed, the standing leg is extended, bringing the hips and torso forward as the knee and waist open. Some ankle flex is maintained, and shoulders stay over or in front of the foot.

Poles are recovered quickly. The hips move up and forward to drive the pole and torso recovery.

F. The skier's core continues forward during pole recovery. This divergence of the core and the gliding ski is barely noticeable at speed when the ski tips are close together but is more obvious when the skis are opened into a wider V.

G. Arms are bent at the elbows as pole push begins. Pole angle varies with speed, but hands are high and elbows outside of the shafts as pole push begins. Effective skate poling mimics the double pole as much as possible.

H. Ski rolls up on edge after poling begins and before push-off begins. To maximize the initial poling force, body weight is placed onto the poles before movement toward the new ski. Movement of the ski away from the core progressively tips it on edge during the pole push, with wide variation in timing and degree of edge angle dependent upon conditions and the skier.

Poling is completed before push-off is completed. The depth and character of upper-body compression matches the time available for poling. More time is available with more glide. With less glide, abbreviated pole strokes may lack follow-through and complete recovery. (Photos A & C)

Push-off occurs with weight still on skating ski. The weighted leg supports the skier until the push-off moves the skier off the ski and onto the next. Weight transfer onto the next ski is timed to prevent the skier from "falling off" the ski before push-off can be completed. (Photos A, B, and F)

inline skating or striding. Find out what works and what doesn't.

There is no one way to skate for every body and for every condition. The ability to feel and evaluate what creates the most consistent glide with the least effort will speed you toward skating mastery quicker than any drill or technique. Get comfortable skating on your skis and relax. Feel the joy of swooping over the snow like a hawk playing on the wind.

POLING PREPARATION

Dan Clausen has worked with hundreds of skiers for over twenty years at Minocqua Winter Park in Wisconsin. Before he introduces the details of poling, he uses this drill to help create the "core discipline" required for effective poling.

As you skate without poles, keep your elbows and arms up and forward (your upper arms should be parallel with the snow). As you move onto each ski, push your elbows as far forward as possible. Feel how your whole body is pulled up and forward as you drive your elbows forward with each skate, especially if you stabilize your core by sucking your belly button toward your spine.

Now, pick up your poles and hold them with the shafts hanging vertically in front of you and repeat the drill. When you can press both pole shafts forward as you skate onto each ski while keeping them hanging loosely in front, then you are ready to work on how to actually use your poles to add power to your legs. The details of where and when you plant your poles vary

with the different skating techniques, but this basic position, with your elbows and core pressing forward, is where each pole stroke should begin.

THE SKATES

Poles and legs can be combined in various ways to match different terrain and snow conditions. These separate combinations are the techniques or "gears" of skating. Shift between them to increase, decrease, or maintain speed and to match power to demand.

The names used for each skate in the U.S. differ from the common terms used by most skiing nations including Canada. Both the U.S. and the Canadian term are used to introduce each skate. After that, only the U.S. term is used.

Poles add power to the skate but can also mess up the good things you have going with just your legs. Make it easy on yourself and do not push too hard on your poles as you figure out the rhythms. Once you get the timings down, then you can apply power to your poles.

As you are learning the different pole timings, it may be helpful to just drop your poles or hold them in the middle of the shaft now and then. Mimic the poling patterns and timing of each technique without using your poles, then try it again with the poles.

THE V-2 (OR ONE SKATE)

In the V-2 you double pole with every skate, which is why the Canadians call it the *one* skate (one double pole push for *one* skate).

The body motion is skate onto one ski, complete the recovery of your arms and poles, double pole, skate onto the next ski, recover, double pole, and repeat. The rhythm on the snow is one ski, two poles, one ski, two poles.

This rhythm—a double pole followed by weight transfer from ski to ski—is the intuitive rhythm of skating that alpine skiers use to skate over flat sections and Nordic skiers unschooled in skating naturally adopt. Some find it a challenge to maintain their balance as they learn the V-2. To help overcome this hurdle Todd Eastman suggests that you approach the V-2 as a double pole with your skis in a V position instead of parallel to each other. Once you have this altered double pole figured out, balancing on one ski between the double poles becomes much easier.

The basic pattern of this altered double pole is simple. With your ski tips slightly apart in a narrow V and your poles planted outside the skis, rise for a double pole and fall forward between your skis while compressing your torso over the poles. As the skis glide apart, pick up one ski and bring it back beneath you to restore the original narrow V. Then repeat the cycle several times to get a feel for the whole movement.

Now back up to build a complete V-2 step by step. Choose a flat or slightly uphill trail where you still have good glide. Begin with a normal double pole *without* your tips apart. During the forward recovery of your arms, lift the tip of one ski off the snow (use your knee not just your toe). Set the ski back onto the snow parallel with the

Lift the tip of one ski as you recover your arms while double poling to prepare for the V-2.

Keep your head, chest, and hips pointed forward and between your skis in the altered double pole.

other one. Then double pole again and as your arms recover lift the other ski. Continue double poling, lifting alternate skis as you recover your arms.

When this is comfortable, open the tips

173

of your skis to form a narrow V and tip your skis slightly up on their inside edges. With your poles planted outside your skis, double pole while keeping your head, chest, and hips pointing forward and between your skis. Both skis will accelerate toward their respective tips as you do.

Before your skis move very far apart, lift one ski and swing that ski and leg back in toward the foot that is still on the snow to restore your original narrow V position.

Shift onto one ski to double pole as glide and speed increase. The left ski is unweighted in the photo.

Repeat, lifting and bringing your other ski back in this time. Continue double poling, starting each cycle with your ski tips apart and then lifting alternate skis to restore your shallow V at the end of each poling stroke. Find a consistent speed and rhythm you can settle into as you pole and then recover with the altered double pole.

As your speed increases, you will be forced to move sideways onto one ski and stay there during your double pole to avoid being stranded between your skis and doing the splits. Remember to push off sideways (perpendicular) to the ski you are leaving and keep the heel on the push-off ski until the last moment. Now you are in the V-2.

It can be very hard to balance on each ski in the V-2 if all you do is stand there and glide. The trick to both balance and to *creating* glide is to stay in constant forward motion. Adjust the timing, tempo, and rhythm of your pole and torso recovery, your poling, and your push-off so you are moving forward and toward your next ski from the moment you skate onto each ski until you skate off of it. Maintain the same narrow V position as you double pole, but now one ski will be off the snow. Focus on moving forward and up the trail from ski to ski instead of balancing over any one ski for too long.

The double pole is the foundation of this technique, so check your basic movements now and then by going back to the beginning of the progression and starting your double pole with both skis on the snow. Be sure to keep your toes and skis turned out from your hips as you pole,

Drive your elbows skyward at the end of your pole push to maintain forward momentum and a higher tempo. (Photo: Fischer Skis)

glide, and recover. Your pelvis should stay facing straight ahead as your skis angle out to the side.

As you gain experience with V-2 pole and leg timing, experiment with different variations. To take your V-2 into hilly terrain, focus on quick, forceful double poles with your hands stopping near your thighs. Recover your poles quickly to keep up with the quick movements from ski to ski. When you are really digging for power, both the pole push and the recovery may be abbreviated.

As speed increases, use deeper, longer pole strokes and recover as you glide on the next ski. If balance is a problem, make sure you are moving your core forward, up the trail, and not just standing on your gliding ski or getting stuck in the middle between your skis. As your hands swing forward past your hips, drive your elbows directly up the trail to raise your upper arms. This will pull your core and upper body forward. Get your poles into the snow as soon as possible so they can help you balance as well as push you forward.

THE V-2 ALTERNATE (OR TWO SKATE)

As speed increases, double poling with every skate in a V-2 gets to be a little much. When you reach that threshold, double poling with every other skate is more efficient. The Canadians call this the *two* skate (one double pole push for every *two* skates).

The body motion is skate onto one ski as you complete your pole and torso recovery, double pole and then skate onto the next ski to begin your pole and torso recovery, then skate back onto the first ski, complete your recovery, and double pole again. The rhythm on the snow is one ski, then two poles, followed by one ski, then the other ski, and then two poles.

This can be as simple as it sounds, but it is easy to miss the hidden power in the recovery of your arms. Drop your poles all together for a moment and skate with the V-2 rhythm while mimicking a pole stroke with each skate. Then drop one of the pole

Halt your forward pole recovery just after skating onto the poling ski.

strokes to move into the V-2A rhythm—pole with one skate and recover with the other. Adjust the timing of both your poling and your recovery so that your hands and elbows come up for the next pole stroke after you have skated back onto the original poling ski. Stop your forward recovery abruptly when your hands and elbows come up. This will transfer the forward momentum of your core and arms to your ski and add to your glide. Then double pole and repeat. Play around with the recovery and the timing without your poles and then try it with them.

FREE SKATE OR NO POLES SKATE

At very high speed, any poling becomes too much to keep up with so pick up your poles and fly! Swinging the opposite arm forward as speed skaters do can add a lot of speed, but direct the swing up the trail, not across your body. Skating without poles is the foundation of all the other techniques. The more time you spend skating without poles, the better skater you will become.

THE V-1 (OR OFFSET SKATE)

In slower conditions, maintaining a consistent speed with the V-2 is difficult. When the snow is slow or the hill is too steep, there comes a time when there just is not enough glide on each ski to recover before the next double pole. Under these circumstances, gear down from the V-2 to the V-1.

The V-1 uses one double pole for every two skates, so the rhythm is similar to the V-2A but the timing is different—the double pole occurs just as you skate onto one ski and not after you have already moved onto it. Because your feet are farther apart at the moment of weight transfer from ski to ski than at other times during the skate cycle, the position of the double pole plant must be altered to avoid placing one basket between your legs. This *offset* pole position gives the V-1 its Canadian name of *Offset* Skate.

The body motion is to double pole just as you transfer your weight onto one ski, skate back onto the other ski as you recover your poles and bring the "poling" ski forward, then double pole again just as you transfer back to the "poling" ski. The rhythm of poles and skis on the snow is both poles and one ski at the same time, then one ski, then both poles and one ski at the same

The pole used in a gliding herringbone becomes the offside pole of the V-1.

time, then one ski. The poling side is called the strong side (or the power side); the non-poling side is called the offside.

The V-1 evolved from the herringbone—Todd Eastman calls it a gliding herringbone with the poling tweaked to enhance glide. To gain some understanding of both the leg and pole motions, herringbone up a decent hill, while adding some glide on each ski by driving your thigh and knee toward the tip. Once you have a little glide going on each ski, pick up one of your poles and fold it out of the way under your arm. As you glide on each ski, continue to pole as you would in a herringbone but use only one pole, keeping the other tucked away.

When you have that mastered, unfold the "underarm pole" and use it with the pole you have been planting to double pole only with every *other* skate. The underarm pole should be planted in line with the trail as you would for a normal double pole. The

original "herringbone" pole should continue to be planted at an angle to the trail or it will end up planted between your feet. Continue to skate off each ski but double pole on only one side with your poles in this offset position.

POLE TIMING

Out of the four things that contact the snow (two pole baskets and two skis), three of them touch the snow at the same time, followed by one. The precise timing of when the poles and skis hit the snow can vary, but the basic pattern is always *3-1*.

To make sure you are using the timing appropriate to V-1 and not V-2A, walk uphill on your edges in a herringbone. Plant both poles at the same time as the strong side ski—this is the three of *3-1*. Then move onto the other ski, which is the one of *3-1*. Continue to climb the hill as you follow the *3-1, 3-1, 3-1* pattern, adding a little glide if you can. If the timing remains elusive, remove your skis and practice the pattern while walking up hill on the sides of your boots. A steep hill works best.

Conventional wisdom says that the V-1 is the easiest skate to learn because it requires less balance than the V-2, but the truth is that most skiers use only an approximation of the V-1 that allows them to hide balance and timing problems while providing some mobility on the trails. An efficient and effective V-1 with a well-timed and complete weight transfer from ski to ski combined with effective poling can be the most complicated skate to master.

Offside hand lower and in front of strong side hand

OFFSET POLING

Oddly enough, the offset position places your offside hand in front of your strong side pole shaft. Even stranger, the offside basket ends up behind the strong side basket.

This may sound complicated, but all you need to do to get it right is to keep your off-side hand lower and in front of your strong side hand as you plant your poles. Keep your elbows forward and outside of your pole shafts and your palms facing slightly inward in the relaxed and comfortable position you would use to pull on a rope hanging straight down.

Because of the position of the pole and the angle of the shaft, your offside pole will help power the glide on the strong side ski. To move your core forward and up the trail, with your poles in the offset position, push on your poles as you would in a normal double pole.

MOVING FROM SKI TO SKI

In the V-2 and V-2A, the leg push and double pole push serve mostly to push your ski forward. To keep your body moving forward, all you need to do is move over to the new ski and go along for the ride. The V-1 is a little different. With your skis in a wider V, the leg push and poling push contribute

Recovery foot and ski move directly forward and up the trail. (Photo: Fischer Skis)

Skate onto the offside ski before beginning your pole and torso recovery.

Drive your thigh and knee toward the ski tip as you skate back onto the strong side ski.
(Photo: Fischer Skis)

more to moving your body forward.

To gauge how wide your V needs to be for this to happen, slide backward on a hill and open your tips in a reverse snowplow until you stop. This tells you how wide your V needs to be. Speed, strength, or technique may allow you to use a narrower V, but you should not need to go wider than this.

After you stop sliding backward in your reverse snowplow, move your core forward by bending your ankles until you feel you are about to fall into the hill. As you skate in the V-1, you can maintain this forward-falling stance by guarding against stepping too far up the hill, which would push you upright and effectively stop your glide. Keep that falling-forward feeling on even

the steepest hills by always moving onto a bent ankle as you move from ski to ski.

Unlike in the V-2 and the V-2A, there is no time for your leg and ski to fall back underneath your body in the V-1. The saddle-sore position of cowboy balance really comes into play here. Immediately bring your ski forward after each push-off to get it into position for the next skate. From where the heel lifts off the ski, your knee and foot should move in a relatively straight line directly up the hill. As the ski contacts the snow, it should be beneath you and your ankle should be bent. Continue moving your core forward as you drive your knee toward the tip to keep the ski moving as you skate on it.

THE OFFSIDE

Weight transfer, pole recovery, and push-off have to happen quickly on the offside since there is no pole push to maintain glide. Complete the power phase of your pole stroke while still on the strong side ski, then push off and move crisply to the offside ski before beginning active pole and torso recovery. Avoid the common mistake of standing up after poling on the strong side ski and then weakly plopping over to the offside ski. As you transfer to the offside ski, drive it forward with your thigh and knee to keep it gliding as you bring your torso, arms, and poles quickly forward. Move back to the strong side with the same crisp and definite push-off.

Bring your arms forward as if you were trying to toss the contents of a cup of coffee held in each hand directly up the trail. The thrown java should make two parallel streaks aligned with the direction of the trail. Snapping your hands and elbows up and forward just as the strong side ski is set onto the snow will add extra glide.

THE MARATHON SKATE

The marathon is basically the V-1 with the offside ski in a groomed track. This technique is not used very often any more, but it is still handy when the tracks are fast or the skating lane is choppy and rough. The marathon is also a good way to pass other skiers clogging up the skating lane.

As in the V-1, the body motion is to double pole just as you transfer your weight

Marathon skating resembles the V-1.

onto the ski that is out of the track. Then skate back onto the ski in the track as you recover your poles and your other ski, then double pole again just as you transfer back to the ski out of the track. The rhythm of the poles and skis on the snow is both poles and one ski (the one out of the track) at the same time, then one ski (the ski in the track), then both poles and one ski at the same time, then one ski.

To get started, bring the untracked ski forward and set it down at a slight angle to the tracks. This would be the strong side ski in a V-1. Pole with the same timing and offset pole position as the V-1. In the marathon skate, the strong side pole is aligned with the track, while the offside pole angles toward the ski that is out of the track. Hand positions are similar to the V-1. Pole with a double pole motion directed up the track.

To ensure weight transfer, lift the ski in the track off the snow as you skate onto the angled ski. Bring it forward as you glide on the other ski. (If the power side ski pulled your airborne ski too far away from the track, adjust the angle of the power side ski on the next skate.) Complete your pole push and move sideways off the angled ski and back onto the ski in the track. Recover as you glide in the track, driving your thigh and knee down the track to keep that ski gliding as you gather for the next cycle.

The extra glide with the ski in the track helps to balance out the lack of a pole push with that ski. This can make the marathon a faster skate than the V-1. The fixed position of the track also forces you to learn how to adjust your timing, weight transfer, and ski angle as your speed changes to keep your offside ski over the track. Explore all the different permutations by using the marathon skate in both fast and slow conditions and both up and down hills. You will learn a lot that will help all your skates, especially the V-1.

DIAGONAL SKATE

The diagonal skate is the down and dirty workhorse of skating and will keep you

gliding when all others fail. It is essentially a gliding herringbone in which you use the pole opposite the ski you are on to help you glide. The body motion is skate on one ski as you push with the opposite pole and recover your other arm and leg, skate onto the next ski as you push with the opposite pole and the other set of limbs recovers, and repeat. The rhythm on the snow is one ski and the opposite pole, then the other ski and the opposite pole.

Transform a herringbone into a diagonal skate by extending your leg and pushing off your entire foot as you shift from ski to ski instead of stepping up the hill from edge to edge. Move onto a flat ski and let it roll up on edge as you pole and continue moving forward. Plant each pole with your elbow up and forward of your torso and outside of the shaft (the pole shaft will be roughly aligned in the direction of the opposite ski).

Move from a herringbone into a diagonal skate by extending onto the next ski to create glide.

SUGGESTED LEARNING ACTIVITIES

- Skate without poles, with your palms on your butt. Press forward with your hands to help keep your core moving forward throughout the skate cycle.
- Try using the same leg skating motions for all the different skates.
- Hold your arms up and out from your sides, like a bird drying its wings, with your elbows bent at a ninety-degree angle and your hands in front of your elbows. Plant, push on, and recover your poles with your upper arms and elbows fixed in this position while your hands and forearms rotate down and back up as if on a pivot from your elbows. This is an exaggerated position that limits your power and range of motion, but time spent skating like this will reveal the benefits of staying up and forward over both your feet and your poles during the entire poling cycle.
- Follow another skater's tracks and try to glide farther on each ski than they do.
- Skate backward. Then see if you can spin around and skate forward with no loss of momentum.
- Develop forward lean while skating by pulling a pulk or attaching a length of webbing to another skier and pulling them as you skate. Keep the resistance low so you can maintain good form.
- Double pole for twenty strokes, then V-1 skate for twenty strokes, then double pole for twenty strokes, then V-2 skate for twenty stokes, and so on.
- To improve your V-2, practice eight or ten quick double poles followed by eight or ten complete and quick V-2 skates. Focus on a quick recovery of your poles and matching the tempo you maintained in a double pole when you switch to V-2.
- To help your V-1 poling, pole with just the strong side or just the offside pole. Then switch which side is which.
- Experiment with a staggered pole plant in the V-1, where the offside basket hits the snow just before the power side basket. See what (if any) amount of stagger helps your V-1 skate.
- Switch from the V-2 rhythm to the V-2 alternate rhythm and back to establish the difference.
- Switch from the V-2 alternate rhythm to the V-1 rhythm and back to establish the difference.
- Play in between the timing of the V-2 alternate and the V-1. Plant both poles before the strong side ski hits the snow. Then plant them when you skate onto the strong side (the conventional 3-1 timing of the V-1), then just after, then a little bit later, then much later, and finally long after you skate onto the strong side ski. When the pole plant gets late enough, just skip it altogether and shift into overdrive, skating without poles.
- Enhance your balance and extend your glide in the V-2 with this drill from Sandy Cook, an instructor at the Silver Star ski area in British Columbia. Get moving in a V-2 and then slightly cross the unweighted ski over the other just prior to your pole plant. As your hands approach your thighs, uncross your ski and move it into alignment for the next skate as you follow through with your poles. Repeat on each ski.

  Remember when doing any drill that accentuates or demonstrates an extreme position ro return to the unexaggerated position and integrate what you have learned.

Use the "working" pole to move up the hill as much as possible even though it is angled across the trail. Swing the opposite elbow and arm up the trail to add momentum as you push off sideways onto the next ski and prepare for the next pole plant.

Another portal to the diagonal skate is through the diagonal stride. Start with the diagonal stride motion and slowly open the tips of your skis into a skating position while you maintain the glide and poling of the stride.

This is a relaxing skate if you keep your motions light and constant. A few strokes of the diagonal skate are often all that are needed to revive sinking speed and energy levels in the V-1. If you start to labor in the diagonal skate, use a wider V and do not try to glide as far with each skate.

CHAPTER 12

Start of the Craftsbury Ski Marathon in Vermont. (Photo: Kate Carter)

Racing and Training

Pain. Agony. Victory. Defeat. Wait—don't flee quite yet. There is more to racing than these common media images.

If you enjoy skiing on groomed trails, if you like people, and if you welcome a personal challenge, it may surprise you to know that there is a good chance that you will enjoy ski racing. Sure, racing is about competition, but that comes and goes so quickly. Beyond the start and finish lines is a rich world.

Racing is about people. It is not unusual to find hundreds at a local race, thousands at a major regional race, and tens of thousands at large European ski marathons.

Racing is a way to become more involved with life. It pulls you into the sport and into association with others with like interests. It takes you to other areas where you discover what skiing is like there. It offers measurable results so you can evaluate the effects of your planning and efforts, and it offers the satisfaction of deciding to do something and then doing it.

The socializing and camaraderie attracts skiers to racing at all levels, but citizen racing is unique in attracting numerous skiers who attend simply for the joy of participating rather than to compete. You can spot these skiers pretty easily—their hats are full of pins from the marathons, races, and other events they have attended, and they are usually surrounded by a large group of friends from years on the local circuit.

CITIZEN RACING

Citizen races are the perfect venue for weekend warriors who have jobs and families. Usually organized by local ski clubs, communities, or Nordic centers, some races are well-established and well-orchestrated affairs, while others are more casual. Men and women usually race together, with separate races for kids at some events. Distances vary, and times are kept, usually according to age group, creating lusty competition over the entire field of participants and not for just the first few to cross the finish line.

Citizen racing also encompasses ski marathons, or loppets, that generally range from 40 to 55 kilometers in length. Because of the large number of participants in some of these events, skiers are assigned to a "wave" based on previous finishes in other recognized races. Those with the fastest times start as a group in the first wave, with the last wave made up of casual skiers and those without any previous marathon finishes.

Weekly citizen series, sometimes held in the evening on lighted tracks, can be a great introduction to racing. The atmosphere is usually low key, and you are likely to meet some folks you can learn from and even travel with to longer weekend races in your area.

PRACTICAL TIPS

If you are just starting to race, here are a few tips that may help:
- Arrive early so you can be relaxed as you get ready to race.
- Race jitters can make you dumb. Pack your clothes and boots and anything else (like food, your wax, and your hydration pack) in one bag well before it is time to leave and then put it in your car.
- Keep your skis and poles in a ski bag to help protect them in a crowded starting area.

Citizen racing. (Photo: Silver Star Mountain Resort, Don Weixl)

- Finish eating three hours before you race.
- Keep drinking water as normal, but be sure to leave time for a bathroom stop before the race starts.
- If it is a classic race, be sure to allow enough time to choose and apply grip wax. If you are new to grip waxing or struggling, ask for help and advice from other racers. If you live where the temperatures are often near freezing, consider purchasing a pair of waxless performance skis.
- Close is good enough for glide waxing, so wax your skis the night before.
- Ski as much of the course beforehand as you can without tiring yourself out, concentrating on the start and finish areas.

- Warm up before the start. For short races, your warm-up should end at a fairly high intensity. For longer races, the start of the race can serve as part of your warm-up.
- Don't start your warm-up too far in advance of the start time and keep your warm-up clothes on as long as possible to avoid chilling down too much. This is when warm-up pants with a full-length side zipper come in handy.
- Do not go out too hard. Aim for a pace that you know you can maintain over the entire distance. If you still feel good once you get well into the race you can always speed up.
- If you think you will be able to stay in the front of the main pack throughout the race, line up in the front lines of a mass start and go out hard enough to get clear of the main pack to avoid entanglement. Once you get in the clear be sure to slow down to a pace you can maintain.
- If you do not think you can stay in front of the pack, line up behind the leaders at the start. The most common mistake made by inexperienced racers is starting too fast.
- If you expect to be on the course for more than an hour, carry your own water. For longer races, carry your own energy source (gel or whatever suits you) or be sure to grab something at a feeding station now and then. Most skiers find it easier to drink from the tube of a hydration bladder than from a water bottle on their waist, but tubes freeze easily.
- Sliced fruit and water are the safest things to request at feeding stations—ingest the other options at your own risk. Avoid candy unless you are within thirty minutes of the finish line.
- If you enhance your water with a powdered sports drink be sure to try it out during training to make sure it will not make you sick.
- Adjust your tempo and choice of technique to match the terrain and the snow conditions. Following an experienced racer is a good way to learn this crucial skill.
- Maintain your pace and tempo over the crest of any hill. This is an easy place to pass others or to leave them behind.
- Rest and ride the glide whenever the course and the competition give you the chance. Tuck when you can, but do not go so low that your breathing or your balance is compromised.
- Maintain as much speed as possible on the downhills, turning or slowing only when necessary. In rolling terrain, bomb the downhills so you can glide as far as possible up the next hill.
- Ski through the corners, not around them—"straighten out the curves."
- In skate races, drafting another skier or a pack is less work than going it alone. Don't attempt this unless you have the skills not to step on the skis or poles of those in front of you and always wear eye protection against flying pole tips. If you draft, it is good manners to take your turn at the front of the pack.

THE BEST LAID PLANS

Ever since I began racing, I have wanted to participate in the legendary Birkebeiner ski race that takes place each March in Norway. In this event, which begins in Rena near the Swedish border and ends in Lillehammer (site of the 1994 Winter Olympics), thousands of racers carrying packs weighing 5.5 kilograms (12 pounds) retrace the route of soldiers who in the thirteenth century skied over two mountain ranges to save the infant prince, Haakon Haakonsson, who eventually became his country's king (the packs represent the weight of the rescued child).

When my wife, Sue, and I took jobs at an international school in England, I knew my chance had come. I would soon be celebrating one of those "decade birthdays," so I had the added incentive of proving that I still had the stamina for 60 continuous kilometers of kick-and-glide. The British Isles don't have much in the way of prepared track, but I was not overly concerned. With the European continent a cheap flight away, and several school holidays on the calendar, I thought I would have plenty of opportunities to train before the race. That year, however, the weather didn't cooperate. Our winter holiday in Austria saw only bare ground, and our plans to warm-up with the Transjurassienne race in France fell through when it was cancelled due to the lack of snow.

My back-up plan was to train with lots of bicycling and some gym time on a ski-simulator. Nordic skiing has little following among the Brits, so finding a NordicTrak in London proved harder than getting a smile from the guards at Buckingham Palace. Bicycling became my exclusive method of training.

Then came the big day. Somewhere around the 45-kilometer mark, the sport-specific muscles of my inner thighs faded. No amount of blueberry soup or spoonfuls of powdered sugar, offered up by spectators along the route, could revive my fatigued propulsion mechanism. If the Birkebeiner had been a multisport event with a cycling segment, I am confident I would have been delighted with my finish. My cardio fitness was at an all-time high, but my ski legs just weren't there when I needed them. As I waved to the Norwegian grandmothers who glided past me, I accepted that there is no substitute for skiing as preparation for a racing competition.

But all was not lost. I still got to savor the sun-kissed beauty of the mountain landscape and the warm hospitality of the crowd.

Steve Walker, citizen racer and adviser to the Outdoor Program
at Western Washington University in Bellingham, Washington

A FEW WORDS ABOUT TECHNIQUE

The nature of racing means that a dispro-portionate amount of time will be spent climbing hills over a varied course. Racers with "big engines" can overpower better technical skiers because they can grunt it out on the hills, but the skier who can cover ground with the least effort is still going to win, all other things being equal.

Skiers who get into racing often watch racing videos and study pictures of racers, looking for tips on technique. This can be useful, but don't fall into the trap of thinking racing is all about mastering a specific form. Good racing, like all skiing, is about glide and efficiency. Practice skiing with smooth, quiet power. When you want to open up the throttle, you will be more than ready.

That said, you can certainly benefit by paying attention to technique while doing your training, whether it's on skis, roller skis, or during dry-land training drills. The areas to focus on are achieving a more timely weight transfer and more forward lean, and eliminating any effort or move-ments that do not move you forward.

SKI TRAINING

Training is a process. As the gurus say, it is the journey and not just the destination that counts. In fact, you need not even want to race to enjoy and benefit from training. On the other hand, you do not need to train to race, but chances are you will enjoy your race a lot more if you do.

Although it can seem like the more you learn and read about training the more confusing the whole thing gets, the main difference between training and just work-ing out is creating and following a plan. To get you started, J. D. Downing, coach of the XCOregon race team and creator of the website *www.xcskiworld.com,* offers these three easy steps to fitness for cross-country skiers.

STEP 1—HAVE A PLAN

No matter what your goals, your age, or your current fitness level, you will benefit from planning the how, when, and why that will improve your fitness for cross-country ski adventures.

How do you start? *Begin by making a list of fitness goals and objectives for the upcoming winter. This list certainly does not have to be (and should not be) limited to cross-country skiing! Go ahead and add other sports and activities, lifestyle items, anything that comes to mind. Make sure that your goals and objectives reflect an honest progression from where you are now to where you would like to be.*

For example, Beth could set a goal of skiing that 30-km tour route she always wanted to do. Her objective would be to maintain a steady fitness routine for six months prior to her target tour date. Another goal could be simply to enter the winter in better shape so she has more fun and can last longer on skis early in the season.

Once you have a rough idea of what you would like to accomplish, make a rough month-by-month outline of all the training/ fitness activities you intend to pursue. This "plan" can be a super-detailed blueprint or it can be a few scribbles on a single sheet of paper. The point is to have something written down that you can refer to, adjust, and expand upon as the year unfolds.

Finally, put your plan in a place where you will be sure to see it on a regular basis. The fridge can be a motivating location. If you keep a fitness journal, that is the perfect spot. Journals are a great idea. Keeping a record of your fitness progress—perhaps a personal best in a strength exercise or being able to do an aerobic activity for 10 minutes longer—allows you to celebrate little victories on a continuous basis. Being able to see written progress is one of the best ways to keep yourself motivated to follow any fitness plan, but combined with activity-specific goals...now that's a recipe for success!

STEP 2—USE A CREATIVE VARIETY OF WORKOUTS, INTENSITIES, LOCATIONS, AND PARTNERS

An easy way to get discouraged and abandon the most detailed and well-intentioned training plan is to go out and mindlessly plug away day after day doing the same kinds of workouts at the same places at the same pace. Bor-ing. Although some folks love a set routine, for most of us, our minds, bodies, and spirits need constant variety.

What can you do to spice up your routine? Go out and try new training methods. Roller skis, for example, can be a great investment for year-round skiing fitness and fun—particularly if you have plenty of paved multi-user paths nearby. Incorporate different kinds of regular strength workouts into your weekly plan. One day you might use circuits. Another day you might work out using traditional weights. Another day you might do plyometrics and body-weight exercises. If you have water nearby, borrow or pick up a used canoe/kayak and go paddling—great for skiers' upper bodies! Instead of just running or hiking, mix things up a bit—jog flats and downhills and hike or bound uphill. Go check out a state park or wilderness trail you have never been to for a weekend workout. Plan a long weekend road trip to a spot where you can have a mini-"training camp" with plenty of different activities. Be on the lookout for different training partners.

STEP 3—THE MORE YOU WANT TO IMPROVE, THE MORE SPECIFIC YOU NEED TO BE

If you are just interested in staying fit year-round for cross-country skiing, the need for specific training methods is pretty low except for the final two to three months prior to the ski season. On the other hand, if you have competitive aspirations or have planned an ambitious tour that is really going to stretch your fitness envelope, you will need to be more specific in order to reach your goals.

A REAL LIFE SKIING FAIRY TALE

Once upon a time, there was an Olympic cross-country skier who lived in western Maine. It had been almost twenty years since she had skied in the Olympics (1984, Sarajevo), and several years since her last race. For a few years, she had gotten away from skiing, and into public education. But nasty non-skiing kids had chased her out of the classroom and back to the snow-covered trails for both her enjoyment and her employment.

Some friends told her about a wonderful weekly cross-country timed event at Great Glen Trails Outdoor Center in Gorham, New Hampshire. At this event, known as the Nordic Meister Series, skiers could ski the 5-kilometer course with either classic or skating technique, either alone or with a group. Besides the chance to race again in a low-key atmosphere, she loved having the chance to meet other adult skiers, talk technique, share waxing secrets, and recount the day's race stories.

At the conclusion of eight weeks of racing, our happy skier was looking forward to the Friday night awards party. On arriving, she found a spot at a table with one of the Great Glen employees, a guy she had spoken to only briefly before. Hot and cold hors d'oeuvres were passed around, and drinks were available. It was a fun evening with friends, families, food, and prizes. She was sorry the series and her weekly trips to Great Glen were coming to an end.

Howie, her new Great Glen friend, had other ideas. He said he'd like to go skiing with her and asked her to return the following week. As luck would have it, when the day came it poured rain. They rescheduled their ski date, but once again the weather didn't cooperate. They got together anyway, went to lunch, talked, skied in the rain, watched a video, and put off saying good-bye for hours.

Five years later, Sue, for that's her name, is beginning her fourth year working at Great Glen, teaching cross-country skiing in the winter, and kayaking in the summer. Howie, her husband of two years, continues to manage both Great Glen Trails and its sister company, the Mt. Washington Auto Road. Each winter, they participate in the Nordic Meister Series (which celebrated its tenth anniversary in 2005) and ski together in the 160-km Canadian Ski Marathon.

Cross-country skiing: it can change your life!

Sue Wemyss

What is specific? *Start by staying on snow as much as you possibly can throughout the year. Most folks don't have the time and cannot afford to travel to glaciers or to opposite hemispheres and most folks do not live in areas with accessible year-round snow, but you can make the most of the snow in your area as long as it lasts.*

Off the snow, your most specific training choices are roller skiing, exercises that imitate skiing, and running in ski-specific terrain. Although in-line skates are an acceptable alternative to roller skiing (particularly if your competitive goals are not all that ambitious or if fitness is the primary goal), more serious skiers should stick with roller skiing. Specific strength exercises in the gym or out in the field are also a critical part of a cross-country skier's fitness routine.

One easy way to stay on top of specific cross-country training ideas is to check out the Workout of the Week posted nearly every week on xcskiworld.com (check out the navigation menu up top). Although the workouts are primarily written for racers, recreational skiers can easily adjust them to a more casual orientation.

As you design a training plan, remember to choose activities that you enjoy. As J. D. says, it is "always better to be happy than to roller ski four times a week when you hate it. Find a way to marry what you love to do with what you have to do to reach your goal."

Training with others is one of the best ways to make training enjoyable. Todd Eastman encourages folks to find the best skiers in their area to ski and train with. Most accomplished skiers will be happy to answer your questions and ski with you if you ask and show commitment.

And finally, be wary of the trap of always training at your limit every time you go out. As former Olympic skier Leslie Hall says, "go easy on the easy days so you can go hard on the hard days."

Many resources are available if you want more detailed information. Books devoted just to training for cross-country skiing are in print, training articles appear regularly in most cross-country skiing periodicals, and the Internet is a rich resource.

DRY-LAND TRAINING ACTIVITIES

This is a catch-all term used to describe a variety of activities used to simulate and train for cross-country skiing away from the snow.

ROLLER SKIS

These are short metal "skis" with wheels on each end. Some use hard, dense tires suitable only for smooth pavement, while others come equipped with pneumatic tires that will roll over packed gravel and dirt roads. Some roller skis are intended for skating only, others come with a clutch that allows them to be used with the diagonal stride.

Think about safety before you hit the road or the trail on roller skis. Wear a helmet, gloves, kneepads, and tight-fitting shorts or pants (to help prevent road rash

Roller skiing

if you fall). Choose quiet roads or suitable trails. Some roller skis come with speed reducers and even brakes, but make sure you know what you are doing before going down any hill—quick stops are simply not possible.

Cross-country boots and bindings can be used without modification on roller skis. Durable pole tips are available to replace the baskets on regular poles. Use a diamond stone to sharpen your pole tips each time you roller ski so they will bite into the pavement.

SKI WALKING

Ski walking is the most accessible specific foot drill for dry-land training. The simplest way to start ski walking is to pick up your poles and go for a hike. As you hike, mimic the ski stride. With no further effort, you have raised your heart rate and are developing ski specific strength and endurance. Ski walking is especially useful when the rains of fall make roller skiing and biking less attractive and encroaching darkness and wet leaves makes trail running a bit risky. After getting accustomed to walking with poles, you can focus on one or more of the details below to improve your skiing when you get back on snow.

Keep your heel down as long as possible as you extend your leg to move forward onto your next foot. Lift your toe toward your shin as you begin to bring your rear leg forward. As your toes start to swish through the grass (if there's grass to swish through), lift your knee and drive it forward to keep your foot from hitting the ground as your body continues to move forward. Land on your heel with a flexed ankle. Simulate the glide phase by extending your rear leg after complete extension as a counterbalance for your upper body as it moves forward. Then flex your front ankle to continue moving forward over the ball of your foot, and then swish your rear leg through again, keeping your other heel down as long as possible again for a long "kick." Always move onto a flexed ankle to prevent over-striding.

Ideally, poles for ski walking should be a bit shorter than those used for skiing. Use them to complement your foot and legwork. Muscling through with your poles will not help your ski walking any more than it helps your skiing.

Ski walking up hills requires only a few modifications. Be sure to stand a little straighter by looking up the trail and not at the ground. Bring your pole through and plant it with a more vertical forearm. Since you basically run up steep hills on skis, you don't need to simulate the glide phase when you ski walk on steep hills. Land on the ball of your foot and keep moving up the hill by instantly deepening the flex of the ankle and knee of your standing leg.

OTHER SKIING-SPECIFIC FOOT DRILLS

A variety of ski simulation drills can be done off the snow to build strength and improve timing and coordination. You can skate walk without poles, mimic poling while skate walking, or do low skate walks and crossovers, among many other options. Another possibility is bounding—ski or skate walking with a focus on explosive extensions. Search the Internet or attend a dry-land training camp for more specifics.

TRAINING RESOURCES

Books

Borowski, Lee. *Optimal Cross-Country Ski Training: Update Your Skiing for the 21st Century.* Waupaca, WI: Waupaca Publishing Company, 2000. Short, succinct and to the point. Full of Borowski's useful opinions.

Gaskill, Stephen E. *Fitness Cross-Country Skiing.* Champaign, IL: Human Kinetics, 1998. Clear and detailed training programs for the casual skier to the competitor. A step-by-step approach.

Websites

www.xcskiworld.com—home of the American Cross-Country Skiers organization and a wealth of information on the sport, including training.

www.fasterskier.com—former U.S. national team coach Torbjorn Karlsen's site. Dedicated to racing and training.

www.nordicskiracer.com—a hotbed of Midwestern racing and training information.

www.nensa.net—home of the New England Nordic Ski Association. Full of useful training information, including a fast and effective stretching program for Nordic athletes and dry-land exercises for classic and skating.

www.usbiathlon.org—home of the U.S. Biathlon Association.

www.mastersskier.com—this site collects back issues of *Master Skier,* an excellent periodical devoted to masters racing and training.

Part III: Skiing for Fun and Adventure

CHAPTER 13

Following the ridgeline. (Photo Steve Barnett)

Backcountry Skiing

Backcountry skiing is defined as much by attitude and intent as by location or equipment. Author and ski instructor Mitch Mode spends a lot of time on groomed trails in Wisconsin, but he also likes to "strap on the backcountry boards and head off into the woods near my home town, slowly plodding along, making my own trail, enjoying the intimacy that off-trail skiing brings." Stephen King of Vista Verde Ranch in Colorado leads backcountry tours in the Rocky Mountains, which he describes as making your own trail and skiing for the purpose of touring, not turning. He says his guests fall in love with backcountry skiing because it goes to the root of what modern humans are missing—being active outside. In West Virginia's Canaan Valley, Chip Chase and his band of merry pranksters maintain a maze of trails at the Whitegrass Ski Touring Center. Some of these are groomed for skating and high-performance skiing, but what brings skiers back time and time again

is the backcountry skiing that can be found between the trails. That is where hillbilly crazies and diplomats from Washington, D.C., whose common motto is "Life is right when it is white," jump off into moss- and fern-covered glades disguised as ski runs by whatever snow is at hand.

Modern backcountry gear has made it easier than ever before to get around in the snowy off-trail world. Walking and striding on skis in the backcountry is not that much different than hiking in the woods. Waxless bases and easy-to-use climbing skins help on the uphills, and shorter and shapelier skis have made going downhill a lot more fun.

Dick Hall, founder of the North American Telemark Association, has spent thirty years spreading the backcountry gospel to over fifty thousand skiers, and what excites him today more than anything is the fit, comfort, and performance of modern equipment. If you are an alpine skier, you can reap the benefits of your existing alpine skills as soon as you clip into modern free-heel backcountry skis. Learning the new skills of climbing and traveling on this equipment offers an attainable challenge to many who thought they were never going to become better skiers or be able to learn much of anything new.

THINGS TO KNOW BEFORE YOU GO

Skiing away from groomed and marked trails is not without hazards, but those hazards are not all that different from what you might encounter on a lonely trail at a Nordic center or alpine resort. The difference is this: in the backcountry you are on your own.

Of course, the best option is to avoid getting into trouble in the first place. This comes down to making good decisions. If your day in the backcountry focuses too much on the goal of climbing a peak, skiing the entire length of a trail, or getting as far from the madding crowds as possible, you may be setting yourself up for unintended consequences. Don't take the wilderness lightly. Do one simple thing—plan your trip to make sure you arrive in camp or back at the trailhead before dark—and you will avoid most of the problems that trip up backcountry travelers.

Even more important, remember that the best-laid plans can go awry. Countless emergencies have been caused when backcountry travelers made bad decisions in their push to get back to the car in time to be home for dinner or to return to work the next morning. There are times when sudden weather changes or other unforeseen events make holing up and waiting for the next dawn more prudent than pressing on. Take enough clothes and equipment with you to survive overnight if you need to. A night out may not be comfortable or convenient, but it may be better than the alternative.

The ability to make good decisions comes from knowledge about the environment and yourself—an awareness that comes from study, practice, and experience. The best approach is to find a respected friend or guide and ski with them for a while. Backcountry ski courses and classes are also offered by a variety of organizations. Regardless of who your companions are, never let their experience override your own concerns or feelings. Learn to hear and to follow your own "backcountry intuition." This sixth sense is not a mystical power, it is a learned skill—the combination of your knowledge, your experience, and your perceptions—and it is one of your most valuable possessions. Respect it.

Skiing alone in the backcountry is not wise. There is a beauty and a distinct appeal in the solitude of going it alone in the snowy wilds, but minor hazards take on a much greater significance. A misstep can take you into a tree well (the steep, inverted cone surrounding the trunks of evergreens in deep snow). Or you may slip into or break through a snow-covered creek or pond. Perhaps a small slide from a tiny slope will bury you under a pile of snow. A competent companion can quickly bail

PATHOS, BATHOS, AND A TOUCH OF THE SUBLIME

In the Northwest, without being too ridiculous about it, you can find snow to ski on for at least ten months out of the year. This breeds a fanatical core of backcountry skiers who just do not know when to quit, or sometimes when to start. A member in good standing of this group, Mark Harfenist shares this story about early skiing on the south side of Mount Baker with an unnamed companion you may come to recognize over the next two chapters:

Two of us meet along the interstate early Sunday morning (fog, drizzle, darkness), ready to ski. We drive to the Schreiber's Meadow trailhead, then sit in the front seat for a while—sometimes peering out the windows at the gloom, sometimes opening a door to poke an arm out in the rain. We make a lot of useless comments designed to stave off despair ("I think it's lightening up a bit; I don't think I could see those trees a few minutes ago," or "Feels like it's getting colder; the snow level's probably dropping."), or to defend against unduly hopeful, upbeat, or optimistic tendencies ("Could stay like this until mid-April for all we know. Shoot, last year it never even snowed at all until early December, and even then it mostly rained.") I get out and wander over to use the large and luxurious pit toilets, then study the posted maps and trail reports, reading all the notices twice. My partner fumbles around until he finds the recliner lever on the seat, gets comfortable, and begins napping.

Then, without preamble, a couple of blue spots appear in the sky. Visibility improves, spirits lift. We shuffle our gear and go trudging up the trail. As soon as the parking lot is out of sight, the blue sky goes to wherever blue sky commonly goes, and it starts drizzling again (more philosophical discussion about this).

Bits of snow appear along the trail below 4,000 feet, and soon there is continuous snow cover. My partner is carrying unreasonably lightweight and floppy waxless skis and wearing SNS-BC boots; he puts on his skis, dances a little jig (it is possible I imagined this part), and cruises happily up the trail. I am carrying giant, stiff skis, massive releasable tele bindings, plush climbing skins, and huge plastic boots. My back hurts and my legs are tired, but I hide this as best as I'm able, pretending that I am happy to be carrying this additional 25-pound load uphill through the slush. We break out of the woods into an area of steep, snow-covered heather, and I hunker down to put on boots and skis. Suddenly it's mid-October, we're skiing, and life is good.

Every ten minutes the weather does a total reversal, from miserable to perfectly tolerable and then back again, but we continue trudging. Heather gives way to moraine, slushy snowpack deepens, and the Squak Glacier comes into view. We climb a line along the glacier's edge through a small cornice above Crag View and prepare to descend.

The skiing is pretty good: eight to ten inches of consolidated (that's a euphemism for "sopping wet") fresh snow over old nevé, smooth and slick for about eight hundred vertical feet. Five hundred feet of half-hidden moraine rocks under seven inches of snow is next, followed by five hundred feet of lumpy heather under five inches. Then a bunch of close-spaced saplings poke through four inches, a narrow trail descends through old-growth trees with three inches, followed by sections of evergreen needles, then deadfalls, and finally gravel under a meager inch. I take my skis off and load them on my pack, but my partner has long since shot off into the distance. Judging by his track, he's leaping over the gravelly streambeds and hydroplaning through sections of waterlogged evergreen needles at a high rate of speed.

Eventually I find him, sitting by the trail, swaddled in a lot of clothes as if he's been waiting for me for a long time. He is polite about this but cannot resist mentioning how pleased he is to have chosen such appropriately light and maneuverable gear (glancing disdainfully at my great and unwieldy load). I am obliged to suggest that his obvious advantage in skill, athleticism, experience, and positive attitude probably contributed substantially as well. I threaten to denounce him publicly to the gear junkies on www. telemarktips.com. This seems to shut him up.

We reach the parking lot under almost cloudless skies, fall colors blazing orange and yellow. I have skied a couple of thousand vertical feet, my more appropriately equipped partner rather more than that. Altogether, this was a very reasonable first ski for the emergent season, informed in turn by pathos, bathos, and a touch of the sublime.

you out of these and other relatively minor jams. On your own, the outcome is less certain. If you wish to ski alone, at least gain some experience with others so you can weigh the benefits against the hazards and make an informed decision.

GROUP DYNAMICS

The trip should match the group. If you start with an intended destination and a proposed route in mind, choose the group to match. If you have already formed a group before you begin planning, match the intended destination and the proposed route to the capabilities of the least-experienced member.

Winter travel requires that the group stick together. Skiers scattered along a trail or slope might as well be skiing alone, and waiting for stragglers to catch up can be a cold business. Staying together is especially important during stormy weather and in avalanche terrain. The correct pace of the group is that of the slowest member.

Choose companions who will agree to these guidelines and use a buddy system as you travel. Planning, routefinding, pacing, and other decisions are simplified by having a leader, but all group members share responsibility for keeping each other happy and safe. This works best when each member is confident and competent and there is mutual respect among the members of the group. A well-matched group of skiers will move forward by consensus and turn back or alter course based on the concern of one member.

PLANNING

In his book *Avalanche Safety for Skiers and Climbers,* Tony Daffern states that a late start and poor routefinding are the two most common causes of mountain accidents, including avalanche accidents. Both can be minimized with advance planning.

Choose a route and estimate how long it will take. Get commitments from your partners to leave home (and the trailhead) in time to allow you to complete your route and return with plenty of time left over. Agree to a turn-around time that everyone will honor regardless of whether your objective was attained. A broken binding, a tired skier, difficult snow conditions, or lingering over lunch can add an extra hour or two to your estimate. Give yourself plenty of time and carry headlights to expand your options if you are benighted.

Leave word with someone about where you have gone, where you are parked, what vehicle you used, the number and names of your party, and when you expect to return. Specifics about whom to call and when to sound the alarm if you do not return are essential.

Check with governmental agencies for backcountry travel regulations, procedures, and any permits that may be required to use public lands. Parking at many trailheads now requires a permit that is often available only at an office or store which is far from the backcountry and only open during regular business hours. Plan ahead and buy the permit, or risk a significant fine or legal wrangling.

Part of planning is checking your own equipment and that of each member of your party. Make sure everyone has adequate clothing, food, water, and ski equipment suitable for the conditions. New or unfamiliar equipment should be tested on short trips first. If you carry avalanche transceivers, make sure everyone knows how to use them. Check the batteries in all electronic devices and lights before you get to the trailhead and carry spares.

ROUTE SELECTION AND ROUTEFINDING

Choose a route that will be fun, safe, and rewarding. Use a map to help maximize your fun and to identify potential hazards. Wind and sun affect the snow differently on different exposures, something that can be determined by reading the contour lines. With a little planning, you can enjoy a warm, easy climb up a sunny and consolidated south slope, followed by a deep-powder descent on the northern exposure. The map may also reveal a gentle ascent up a watercourse to your intended destination, which can replace the punishing route that is more obvious from the trailhead.

Snow and wind can quickly erase any

sign of your passing, and changing weather can hide landmarks. Keep track of where you are on the map as you go along. Whenever anyone becomes concerned or confused about the route, stop, dig out the map, and consult with others. Ask for advice and turn around and retrace your steps if you have any doubts about continuing. Remember that your ultimate goal is to return to where you began or to set up camp well before darkness descends. This means that midwinter ski trips can be kind of short.

DEVELOPING MAP SKILLS

If you are new to maps, before venturing into the backcountry you should get a map of a nearby area that you know (snow-covered or not) and follow along on the map as you make your way through familiar terrain. Study the map to learn how changes in elevation, streams, roads, buildings, and other features are rendered. Learn to visualize the ridges, valleys, cliffs, plateaus, and meadows described by the contour lines.

Maps are available at outdoor shops and some bookstores, from the U.S. Geological Survey (*www.usgs.gov*) and other suppliers, and on CD from various sources. If you print a map on your home printer for use in the field, be aware that most printer inks are not waterproof.

COMPASS, GPS, AND ALTIMETER

A compass alone cannot tell you where you are. If you do know where you are, and you know how to read a map and how to use a compass, then it can point you toward where you want to go. Find a book or attend a class to get your bearings and to understand magnetic north, declination, triangulation, and so on. Ski orienteering, the winter version of the increasingly popular summertime pursuit, is an excellent way to practice these skills.

A GPS (Global Positioning System) receiver can provide your latitude and longitude, but in the backcountry it will be up to you to interpret these coordinates and find your location on a map. Excellent and affordable handheld GPS units are available. Be aware that deep forests and valleys can interfere with reception and, of course, batteries do run down. Study GPS manuals or books or enroll in a class to learn how to use one. Practice with it before you need it and carry a compass as a backup.

Altimeter watches are now readily available at prices that the casual adventurer can afford. These watches track how much elevation you have gained and lost and some even chart your rate of ascent and descent. These functions are fun to play with, but an altimeter can also help you navigate.

Knowing your elevation gives you one more way to confirm that where you think you are on the map is where you actually are. It is also extremely helpful when you are traversing a slope in poor visibility and want to avoid steeper ground above or below you or you need to go up or down a certain amount of elevation before changing course.

Altimeters determine elevation by measuring changes in atmospheric pressure. As you go higher, the atmospheric pressure

Ski tracks on Maple Pass in Washington's North Cascades. (Photo Steve Barnett)

goes down. Weather changes, since they involve changes in atmospheric pressure, also affect the readings from a stationary altimeter, which can cause them to vary by hundreds of feet from the true elevation. This means you cannot trust the accuracy of a reading unless you have adjusted your altimeter to match a known elevation under current weather conditions. A relative elevation change reading, however, will be accurate, if it says you climbed one thousand feet in the last hour, you have.

Some altimeters are able to track changes in atmospheric pressure over time—a valuable function that enables you to review the trends (up or down) to gain more

information on upcoming weather conditions. Even without a pressure tracking function on your watch, if you notice that your elevation appears to have decreased but you have not moved, then the pressure is going up and perhaps fairer weather is approaching. Of course, when your elevation climbs but you do not, the opposite is true and bad weather may be on its way.

AVALANCHE TERRAIN

Avalanches do not threaten all backcountry skiers. If there is no snow hanging above or below you, then there is no avalanche danger. On the other hand, six inches of snow sliding off a short, steep slope is more than enough to bury you if the terrain concentrates the slide. You can reduce the risk of avalanches by learning to identify and to recognize avalanche hazards and by understanding how to avoid them.

The information in this chapter is intended to provide a very basic outline of what you need to know about avalanches to ski in the backcountry. However, if you intend to travel where avalanches may strike, the best thing to do is sign up for the next avalanche awareness and education course you can find (see sidebar).

WHAT CAUSES AVALANCHES?

To vastly oversimplify a complex phenomenon, two things are needed to create an avalanche: an increase in the weight of the snow and/or a weakening of what supports it, and a slope steep enough that an unsupported mass of snow will slide.

You can watch these basic principles in action by observing the snow on various kinds of roofs. Snow on a relatively flat roof is unlikely to slide, and very steep roofs constantly shed snow and fail to build up any accumulation. Roofs in between these two extremes build up snow, which then avalanches in successive cycles. Snow on smooth metal roofs slides more easily and more often than that on rough-surfaced shake or shingle roofs.

The same principles apply in the backcountry, snow on smooth, grassy slopes slides more easily than snow on slopes covered with rocky outcroppings or scattered brush, stumps, and other anchors, at least until additional snowfall or drifting smoothes everything out.

Slopes over 55 degrees constantly clean themselves with smaller, loose-snow avalanches called point-release avalanches. Even steeper slopes shed extra material almost immediately. Shallower slopes tend to build up snow and then release it in periodic cycles.

The most destructive point-release avalanches occur in the spring, when small wet-snowslides gather large quantities of snow as they ooze downward. These avalanches move slowly but can create massive damage, uprooting trees and mangling skiers. Be very wary of south-facing slopes in the spring or when the weather is warm, especially in the afternoon. Warming weather is also notorious for causing snow on rock walls and trees to drop onto the slopes below, which in turn can cause a slab to fail or trigger a wet-snow avalanche.

Slopes under 20 degrees seldom slide except in very wet snow conditions. The vast majority of avalanches occur on slopes between 30 and 45 degrees, with the most activity observed in the 35 to 45 degree range. Since it is hard to accurately judge the pitch of a slope without an inclinometer, keep it simple and stay off steep slopes if you are concerned about the avalanche hazard.

A variety of unseen processes can weaken the bonds that hold snow to a slope, causing it to suddenly let loose without any external trigger. These dangerous and unpredictable avalanches are most commonly encountered in the Rocky Mountains and other interior ranges around the world dominated by continental climates that produce extended periods of cold, clear, and dry winter weather in conjunction with a variable, usually shallow, snowpack.

Wind and other forces can create bonds that connect parts of a slope into a larger whole. If a portion of this slope becomes too heavy to be supported by the underlying layers of the snowpack, that section will break loose from the rest. This is called a slab avalanche and often produces a "whoomp" or sharp crack as the underlying layers fail. Slab avalanches are especially

AVALANCHE EDUCATION COURSES AND FURTHER READING

The organizations listed below all provide resources to guide you to a qualified course or online tutorial.

The Canadian Avalanche Association
P.O. Box 2759
Revelstoke, BC V0E 2S0
(205) 837-2435
www.avalanche.ca

American Avalanche Association
P.O. Box 2831
Pagosa Springs, CO 81147
(970) 946-0822
www.avalanche.org

American Institute of Avalanche Research and Education
P.O. Box 2206
Crested Butte, CO 81224
(970) 209-0486
www.avtraining.org

Daffern, Tony. *Avalanche Safety for Skiers and Climbers*. 2nd ed. Seattle: The Mountaineers Books, 1999.

Fesler, Doug, and Jill A. Fredston, *Snow Sense*. 5th ed. Anchorage: Alaska Mountain Safety Center, 2001.

LaChapelle, Ed. *Secrets of the Snow: Visual Clues to Avalanche and Ski Conditions*. Seattle: University of Washington Press, 2001.

LaChapelle, Ed, and Sue Ferguson. *The ABC's of Avalanche Safety*. 3rd ed. Seattle: The Mountaineers Books, 2004.

McClung, David, and Peter Schaerer. *Avalanche Handbook*. 2nd ed. Seattle: The Mountaineers Books, 1993.

dangerous since a large mass of snow can break loose and begin to slide all at once. Individual blocks often form within the larger slab, creating additional dangers as they rumble down the slope.

The easiest aspect of avalanches to understand might be called the "disturbance principle" (*direct action* is the technical term).Warm things up, pile on more snow (by wind or snowfall), wet things down, ski or jump onto a slope, or drop a cornice or point-release avalanche from a cliff onto a slope, and you may cause that slope to slide.

The point where an avalanche starts is called the start zone. The path an avalanche follows down the slope is called the avalanche track or the slide path. The area where the snow slows and accumulates is called the run-out zone or the deposition zone. Understanding this anatomy is crucial, because staying out of the start zone is by far the most effective way to avoid being caught by an avalanche.

Slab avalanche. (Photo: Don Svela)

Fig. 13.1 – Start zone, avalanche track, and run-out zone

Large slide paths are easy to see—they often have smaller trees in the middle with larger timber defining the sides of the avalanche track—and some run-out zones are easily spotted in the summer because they are full of mangled trees and other debris.

Heavy timber usually provides an area of safety, but only when it is dense enough to be very hard to ski through. Studying the size of trees growing in paths where avalanches obviously run will make you think twice about how safe skiing in those trees might be.

This quick and oversimplified survey of avalanches can help you recognize when avalanche danger may be high, but it is completely inadequate for determining if a slope is safe or not. Any attempt to outguess the snowpack and local avalanche forecasts is foolhardy indeed. Mastering the skills and the art of routefinding takes time and experience. Stay alive by avoiding steep and open slopes as you learn to identify start zones, slide paths, run-out zones, and areas of safe travel.

TRAVEL IN AVALANCHE TERRAIN

Safe travel in avalanche terrain starts with learning the topography, the local weather patterns, the history of the snowpack, and the current avalanche conditions for where you will be skiing.

Research where you want to go with maps, guidebooks, and by talking with others who have been there before. Avalanche reports for most backcountry areas in Canada and the U.S. are available on the Internet and through local telephone numbers. If you are traveling on public land, check with the administrating agency for information on current weather and snow conditions. They will be able to provide you with the telephone number for the local avalanche report. Local ski patrols, newspapers, and radio reports are other possible sources for information on avalanche conditions.

To make informed decisions on where to go and how to travel you need to know the local history of seasonal weather patterns and the snowpack. A ski shop or a bar in the closest town where the locals hang out can often be your best source of this information, although a bit of skepticism will be useful in sorting out the truth from the exaggerations.

ROUTE SELECTION

If the day of your trip coincides with a forecast of high or extreme avalanche danger, plans that involve crossing over or under any slopes steep enough to avalanche will have to be scrapped. Anytime you venture out beyond the boundaries of a controlled area make sure that your terrain objectives match the avalanche conditions. Michael Jackson of the Alpine Safety Awareness Program compares matching objectives with the level of avalanche, or "avy," danger to balancing on a teeter-totter. High avy risk must be balanced with low-angle terrain and high-angle terrain can only be balanced with no avy risk. Most days spent in the backcountry fall somewhere between these two extremes.

Winter weather can change in an instant, bringing a storm that completely reverses the avalanche forecast you picked up before leaving in the morning or invalidating your own assessment of the conditions. Wet and warm storms are an extreme example of this scenario. Wet snow, and especially rain, will often begin to trigger slides soon after the storm begins. Only the very safest of routes become reasonable options in such conditions.

Some signs of increasing instability are "whoomps" coming from the snowpack as you ski across it, snow falling from cliffs and trees, pinwheels rolling down slopes, cracks spreading in front of you across the snow, and of course, fresh avalanches.

When the weather changes unexpectedly, or you begin to notice these and other signs of instability, you may have to drastically alter your route or turn back. Long and difficult detours may be needed when changing conditions prevent you from retracing your steps across slopes that no longer present a reasonable level of risk. It takes far more confidence and courage to turn back than to forge ahead, so let no one talk you out of it. In extreme conditions when the danger becomes high and no safe routes exist, you may have to find a safe spot and stay put until conditions improve.

In over 90 percent of avalanche accidents, victims or a member of their party triggered the slide themselves. It is rare that a natural slide or an avalanche started by another party traps someone. This is why route selection in avalanche terrain is so crucial. The safest routes avoid any slopes over 25 degrees and follow ridge tops above start zones or are along valley bottoms far from the run-out zones of any slide paths.

Skiing in avalanche terrain is never completely free of danger. The more you ski in such areas, the more the odds begin to stack up against you due to repeated exposure. The best option is to find and

SETTING THE TRACK

If you are the first skier putting in an up-track after the last snow, the responsibility for setting a safe, user-friendly and aesthetically pleasing track goes right along with the extra work of breaking trail. The art of routefinding takes years to refine, but seemingly insignificant choices can make the difference between easy walking and flailing, or even life and death. Follow these tips to set a trail that will make your friends want you to break trail all the time:

- On easy terrain, go straight up. The steepest slopes that skins can grip are in the 15–20 degree range under most conditions. If it's easy to be direct, you will save energy by breaking less trail. As the terrain steepens, veer off to one side or the other. Rule of thumb: if you are slipping in the front, someone behind you will be too. Slipping, falling, or just recovering, all of these zap energy that could be better used for climbing.
- On steeper ground, use switchbacks to keep the gradient, or angle of climb, consistent. Try to make each switchback as long as practical to minimize the number of kick turns; if possible place your kick turns on flatter areas between the switchbacks. Other skiers, especially those less skilled at kick turns, will appreciate it.
- Avoid flat-tracking in the middle of a climb, except to avoid avalanche hazards. The work of breaking trail is best dedicated to upward travel. Anticipation and planning will enable you to maintain the most constant gradient possible, so look ahead as you slog along.
- On a windy or snowy day, set your track through trees instead of out in the open to keep everyone warmer or drier. Climb up the side of a ridge that is less exposed to wind, but be wary of avalanche-prone leeward slopes that may be wind-loaded.
- If you intend to make multiple laps, think ahead to where you will end up after that first powder run. If it's convenient, ski by the "finish zone" on your way up. You will have a ready-made track waiting to take you back to the top.

Scott McGee, guide for Exum Mountaineering and a two-term member of the PSIA Nordic Demonstration Team

follow the safest route available at all times, even if the danger is low.

AVALANCHE TRAVEL PROTOCOLS

Surviving an avalanche burial in the backcountry is dependent on the actions of the members of your party. By the time any outside group can reach you, any rescue is likely to be a body recovery. Your buddies cannot help you if they are buried too, so the first rule of travel in avalanche terrain is to spread out and cross any suspect area one at a time.

Post a spotter to warn of any slides coming down from above while the party crosses a run-out zone. Decide in advance on a point of no return, where you will push on to the other side instead of turning back if the slope above does begin to slide.

During a storm pay particular attention to the terrain. Whiteout conditions can make it easy to wander into dangerous areas. Ski groups also tend to bunch up in storms, making a bad situation worse by exposing everyone at the same time to any dangerous slopes you happen to cross over or under but are unaware of due to limited visibility.

It is much easier to recognize the conditions that lead to snowpack instability than it is to determine the stability of a particular slope at any given time. To thrive and survive as a backcountry skier, you need to recognize hazardous situations. Some of the things to keep in mind:

- Open slopes, chutes, and other obvious avalanche paths on slopes between 20 degrees and 50 degrees hold the most potential for avalanches.
- Ridge tops are the safest and valley bottoms are second best. Avalanches do not stop immediately when they reach the bottom of the slope. Detour around the bottom of any open slope or other potential slide path.
- Do not stop for lunch, take a break, or set up camp beneath a slide path or a cornice (ridgetop snow drift) or in the middle of an open slope that could potentially slide. This is a common mistake.
- Heavy forest that would be hard to ski through is much safer than open slopes but not a guarantee of safe passage.
- Small point-release avalanches become

serious when they sweep you over a cliff, into trees, or pile up in a gully or creek bed. Be on the lookout for these "terrain traps."

- The periods during and just after heavy snowfalls and persistent high winds present the greatest danger. Subsequent cold temperatures may prolong the danger. Stay out of avalanche zones when these conditions exist.
- Wind can deposit snow on lee slopes and build cornices on the ridge tops. Wind-loaded slopes are likely candidates for slab avalanches, and cornices can fall without warning, triggering larger slides or posing their own dangers. These dangers are often overlooked as they can increase in periods of sunny but windy weather.
- Warming temperatures can weaken a cornice or a slab, creating hazardous conditions during sunny, calm weather.
- North slopes are sheltered from the stabilizing effect of the sun's warmth, which is why they hold the best powder. Resist the allure unless you are confident of the slope's stability.
- In the spring and during any winter warm-ups, sun-baked slopes are prone to wet-snow avalanches in the afternoon.
- Small variations in the aspect of the slope (the compass direction it faces) can have large effects on the snowpack. Pay careful attention to how the terrain changes as you ski over it and avoid the common mistake of assuming that because one slope was stable, a similar slope will also be skiable.

Many reports of the second or third or even the thirtieth skier crossing a slope and setting off a slide have been recorded. Tracks on a slope are not an assurance of safety or stability.

EQUIPMENT

As in any other kind of cross-country skiing, having the right equipment for the backcountry can add immeasurably to the quality of your experience.

PACKS

A pack in the 1,500-cubic-inch range should do for day trips, and a 3,000- to 4,000-cubic-inch pack will see you through most overnight excursions. A pack that is too big invites you to fill it with things you do not need, while overstuffing a small pack will make it feel like a football on your back.

To minimize movements of whatever you'll be carrying, choose a pack with load control straps on the bag itself and with well-designed shoulder straps and a waist belt to secure the pack to your back as you ski. Side straps for attaching skis to the pack are crucial and help to compress the pack's volume when it is not full. A loop on the back or some other means of carrying a shovel with the blade on the outside is handy. A tough and waterproof bottom will help keep your gear dry and extend the life of the pack. Most packs sold as climbing, skiing, or snowboarding packs work well because they have these features and little more. They also tend to be tall and thin, allowing your arms to swing freely as you pole.

The exact content of your ski pack needs to be determined by you. Ask your ski buddies what they carry and then start out with a good selection of the basics. Over time, you will adjust the contents of your own pack to include the essentials of what you need to be safe and comfortable. Don't forget to include any additional spare parts that may be needed for your particular brand of binding, pole, or other equipment, and make sure you have extra batteries for any electronic gizmos.

In addition to the items that always stay in my pack (see sidebar), I add food and water for the day, and maps and photocopies of the pages of any guidebooks that I might need for the specific objective of the trip. In the winter I usually carry a few more items of extra clothing. I carry extra socks more often in warm weather than in cold—a change into dry socks can do more than anything else to make your feet less likely to blister.

You may choose to go lighter by carrying garbage bags in place of my emergency tube tent, or you may want a larger margin of safety and choose to carry a light sleeping bag, a lightweight tarp, and some nylon cord to set it up with. I carry devices to prevent the loss of my hat and sunglasses. You may choose to carry extra hats and sunglasses. The first-aid supplies I carry are certainly not inclusive of everything you could include.

Previous tracks are not a guarantee of stability. (Photo: Don Svela)

MY PACK AT THE END OF THE SEASON

Here in the Northwest, the first skiable snowfall usually graces the Cascades sometime before Halloween. By that time, my ski pack has been used as a hiking pack, a climbing pack, a haul-stuff-to-the-beach-for-an-evening-picnic pack, and who knows what else. It takes a few hours of rummaging around to get packed for that first trip. Then it stays packed and slowly returns to its proper glory—finely tuned to the essentials. Here's what I include:

Top Pocket

Zippered pouch containing:

- butane lighter
- self-adhesive nylon repair patches from Gore-Tex (because they stick the best on any synthetic material)
- a small sewing kit like those found in swanky hotel rooms
- New Skin, a blister prevention/repair liquid that is painted right on the skin for protection; it hurts but it works
- water treatment tablets
- pieces of moleskin and molefoam
- eight adhesive bandages
- eight safety pins

(All numbers in this list are approximate.)

A small wide-mouth stuff sack containing:

- waterproof tape (Johnson and Johnson sticks best)—use on heels prior to a trip to prevent blisters, to keep blister treatments on during a trip, for other first-aid applications, and for securing skins to skis when the glue fails
- anti-fog cloth for glasses and goggles
- another lighter
- strike-anywhere matches in a waterproof container
- lip balm
- sunscreen
- bug juice (for summer skiing)
- hat clip—attaches ball cap to collar so that wind does not blow away crucial sun-protection device at inopportune time
- small and lightweight headlamp with one battery reversed to prevent accidental draining
- extra batteries for my small headlamp and my avalanche transceiver
- whistle for emergency signaling
- simple compass
- an extra elastic restraining strap for sunglasses
- spare pole basket
- spare tip for climbing skins
- ratcheted driver with proper bit to tighten loose binding screws

- four small hose clamps and a half-round pole repair sleeve (hose clamps can be used for pole repair, as a substitute for a broken boot buckle, or possibly to help hold a binding onto a ski)
- wire—to repair a boot, binding, or pole
- extra cable for my binding

A small roll-top waterproof bag containing:
- a dozen or so ibuprofen tablets
- a blister pack of Benadryl for anaphylactic reactions
- several gauze pads
- more adhesive bandages, including larger sizes
- butterfly bandages
- blister treatments such as *2nd Skin*
- cotton swabs
- alcohol wipes
- antibiotic lotion
- elastic wrap for sprains
- folding scissors
- another lighter
- small tweezers

Bandana—for sun protection, to clean glasses, or to be used as a triangular bandage or a sling
Small multitool with pliers, wire cutter, and knife. If this tool had a posidrive screwdriver and scissors, the folding scissors and ratcheted driver could be left at home.
Ziploc bag with TP and yet another lighter
Sunglasses

Main Compartment
emergency tube tent
piece of old inner tube to be used as a universal binding-cable replacement, as a cinch for a broken boot part, etc.
extra gloves
gaiters
extra hat
synthetic puffy jacket
wind and rain shells for top and bottom
extra lightweight fleece
avalanche probe
avalanche transceiver
shovel
skins/wax

have an avalanche probe or a thin snow saw stashed in the handle.

Backcountry and avalanche shovels are specialized tools. Using them to dig out your car or to chop ice will eventually ruin them. Put a separate shovel in your car for roadside use and carry ice tools if you expect to chop steps.

CLIMBING SKINS

Climbing skins help you grip the snow when you do not want to mess around with grip wax or the route you wish to follow is too steep for wax. They are called skins because they originally were made from animal hides.

Today almost all skins are synthetic. The side facing the snow is a carpet-like material that stays smooth and flat as the ski slides forward. As the ski slides back, the fibers of this material rise up to provide traction, much as a cat's hair rises up when you pet it in the wrong direction. The backs of most climbing skins are layered with an amazing adhesive that almost never wears out. If it does, you can apply more glue.

Some sort of tensioning device is used at either the tip or the tail to help keep the skin in place. Partial skins that attach just under the foot are also available; use these as back-up traction for tours during which you will be using grip wax the majority of the time.

A few tricks can make skins work better. Always apply your skins to a dry ski. If your ski is wet, wipe it off as best you can or set it in the sun to dry. If it is very cold, carry your skins inside your jacket to warm

Snow shovel and snow saw

SNOW SHOVELS

Shovels need to be strong and light. Size also matters, especially if you have to move a lot of snow to excavate a snow shelter or to dig out an avalanche victim. Aluminum grain scoops with the handle cut down can work, but specialized shovels available from a variety of manufacturers are usually a better choice. They are light, strong, and come apart, making them easier to carry. Some

the glue so that they stick better. Never let the glue side touch the snow or any other contaminants. If your skin slips off at the tip or tail, stop immediately and reattach it. If it will not stay on, tape it to the ski with duct tape or waterproof first-aid tape.

To help the fuzzy side slide better and absorb less water during warmer tours, apply bar wax or a liquid treatment sold for this purpose. When you stop for lunch, set your skis in the sun or, if you will be descending after you eat, remove your skins and hang them to dry. When they're not in use fold your skins back on themselves to keep the glue from picking up contaminants in your pack (like stray peanuts and cookie crumbs).

Choose the right width of skins for your skis—only the metal edge and no more than an eighth of an inch of base in the middle of your ski should be left uncovered. For shaped skis with narrow waists and wide tips and tails, buy skins that are wider than the waist of the ski and trim them to follow the shape of the sidecut.

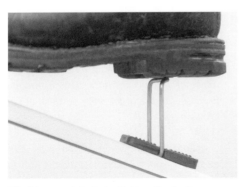

Climbing posts help to flatten the incline.

If your glue wears out, talk to someone who has had good luck with a particular brand of skin glue, buy what they use, and follow the directions on the container. To remove old, dirty glue, lay your skins glue side up on a bench. Set a waxing iron to waxing temperature and place one layer of a brown paper bag on the glue. Place the iron on the bag. The heat will pull the glue into the brown paper. Be sure to clean your iron after using it to remove skin glue. Solvent that will remove dirty glue is available, but it is toxic and very messy to use.

CLIMBING BARS OR POSTS

These devices support your heels, helping relieve the strain on your calves and hamstrings when you are climbing up steep sections. They also help you to stay forward and over your feet for better grip. Climbing bars that flip up from the heelpiece on the ski are the most convenient. If your heelpiece does not include a climbing bar, you can retrofit a heelpiece that does, or you can use a climbing post. Climbing posts are chunks of plastic held in place around your ankle with an elastic cord. When you want a heel lift, you slide it into place beneath your heel. When you do not want it, you slide it around to the front.

CLIMBING ON SKINS

Scott McGee is not only a guide for Exum Mountaineering, he is also Nordic director at Jackson Hole in Wyoming. He offers these suggestions for using skins:

Keep your head warm and your skins dry.

CLIMBING

There is a limit to the steepness that skins can climb. However, technique can make the difference between smoothly ascending and slipping backward. Proper stance, positive stepping, un-edging, and careful placement can get skins to grip that would otherwise slip.

Stance: *Walking uphill is easiest with a fairly upright posture with rounded shoulders and relaxed arms. Stand in the center of the ski and the middle of the skin will grip better. Bending forward moves the hips back and may lighten the pressure on the front of the skis causing them to slip. Use climbing posts or heel lifts to optimize posture and grip.*

Positive Stepping: *Two benefits result from stepping firmly onto a ski after moving*

it ahead of the other ski. First, the fur on the bottom of the ski will engage better if the ski is pressed firmly into the snow. Move the ski ahead and step up onto it in one move. Second, a skin can only grip the snow that it touches. If the surface is uneven, stomp the ski to deform the snow surface to match the bottom of the ski, maximizing skin/snow contact, and therefore grip.

Un-edging: *Skiers are accustomed to pressing their uphill edge into the slope to keep their skis from slipping down the hill. However, this lifts the downhill section of the skin off the snow. When ascending a slope in a climbing traverse, flattening the ski aids grip by increasing the contact surface of the skin to the snow. Practice this counterintuitive technique and learn to trust the grip of the skins instead of the edge. Edging too much will provide immediate feedback in the form of an unwanted slip.*

Careful Placement: *Finding a good place to put the skins down is a very effective way to increase grip. Since the metal edges are slippery, and the skins grip, try to place the center of one ski on the small ridge of snow between ski tracks, stepping the other ski above or below the tracks. This technique is especially useful for short sections of icy or steep track.*

The above techniques in combination with good cross-country skiing technique will help you get to the top with more energy and time for more runs.

REMOVAL

Once you've made it to the top, you're ready to peel. The easiest method is to take your skis off, release the tensioning device, peel the skin off the base, and then carefully fold the skin to itself such that no glue is left showing. Slightly quicker, but infinitely more difficult, is the method of peeling the skins without removing your skis. This task is best accomplished with rubber skin tips or tails that stretch, allowing the skier to pull the tip or tail off without releasing the glue first.

First, kick one ski up, placing its tail even with the other ski's tip. Pull the tip of the upright ski back toward you until it is within easy reach. Warning: this requires good balance. Use an uphill pole plant braced against your hips if you're worried about toppling over. Stretch the tip clip over the ski tip, and in a quick whipping motion, peel the skin away from the ski. Skins with new glue may require a few extra tugs to release the glue all the way down. If you have tail clips, lift your tails, being careful to keep your skin glue out of the snow as you rip it off the base.

OVERNIGHT TRIPS

Spending the night out in the snow is fun and challenging. If you have backpacked without snow on the ground, you already know most of what you need to know and you probably have most of the gear.

There are many good books on snow camping. Books on climbing, mountaineer-ing, and backcountry travel also offer a wealth of information and suggestions on staying alive and comfortable in the cold and the snow. I will not attempt to repeat that information here, but there are a few things to consider on an overnight back-country ski trip.

You'll need the same clothing for an overnight trip as for a day tour, plus ad-ditional dry socks, underwear, and top and bottom next-to-the-skin layers to change into after you set up camp. Hanging around camp during the milder days of spring requires no more clothing than what should already be in your pack for a cold and windy lunch stop or an unexpected emer-gency. (This includes extra outer layers for wind and water protection, extra insulation layers, extra warm gloves or mittens, and an extra warm and windproof hat.)

For midwinter trips, add thick mittens and mukluks or overboots to wear over your dry socks while you accomplish any chores you are forced to do outside your tent or snow shelter. Otherwise, arrive in camp, set up your shelter, and climb inside. During the dead of winter, there is no reason to hang around outside in the dark and cold.

Fires can of course make camp a warmer and friendlier place to pass the night, but harvesting wood for your evening pleasure is seldom recommended in the over-trav-eled areas that most backcountry skiers frequent. In deep snow, preventing the fire from melting deeply into the snowpack is another problem, as are sparks that can quickly melt rather large holes in your expensive clothing and tent.

Snuggled into the snow under a floorless tent. (Photo: Steve Barnett)

Respect the environment wherever you travel and leave no trace of your trip. Cutting branches to sleep on is definitely out. Be aware of where you deposit your waste, and keep it far away from streams and other water sources to avoid contamination when the snow melts. Pack out all garbage, including toilet paper, unless you can get it to burn.

SHELTER

Freestanding tents constructed to withstand wind and snow loads are the simplest way to provide overnight accommodation, but they are also heavy and expensive. In the winter tents also suffer from condensation and icing problems on the inside and offer only a small and cramped area in which to spend the long winter nights.

Constructing a snow shelter for the night takes more time, but the payoff can be great. Snow caves are popular among Boy Scouts and other groups, but after building one or two, most folks opt for a different solution. The main problem with building a snow cave is that you spend an hour or more rolling around in the snow. By the time you are done, your hat, gloves, and all your clothes are soaked from both sweat and snow. This is a real problem when you are out for more than one night, since the inside of a snow cave is not a great place to dry things out.

A better solution is to carry a waterproof tarp sized to fit your party and your shelter ambitions. With the shovel you already carry for safety and convenience, you can dig a trench horizontally across the slope and use the tarp to cover it. A snow saw, a thick aluminum blade usually about a foot and a half long with large serration along one edge, can be used to cut snow blocks out of consolidated snow to construct walls, or even gables, to stretch the tarp across. Some backcountry shovels come with saws cleverly hidden within the handle. These are convenient for certain avalanche stability tests but may be a little wimpy for serious snow shelter work.

If you are the no-fuss no-muss type, tarp and snow shelters may not be for you. I love them, both for the weight savings of leaving the tent behind and for their comfort. A tarp and snow shelter is warmer than a tent and, if properly constructed, much more storm-proof. It can easily be fairly roomy, and the interior walls are bright and reflective, permitting one candle to illuminate the entire space. Crawling into a tent to remove clothing and boots inevitably brings snow into the tent as well. A well-made tarp and snow shelter includes a covered entryway with a snow floor, keeping the ground tarp in the rest of the shelter snow free. You can dig fresh snow out of one corner to melt while you pour your dishwater in the opposite corner. With the approval of your mates, a third corner can even be designated for middle-of-the-night liquid relief.

Other lightweight and roomy solutions include various floorless tents and tarps that offer many of the same advantages with less set-up effort. Skis, poles, and shovels all make great anchors to support your tarp or tent. With skis you can just jam the tail into the snow and tie the guyline to it. Digging a trench perpendicular to the guyline and burying the anchor will make it stronger. Dig a smaller trench for the guyline so that as it is tensioned it does not lever the anchor out of the snow. Be aware that in some snow conditions, your anchor may freeze in so well that removing it will be difficult.

There is one problem with using skis, poles, or shovels to anchor your tent—you cannot go skiing or use the shovel without compromising your home away from home. Lightweight nylon stuff sacks filled with snow are a simple solution to this problem. For the ultimate lightweight anchor, try this stuff sack design by Brent Harris, designer for Brenthaven of Bellingham, Washington (Figure 13.1 on page 222).

Experiment with your first snow shelter on a day trip so that you do not find yourself homeless if things go awry. To begin with, make sure you are not settling in for the night beneath an avalanche path or underneath trees overburdened with snow. If you dig a snow cave, be careful of soggy conditions or other types of snow that may collapse on you while you are inside. Be sure to always slope the entrance of any shelter downward to drain the cold air away and provide some means for fresh air to be drawn in from above. A snug snow shelter can be quiet and comfortable, so be careful that you do not climb inside and forget about the outside world and get snowed in.

A shallow snowpack or the loose and unconsolidated snow common in drier climates makes it very difficult to construct a snow shelter. If there is any chance of encountering these conditions you should carry a tent.

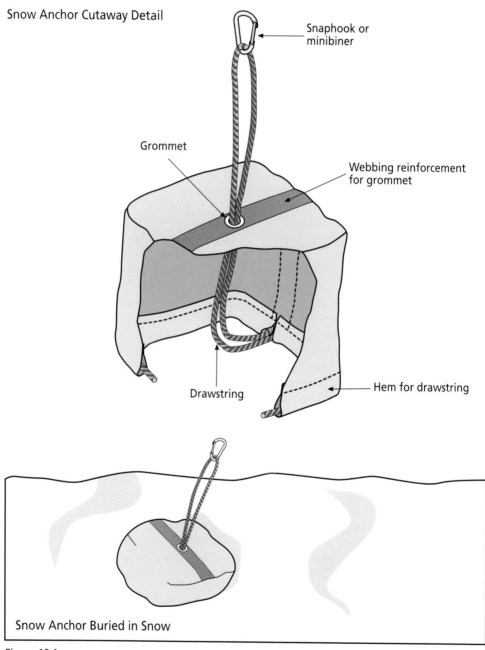

Snow Anchor Cutaway Detail

Snaphook or minibiner

Grommet

Webbing reinforcement for grommet

Drawstring

Hem for drawstring

Snow Anchor Buried in Snow

Figure 13.1

COOKING AND WATER

Cooking in foul weather is always tricky. Cooking inside a tent, however, is dangerous. Combustion uses oxygen, tents can catch fire, and most fuels emit noxious gases as they burn. A snow shelter is a better place to cook since it is nonflammable, but exhaust gases from the stove can still deplete the oxygen inside if you are not mindful of what you are doing.

One solution is an alcohol stove, which emits only carbon dioxide and water vapor. No matter what stove you use, be sure to provide plenty of ventilation and pay attention to what you are doing.

On any extended winter trip, fuel will be one of the heaviest things in your pack, since you have to carry enough to melt all of your water. To reduce your need to melt water, put a little snow in your water bottle during the day, provided you can keep it warm enough to melt the added snow. Keep your water bottle (closed very tightly!) inside your sleeping bag at night so that it does not freeze. Fill it with warm water for an extra treat.

To save fuel while cooking dehydrated food, put the food in a bottle with some water in the morning so that the food will rehydrate during the day (as long as the water does not freeze).

If you do come across an open stream, it can be a challenge to get to the water. One method is to grab a pile of snow on your pole basket and dip it into the water. The snow will absorb quite a bit of water, which you then can drain into a pot or suck directly from the snow. Giardia and other nasties may still be around in the water source, so follow whatever precautions you would observe in the summertime. If you have a pump-type filter with you, the intake hose can be handy for reaching the open water between the snow banks. Iodine tablets can also be used to treat water, but be aware that it takes iodine much longer to work in cold water.

WINTER CAMPING INFORMATION

Howe, Steve, and *Backpacker* magazine. *Making Camp: The Complete Guide for Hikers, Mountain Bikers, Paddlers, and Skiers.* Seattle: The Mountaineers Books, 2001.
Lanza, Michael, and *Backpacker* magazine. *Winter Hiking and Camping: Managing Cold for Comfort and Safety.* Seattle: The Mountaineers Books, 2004.

CHAPTER 14

Parallel and Telemark Turns

The step, skating, and wedge turns described in Chapters 2 and 9 will be sufficient for most touring and track skiers, but if you want to tackle steeper hills or are going to ski the backcountry, you'll have a lot more fun if you learn how to make parallel and telemark turns.

Backcountry skiers use a variety of equipment to cross the country—from lightweight skating equipment on a spring crust to burly telemark gear. The key to turning is to understand the fundamentals of your own equipment and how to make it do what you want it to do without taking a tumble.

Making turns with narrow skis designed only for touring, which have a lot of camber but little sidecut, requires a lot of effort and very quick feet. Dick Hall, founder of the North American Telemark Association, describes the antics of a skier in challenging conditions on this type of equipment as a scarecrow flailing around with hot sauce down his pants.

In contrast, modern telemark equipment allows skiers to control and direct their skis with subtle movements of their hips and core, with the result that they will ski very much like alpine skiers, especially on groomed snow. Hall likens skiing on this type of gear to dancing with a partner that you have enjoyed dancing with for years—quiet and subtle interactions create instant and graceful responses.

Skiers on light but supportive boots and modern skis designed to both tour and turn fall somewhere in between. This equipment does not require the hot sauce dance of the scarecrow, but neither does it allow for the subtle finesse that is possible with wide, heavy-duty telemark equipment. Hall compares skiing on this less restrictive gear to dancing with your twelve-year-old niece at your cousin's wedding. After a few attempts to guide her gently through the dance steps or to teach her how to follow your lead, you just pick her up and show her how to do it with her feet held off the floor. In other words, skiing on this in-between gear sometimes requires picking up your skis and putting them where they need to go.

The ideal backcountry equipment for you will be whatever suits your tastes and your desires. Personally, I like gear with enough heft, support, and sidecut to avoid flailing around like that scarecrow but which is still light enough to make the flats and uphills a pleasure.

LEARNING TO TURN

If you have never made turns on any type of equipment, the quickest way to learn is to spend a day or two at an alpine ski area. Rent a set of alpine gear, buy a lift ticket, and make sure you know how to load and unload from the lift before you jump on it. Grab an instructor and work on getting comfortable, relaxed, and balanced while sliding downhill. You will make more turns in a day of lift riding than in two solid weeks of hiking for your turns. Stay on terrain where you can relax, stand over your feet, and allow the skis to turn for you. If you stray onto a slope that is too steep before you are ready to tackle it you will develop defensive habits that will screw up your skiing for years.

If you do not want to mess with alpine gear but would still like to ride the lifts, rent some backcountry skis with metal edges and spend a day or two at the ski area with this gear. If alpine skiing or riding a ski lift is simply not for you, consider spending some time skating at a Nordic center to shorten your downhill-turning learning curve. Moving from ski to ski, balancing on skis going in different directions and edging skills are just a few of the many basics that can be picked up quickly while learning or perfecting your skating skills.

START WITH STANCE

Easy turns start with an active and balanced stance. You can call this a ready stance, an active stance, a fighting stance, or whatever term you like that evokes an image of an athlete or an animal ready for action.

Once you're moving, the trick is to stay relaxed, ready, and over your feet as forces jolt, jar, and jostle you and for that you will need to use your core muscles (see Chapter 9 if you need a review of these basics). Keep your core muscles strong and active, and do not give in to the forces of evil that seek to fling you off your skis!

Fight to retain and regain your "ready stance" when things start to go downhill. As Scott McGee, Nordic director at Jackson Hole reveals, "Don't think that great skiers are never out of balance. They are just quick at getting it back."

HOW TO FALL

A fall should not be your first reaction to a bump in the road, but trying to save a lost cause can lead to injury. Once you have been knocked out of your ready stance and know you are going down, relax and take the stress off your joints. Be especially wary of a fall straight back onto the heels of your skis. This is how skiers tear the ligaments

QUICK START TURNING TIPS

Street and ice skaters—If you can turn on skates, you will be able to turn on skis. The big difference is dealing with gravity. To do so, let your legs turn and tip more than your torso, something that aggressive street skaters will already know how to do if they have done any turning on hills.

Snowboarders, skateboarders, and other board riders—If you are a boarder, the weirdest thing about skiing is sliding in the same direction as your feet are pointing. Once you get over that, work on doing the same thing with both your feet. If you do different things with them, they will go in different directions.

Like boards, skis go straight when they are flat, and turn when they are tipped onto their edges. The trick, just like when riding a board, is to stay in balance over your feet as the skis go straight or as you tip them to turn.

What is nice is that there is neither a toe side nor a heel side—your joints and everything else work the same whether you turn to the left or to the right. What you will not have, however, is the stopping power of your heel side. Choose a mellow slope to start with.

Groomed trail or tour skiers—Balance will be easy with the bigger boots and wider skis of backcountry equipment, but dealing with gravity will grab a lot more of your attention. Trail and tour skiers typically shy away from facing the bottom of the hill and love to sit back, recoiling from the yawning chasm below. This makes turning about as easy as driving a car from the back seat.

Backcountry and telemark equipment is powerful, so back off and let it turn for you. Feel how skis turn simply by tipping them on edge. Reduce the amount of body English you use. Turning on equipment designed to turn is a sport of balance, not strength.

Alpine skiers—On alpine gear, you can lean into the fronts of your boots to stay forward. On free-heel equipment, flex your ankles to stay forward and keep up with your skis. Pushing into the front of cross-country boots will result in spectacular face plants, since cross-country bindings are just a set of fancy hinges.

Adapt your alpine skills to your new equipment before attempting to add the telemark to your repertoire. You will find telemark equipment similar to alpine equipment, cross-country touring equipment less so. Explore the similarities of cross-country and alpine equipment instead of the differences. Choose slower speeds, mellower terrain, and easier snow.

Poles. For all newcomers to turning, poles are handy accessories, but not essential. If you find them hopelessly confusing, grip them lightly and let the baskets drag in the snow.

SKIING IS BELIEVING

Falls are due to a lack of will power. There is an element of volition in ninety-nine falls out of a hundred.

Never lie down until you are thrown. The man who is determined never to fall until the ground gets up and hits him between the eyes will soon make a skier.

Of course, there are rare occasions on which an intentional fall is justified, for example, if you are heading for a cliff or an open crevasse or a judge of a ski test which you are hoping to pass.

Most falls, however, ought to be and can be avoided. A bad runner always assumes that he is under a positive obligation to fall if anything unusual occurs. If one ski parts itself on an icy rut, the bad skier promptly sits down. He doesn't even wait to fall. Etiquette, he seems to think, demands a prompt surrender.

The bad runner does not realize that even a forward fall is frequently a sign of pure funk. If he pitches forward on a sudden patch of soft snow, he feels virtuous, he assumes that there can be nothing intentional about a forward fall. He is wrong, for the will to stand would probably have saved him. The really determined runner instinctively braces himself the moment his leading ski drives through the resistance. The bad runner, instead of bracing himself, goes flabby, and his muscles and his will to the unforeseen check and over he goes.

It is amazing what one can survive in the way of changes of gradient or of snow if one is feeling really good. Even when you believe a fall is inevitable, try to stagger on for a yard or two. "I'm going to fall of course, but I'm jolly well going to wait until I'm thrown down. I don't object to falling, but I do object to lying down." If this be your attitude you will get away with it time and time again. Your ski gets in a rut. Set your teeth and drag it out of the rut. You strike a bump and fly into the air. A bad runner, of course, will at once assume that he has the legal right to lie down once his ski leaves the ground. If a man who jumped seventy meters stood, surely you can manage an impromptu five meters without collapsing.

From The Complete Ski-Runner *by Arnold Lunn,*
president of the Ski Club of Great Britain, 1928–1930

in their knees. If you feel yourself starting to fall back over your heels, slide your butt sideways and sit down into the hill. Once your hips are well behind your heels never try to save a fall by pulling yourself back into position with your legs and core muscles. Skiers also injure themselves when they attempt to stand back up before they are over their feet. Wait until you have come to a stop before getting up.

GETTING READY FOR PARALLEL TURNS

By the time you are ready to tackle parallel turns, you should have mastered step turns and wedges (see Chapter 2 for a review). One additional skill and some knowledge of how skis turn will also be helpful.

SIDESLIPPING AWAY

Sideslipping—sliding sideways down a slope while your tips and tails point across the hill—is a skill that every skier needs. Once mastered, sideslipping can get you through tight places and other spots where conditions or exposure make turning unpleasant.

Find a smooth, firmly packed surface to learn on. Stand with your skis positioned across the fall line on a moderate slope (the fall line is simply the most direct path down a hill). To remain stationary, tip your skis into the hill so that they are level from side to side (if they were carrying a cup full of water it would not spill). To release your edges and start sideslipping, roll your ankles, knees, and hips downhill (spill water over the downhill side of the cup). This will flatten your skis in relation to the slope, and you will start sliding sideways down the hill.

Caution: If you move only your ankles, your skis will slide out as your edges lose their grip and you will fall on your hip. This rolling of ankles, knees, and hips out and toward the yawning jaws of gravity is not an intuitive movement. In fact, most skiers hesitate a bit as they roll their skis downhill. As a result, they move forward

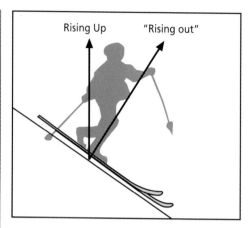

Fig. 14.1 – Rise out

Stay over your feet as you roll your ski into the hill by "pinching at the waist."

or back as well as sideways down the hill, depending on where their weight is on their skis. This is not a bad thing, since sideslipping while moving forward or back is a great way to negotiate tight spots. However, learning to intentionally move directly downhill, or back and forth across the hill, in a sideslip will allow you to make quick and easy turns all over the mountains.

Rising out. The key to slipping directly sideways down the fall line is a move known as "rising out." To rise out, extend your legs and push yourself away from the slope (not up) as you roll out to flatten your skis. Rising out keeps you on top of your skis as they sideslip downhill.

To slow or to stop your downhill sideslip, roll your edges back into the snow by moving your hips into the hill. Move only your hips, leaving your head and shoulders over your feet. This will create a "pinch" at your waist. As you edge your skis, imagine you are trying to hold an orange or a grapefruit between your ribs and your hips on your downhill side. To get your skis sideslipping again, un-pinch, straighten at the waist, and rise out.

Add *intentional* forward or backward motion by moving your weight forward or backward over your feet. Move onto the balls of your feet to sideslip forward and sideways. Conversely, moving onto your heels will direct your skis backward as you slip downhill. Always keep your ankles flexed while sideslipping in either direction or directly downhill.

TIPPING TO TURN AND TWISTING TO TURN: CARVING AND SKIDDING

Modern backcountry skis with softer cambers and deeper sidecuts will turn automatically when you tip them on edge—all you have to do is balance over them and go along for the ride. Using your skis like this is called carving a turn. In a carved turn, the tips of the skis always point toward where your skis are going and the tails follow the same track as the tips.

At the other extreme is a skidded turn, in which you use your feet and legs to physically turn the skis. In a skidded turn, the skis move forward and sideways at the same time (think of sliding across a slick floor in your socks with your feet turned sideways to the direction of your slide) so the tips are not pointing in the direction you are traveling.

Practically all turns are a combination of carving and skidding, but modern skis with deeper sidecuts allow for more carving, while straighter, touring skis will require you to rely more on skidding.

As you attempt the moves described in this chapter, keep in mind the kind of ski equipment you are using. You may need less movement than what is described to make your skis work if they have a deep sidecut and a turning camber. If you are on skinnier skis with little sidecut and a stiff camber, more up-and-down motions will be needed to start and finish each turn, and you will have to twist your feet and legs more than indicated.

MOVING FROM WEDGE TO PARALLEL

Most people learn how to turn by using the wedge. The wedge is a good choice for beginners because its wide and stable stance protects them from the consequences of a misstep—one ski is always there to catch them when things go bad. The price you pay for this stability and forgiveness is the constant attention and effort it takes to get wedged skis to go in the same direction.

Turning with both skis parallel to each other and tipped on corresponding, rather than opposing, edges is much easier once you get the hang of it. The first step in turning a wedge turn into a parallel turn is to slide your skis together after beginning your turn. This is much easier if you first move your core toward where you want to go. From a gliding wedge, start a turn to the right by moving your core toward where your *left* tip is pointing. This will cause your left ski to edge more, and it will start to carve a turn to the right. It also moves your body over your right foot and flattens your right ski, making it easier to slide it into position parallel with your left ski as you complete the turn.

Fig. 14.2 – Opposing and corresponding edges

The ski that tips up on edge at the beginning of a wedge turn is called the outside ski since it is on the outside of the turn as you cross the fall line. As the turn progresses, the outside ski will be on your downhill side, which is why the outside ski is also called the downhill ski. The other ski is called the inside or uphill ski. If the concept of inside and outside confuses you, imagine you are straddling a very low fence that encloses a circular horse corral. The curving fence in front of you traces the turn you are making. Your outside ski is outside of the corral, and your inside ski is inside of the corral. If you turn around and straddle the fence in the opposite direction the fence now traces a turn in the opposite direction and your inside and outside skis will be reversed.

In grabby snow or with less subtle gear, you will need to add extra up-and-down movement to make wedge turns with a parallel finish. Quick up-and-down movements have the effect of alternately unweighting and weighting your skis. When you reach the top of your up motion, your skis get lighter (the quicker you extend or "get tall" the more your skis will be unweighted). At the bottom of the down motion after flexing to "get small," your full weight and more presses the skis into the snow when you extend to "get tall" once more.

On stiffer skis, it is easier to roll your skis from one set of edges to the next at the top of the motion when there is less pressure holding them in the snow. Pushing your skis back into the snow at the bottom of the motion helps bow them into a more

Rise out and toward the next turn. (Photo: Steve Barnett)

of a banana shape, or reversed camber, to help make them turn.

The up-motion to start the turn consists of pushing the triangle defined by your belly button and your shoulders (your torso triangle) up and away from the slope as you extend (rise out) toward the next turn. To finish the turn, push your inside knee across your inside or uphill ski and into the hill so that the edge does not catch as you slide into a parallel position after crossing the fall line. If that does not work, pick up the uphill ski and move it into position, parallel to the downhill ski. Flex at the waist, knees, and ankles to complete the turn and

to prepare to extend into the next direction with your next up-and-out motion.

To eliminate the wedge altogether, start your wedge turns with less distance between your tails and slide your inside ski into the parallel position sooner. A series of small wedge turns at a slightly faster speed will often make this happen automatically, especially on a smooth surface.

Picking up your uphill ski to move it into position is a great survival tactic, but learning how to make smooth parallel turns with both skis on the snow will quicken your turns and reduce the physical effort of turning. To develop this subtlety and finesse, think of flowing through a series of turns. To avoid getting stuck in the past, do not cling to the hillside at the end of each turn. This will allow you to ski downhill with confidence and grace. If this seems impossible, back up to gentler terrain where you are willing to let go of the hill at the end of each turn.

Rising out and flowing from turn to turn with continual motion down the slope is easy to talk about but harder to do. Start by pushing your knees from one turn to the next instead of worrying about your entire body. To turn with your knees, roll both of them from one side of your skis to the other in a single smooth motion. Rise out and extend as you roll your knees. Be sure to keep your ankles flexed and your knees "pointy" to help you stay over your feet so you can guide your skis into and then out of the fall line during each turn. This is a powerful technique used by good skiers in stiffer snows and on lighter gear.

The ultimate goal is to learn how to coax the skis from turn to turn with movements starting in your feet. With compliant snow and skis, it is possible to start each turn by simply using the soles of your feet to press the "new" inside tips of both skis into the snow. Turns started with such subtle movements flow from one to the other like thought.

CONTROLLING YOUR SPEED

When you are facing the fall line in a wedge or wedge turn, you have complete control over how fast you are going from moment to moment. When you are facing the fall line in a parallel turn the opposite is true—gravity has complete control over you for that instant when the tips of your skis are pointing straight down the hill.

At this point many skiers tend to panic and throw their skis sideways to scrub speed and regain control. This creates an erratic and exhausting (both physically and emotionally) fast-slow-fast-slow descent. Leaving the wedge behind as you approach parallel skiing requires letting go of the natural urge for complete control. This is not easy, but there is no choice—mere humans cannot control gravity.

Instead of helping you control your speed, hanging onto the end of each turn actually creates a sudden and scary burst of acceleration when you finally let go to start the next one. Although it is counterintuitive, letting go sooner will result in a more constant pace and avoid increased speed at the beginning of each turn. A quick way to learn to let go earlier is to start some turns from a sideslip.

Sideslip to Turn. With your skis across the fall line and edged into the hill, turn your torso triangle toward the bottom of the hill as you did in the sideslip drill. To allow gravity to start your turn, make a confident rise out movement as you flatten your skis. As you sideslip, add a little pressure to the balls of your feet. This will swing your tips into the fall line.

This is the crucial and transformative moment. If you stay relaxed and keep your ankles flexed and your knees pointy to remain centered over your skis, then you will be ready to roll your skis either way to turn them back across the hill. What is more likely to happen on your first few attempts is that your skis will jet out from under you and down the hill. If this is the case, there is nothing wrong with you except that you have chosen too steep a hill to learn on.

Set yourself up for success on a gentler hill. Once you can swing your tips down-hill while keeping your weight centered over your feet, then you can roll your skis onto the next set of edges to complete the turn. Be patient and wait for your skis to slow you down as they turn across the fall line and back into the hill. Come to a stop and then repeat, moving from a sideslip into a turn by letting your ski tips seek the fall line and then rolling your skis on edge in the opposite direction. To link turns, roll from one set of edges to the other, remembering to keep the skis on edge and turning long enough to turn into the hill and slow down. It may be helpful to scream to release tension and anxiety when gravity grabs your tips at the start of each turn, then sigh in relief as your skis turn back across the hill. The goal is to feel a little thrill or even a little panic at the start of each turn. As you gain confidence and

Push both hands down the hill and across your skis to keep your chest over your feet in the hockey stop.

learn to trust the rest of the turn, this little thrill becomes one of the sensations that makes skiing downhill so addictive.

The Hockey Stop. Hockey stops are how you stop *now*. To hockey stop on skis, swing your tips into the fall line, get up some speed, and then rise out abruptly to unweight your skis. Turn both skis sideways (across the hill) by rotating your legs and turning your feet, while keeping your torso triangle facing straight ahead and down the hill. As your weight comes back onto your skis, push your hips into the hill but keep your nose over your feet as you press the uphill edges into the snow to slow down. This position helps you resist the quick deceleration of the hockey stop.

The hockey stop is a fun and effective way to stop, and a great way to gain further experience with turning your legs and feet more than your torso and pinching at the waist to stay in balance over your skis as you sideslip. Practicing the hockey stop is much, much easier when the snow is firm and smooth.

USING YOUR POLES

Poles play a supporting role to a good stance and effective movements of your legs and torso. How you hold them can help you balance and how you use them can help keep you moving from turn to turn as well as providing some extra turning power.

Hold your poles for better balance. An easy way to determine where to put your hands for better balance is to keep them where you could see them through the lens of a pair of sunglasses or goggles while looking ahead.

Swing the basket to plant your pole. When you pick up your poles, hold the grips in the waist-high position described above and cock your wrists so that the baskets are behind the grips. Swing the basket forward with your wrist and not with your arm and shoulder. This will keep your hands in a good position and reduce the motions required to plant your poles. Gripping the handle lightly between your thumb and forefinger makes this a lot easier to do. It is easier to swing the baskets forward with wrist motions if your poles are shorter than typical touring length. To plant longer poles with wrist action, swing the basket out to the side as you swing it forward or choke up on the pole and hold it below the handle.

Practice planting your poles by swinging the baskets forward with your wrists as you ski down a very shallow slope without making turns. Minimize the movements of your arms and shoulders and see how quickly you can make pole plants. You can turn as fast as you can pole, so practice until you can plant accurately and rapidly.

Use poles to pull yourself into the next turn. Imagine that there is a string attaching your pole basket to your hip. To start a new turn, reach downhill with your pole basket. The string will pull your hip from the uphill side of your skis to the downhill side and the next turn will begin. Practice until you have internalized this movement of your hip with your poling and

Reach toward the next turn with your downhill pole basket.

you will find that simply planting the pole will pull your body into the next turn.

Use poles to push yourself into the next turn. This is the obvious way to use poles. You can use either one or both when you want to jump up or out of the snow or simply need to lighten your skis to help them turn. Since you are using your arms as well as your legs to move your body, this can be a physically demanding way to ski.

To make it less demanding, time your pole plants. When you jump on skis they bow into the snow and then spring back, just like a diving board or trampoline. Time the push-off of your pole plant to take advantage of this rebound.

If you habitually rely on poles to push yourself into every new turn then you probably have a balance and stance problem or you have trouble committing to the fall line. To break this habit, go back to gentler terrain, where you can practice moving from turn to turn without any assistance from your poles. At the start of each turn, just lightly touch the snow with your downhill pole tip. When this becomes a habit you are

237

Use your poles to push yourself into the next turn. (Photo: Steve Barnett)

Hold your torso steady with your pole and let your skis turn as your legs unwind.

ready to move back onto steeper terrain.

Blocking pole plants. Blocking pole plants can be used to help you make quick and snappy turns in deep and resistant snow or in steep terrain. With your skis turned across the hill and your torso facing directly down the fall line, your downhill pole or sometimes both of your poles can be planted to "block" your upper body, holding it in place. When you rise out to start the next turn, your legs will untwist to realign with your upper body and your ski tips will immediately swing into the fall line. Try this on mild terrain and in easy conditions before attacking the steep and deep.

Poling simply enhances what your feet, ankles, and legs do. Work on the basics of standing in the center of your skis and using your skis and your lower body to make turns before you concentrate too much on pole use.

DETERMINING YOUR FUTURE

A calm and quiet upper body makes it easier to stay over your feet in any turn. Your upper body should not turn as much as your feet and legs while you are making turns. What it should do is to anticipate where you soon will be, always moving toward the future.

Where you soon will be changes when you are making long turns as opposed to short turns. When you are making long and relaxed turns your future lies across the hill in the direction you are going. Short, rapid turns constantly move you down the fall line so your future lies directly downhill, especially in steeper terrain.

On a steep hill, your natural reaction will be to turn your chest and arms up and into the hill as your reptilian brain sounds the danger alert. Tame your inner reptile

Keep your palms facing downhill as your feet and skis turn.

Face your chest and hips down the hill and across your skis as you did when the poles were across your shoulders.

by taking your poles off and holding them horizontal to the snow and across your body in front of you. Grab them with your palms facing down and lift them over your head. Place them behind your neck and across your shoulders, palms now facing forward. As you make parallel and telemark turns, keep your palms facing downhill to keep your upper body facing your future. Keep your core in line by directing your belly button in the same direction as the rest of your upper body.

Spend some time with your poles across your shoulders for practice. Then maintain the same discipline while holding your poles as you normally would. Many skiers tend to cheat at this stage—facing their shoulders uphill of their skis and toward the imagined security of the slope while keeping just their hands and poles aimed downhill. Make sure you are pointing your shoulders and belly button down the hill and across your skis instead of just your hands and arms.

BEND TO BALANCE

Although you can tip a ski on edge with only your ankle, tipping skis on edge with your legs is more powerful and effective. That's the good news. The bad news is that tilting your leg pushes the rest of your body away from your feet, making it hard to avoid sliding out and landing on your hip. To stay in balance bend sideways at the waist, bringing your chest, shoulders, and head back over your feet.

Tilting your leg to edge your ski while keeping your body straight is called banking. Banking is no big deal on shallow terrain and in deeper snow. In fact it can be kind of fun to swoop down the hill like a hawk or a hang glider. The problem with banking, however, is that once you have tilted your entire body into a turn, you are relying on the relationship between your ski and the snow to stay constant throughout the turn. If that changes, such as when your skis slip or skid out sideways, there is nothing you can do to recover. If your hips are sore from falling on them, you are probably a banker. Bend sideways at the waist to bring your head and shoulders back over your feet. From this position you can recover from a slip and avoid a fall because your weight is over your feet.

At the end of a turn on icy or steep terrain or at speed, combine this pinch or sideways bend at the waist with anticipation of the next turn. You should look and feel like you are ready to dive over the side of your downhill ski and into the next turn. This is a position that develops over the course

Pinch at the waist as you anticipate the next turn with your torso.

of the turn as your skis turn across the hill more than your torso. It is not a position you contort your body into just before the next turn begins.

THE TELE TWEAK

Sooner or later while making parallel turns with your heels unattached to your skis you will hinge forward from your toes, plant your face into the snow, and decide it's about time you learned about telemarking. In a telemark turn, the outside or downhill ski is positioned in front of the inside or uphill ski, with the heel of the rear foot raised and the knee dropped toward the ski.

On wide skis with a lot of sidecut and in tall supportive boots, the main purpose of the telemark is to provide front-to-back stability. On skinnier skis with less sidecut and lower boots, the telemark is a both a position of stability and a way to help make the skis turn. With the tip of the rear (or trailing) ski held near the binding of the front (or leading) ski, the two skis act as one long ski with a sidecut that can be adjusted by moving the tail of the rear ski in or out. To turn, the skier puts both skis on their inside (corresponding) edges and rides the curved runner created by this edging through the turn.

With modern telemark gear, starting a telemark with one ski pointing toward the other foot does not work out as well. Telemark turns on this type of equipment work best when both skis are kept parallel to each other while in the dropped-knee position.

If you are interested in skiing on modern telemark equipment, two excellent guides are *Free-Heel Skiing: Telemark and Parallel Techniques for All Conditions* by Paul Parker (Seattle: The Mountaineers Books, 2003) and *Allen & Mike's Really Cool Telemark Tips* by Allen O'Bannon and Mike Clelland (Helena, MT: Falcon, 1988). Another option is to view one of Dick Hall's effective and entertaining videos available at *www. telemarknato.com.* The remainder of this chapter will focus on telemark turns on lighter equipment. Making any type of turn on light equipment becomes a dance that requires quick footwork and quick reactions.

THE TELEMARK STANCE

If I came up beside you and shoved you sideways, you would step your feet apart from side to side to avoid falling over, before turning to give me an earful about being rude. If I came up behind you and gave you a shove, you would step your feet apart from front to back, before turning to chastise my bad manners. This second position, with your feet split apart from front to rear, is the telemark position or stance.

Moving your feet apart adds stability only if you have some weight on both. It is a common mistake to try to stride into the telemark stance, but doing this places most of your weight on the front foot. To keep some weight on both feet as you move into the telemark stance, drop your rear knee directly toward the ground, while keeping it close to the calf and heel of your front leg.

Your back ski should move back as much as your front ski moves forward as you settle between them. Another way to keep some weight on your rear ski is to mimic the movement used to scrape a canine waste product off the sole of your shoe as you draw your rear foot back.

This is an odd position, so take some time to get used to it. It is easy to come close to the proper telemark stance but hard to actually nail it. Here are some checkpoints to help out:

- Your hips should be between your feet to weight both skis. Your rear thigh should be beneath your hip and more vertical than your front thigh.

- Keep your front ankle bent so that your knee is above your toes. Your front shin should remain in contact with the cuff of your boot at all times.

- Your front heel should remain firmly on the ski. If your heel lifts off the ski every time you try to move your front knee forward, you need to move your hips back and weight the rear ski, too.

- Weight your rear ski through the ball, not the toe, of your foot. Crunch your rear boot to apply pressure to the ball of your foot by driving the top of the tongue toward the toe of the boot with your shin.

- Avoid squatting over your rear foot by

Stay centered between both feet in the telemark position.

keeping your core muscles firm so that you do not fold at the waist.

- When your rear thigh begins to burn, you'll know you're getting it.

On the flats try moving in and out of the telemark stance without sliding forward. When you start to feel like you are getting it, check that you are balanced between your feet with weight on both skis by making a small jump straight up in the air from the telemark position. If both feet are equally weighted, both feet should leave and return to the ground at the same time. If not, the foot that leaves the ground last is the foot with more weight on it. If this is the case, readjust your stance and jump again. When you can jump off and land on both feet at the same time, focus on putting spring into your legs while in the tele stance so that you land softly and quietly. After that, make a small jump and switch lead skis while in the air. When that is comfortable, keep reducing the height of your jump until your skis stay on the ground but remain weightless as you switch.

Put your telemark stance or position into motion on a gentle slope that you would be comfortable descending without making any turns. Without switching lead skis, flex up and down while remaining between your feet. Drive your rear knee to the ski to keep your thigh beneath your hip as you flex deeply. Bring your skis together as you rise up and then drop back into a telemark position. Climb back up and practice switching lead skis as you slide down the same gentle slope. Concentrate on bringing the front ski back instead of

the rear ski forward. Spend some quality time on this, since feeling truly comfortable while genuflecting to the snow gods requires devotion.

THE BASIC TELE TURN

To make your first tele turns head straight down a very gentle hill while switching lead skis to make sure your weight is between your feet. To make a turn to the left, start in the telemark-position with your right ski in front. Roll your right ankle toward your right big toe, and aim your right knee into the hill and across the tip of your rear (left) ski. Be patient and wait for your front ski to turn to the left. Ride it until you turn far enough across the hill to stop. Go back up and reverse all of the above directions to make a turn to the right.

Get both skis to turn at the same time from the telemark stance by repeating the above directions with one addition. For a turn to the left (with your right ski in front), roll your right ankle toward the big toe on your right foot and aim your right knee across the tip of your rear ski and into the hill as you did before. At the same time, roll your left (rear) ankle toward your left little toe and push your left knee into the hill. Wait, be patient, and both skis should turn to the left and into the hill. Repeat with your left ski in front, reverse all the directions, and make a turn to the right with both skis.

Once you have some success with assuming the telemark position first and then tipping your skis into a turn,

TELEMALARKY

In case you have not noticed, telemarking is a religion and not just a sport. Adherents to this cult follow a creed of serial infidelity, total commitment, and complete forgiveness. No sacrifices in the present are required for future rewards. In fact, the religion of Telemalarky delivers the goods immediately—sweet turn after sweet turn.

To reap your well-deserved earthly rewards, follow the teachings of the high priests and priestesses of snow genuflection: get out of each turn while the getting is good. In fact, abandon your relationship with a turn at the first sign of trouble! Milk it for all the fun, thrills, and pleasure you can, then jump into the next turn as soon as the bloom on the rose begins to fade. Do not talk about it, work on it, or start to analyze it when things go sour. By all means do not buy a self-help book on the subject. Just move on.

Move on with total commitment to the next turn, which lies in front of you and down the hill. After all, any problems you were having with the last turn were not your fault. Throw yourself into the next turn with passion and abandon. Hey, if things go bad with that turn there are plenty more waiting for you just down the hill.

In fact, do not even wait for things to go bad in each turn. Let go of any issues that come up in each turn, quit grasping so hard at reality, and stop trying to totally control everything that you are involved with for heaven's sake.

If you practice this *religiously,* all the sins of past and present turns will be forgiven at the start of each and every turn. Do not dwell on the past! Jump into the snowy and forgiven future!

practice rolling or tipping both skis onto edge as you slide and settle into your telemark position. This should make your turns happen quicker. Edge both skis equally by pushing down on the big toe side of your front ski and the little toe side of your rear ski.

The next step is to link one turn with another. On a mild pitch, slide and settle into a telemark position as you roll your ankles and tip your skis onto their corresponding edges. As soon as you feel the skis begin to turn, rise out toward the bottom of the hill and move into the next turn by rolling over to the opposite set of corresponding edges as you switch lead skis. Link together as many turns as you can by doing this over and over again.

THE RULES

Here are two rules that will help you flow down the hill while making telemark turns:

Turn Before You Tele. Skiers often struggle to link telemark turns for the same reason that they struggle to link parallel turns—hanging onto the last turn in a search for security and speed control. Tele skiers often fool themselves into thinking they are moving on and starting a new turn by switching lead skis, but this is not true. Switching your lead skis before flattening your skis only delays the start of the next turn. The next turn only begins when both skis are flattened and guided downhill. Switching lead skis while your skis are across the hill also puts you in a very sketchy position on steeper slopes, since the long and narrow telemark position is inherently unstable from side to side.

Skiers who tele (switch their lead skis) before they begin to turn their skis downhill usually respond to this instability by wedging the new front ski uphill for support. This creates another impediment to getting the turn started since you now have to move across the hill and onto the wedged ski before you start to go around the corner.

Move directly into the next turn by turning before you tele, which means you need to roll and guide your skis down the hill and into the next turn before you switch lead skis. To practice, hold the telemark position from the last turn until you are completely in the fall line and facing directly downhill. Then switch lead skis as you continue to tip your skis on edge and guide them through the bottom of the next turn.

If this seems impossible, back up to a shallower hill and review the sections on sideslipping, rising out, and sideslipping to turn earlier in this chapter. Go through the suggested activities in these sections in the telemark stance instead of the parallel stance.

When you are ready, turn your tips downhill without changing your lead skis

by starting the next tele turn from a tele sideslip. Once the sideslip gets going, move your weight slightly forward to swing both ski tips down the hill. Resist the urge to switch your lead ski until you are facing directly downhill. Then switch your lead ski and roll onto the next set of edges to turn back across the hill in a new telemark position. Congratulations! You have just turned before you "tele'd."

Another trick to help you turn before you tele is to take your downhill hand and grab your downhill knee to start the next turn. Open your downhill knee with your hand and push it across your ski to roll your old front ski from edged to flat. Follow your front knee and ski with your rear knee and ski until everything points downhill. Then switch your lead ski and complete the turn.

Once you have developed the habit of turning *before* you tele, start to blend the two so that you turn *as* you tele. To blend both motions, time your movement from one set of edges to the next so that your skis are flat on the snow as your feet pass while moving from one telemark position to the next.

Keep Both Feet Beneath You. Many problems in the telemark turn and the telemark position can be traced to favoring either the front or the back foot. To stay in the middle, avoid splitting your feet too far apart.

If you just cannot seem to prevent your skis from being pulled apart from front to back during each turn, the solution may be in how you start your turn (see above). A strong move onto your front ski (often caused by switching lead skis before guiding your skis into the next turn) will start your new front ski into the turn before your other ski. When this happens, your rear ski is left behind and your feet get pulled apart. Learn to turn before you tele and you will find it easier to keep your rear toes closer to your front heel.

Skiers new to skiing downhill on any type of equipment often favor the rear foot because they are hesitant to give in to the pull of gravity during the transition between each turn. If you find that you camp out over your back foot, move to a gentler slope where you can focus on flexing your front ankle to drive your knee over your foot. This will pull you forward and between your feet where you belong. Once you are balanced between your feet, you will be able to turn quicker, spend less time in the fall line, and feel more comfortable on steeper slopes.

Accomplished alpine skiers comfortable with going downhill often suffer from the opposite affliction—too much weight on the front foot. These suave skiers pretend they are in the telemark stance by holding the inside foot and ski behind the front ski while actually skiing with all of their weight on the front foot. This is commonly called the fake-a-mark.

With most of the weight on the front ski in a fake-a-mark, the rear often seems to have a mind of its own. Skiers who are light on their rear ski are easy to spot because they often hold it close to or against the front ski to keep it from causing too much trouble. Another telltale sign of a skier

overbalanced on their front foot is an air space between the front heel and the ski.

A quick fix for front-foot-reliant alpine skiers is to exaggerate each telemark position. Drop into a deep telemark stance, touching your rear knee to your rear ski. This exaggerated stance is not how you want to ski, but it will force you off your front foot during each turn. This remedy can be much worse than the original disease, so use it only as long as your symptoms persist. Once you have broken the front foot habit, return to a more functional telemark stance.

ADVANCED TELEMARK TURNS
The only rule concerning ski technique while skiing in the backcountry is that there are no rules. Anything goes when you are out back of beyond and need to get down the hill. Turns with your skis angled to each other, turns where one and then the other ski is stepped into the next turn, turns where you jump up and turn in the air, and many, many more variations are all fair game. Below are just a few of the many varieties that may prove useful.

The Sneak-a-mark. The older style telemark with the rear tip near or against the front boot as the front tip moves into the new turn is very useful in many backcountry situations. Think of it as a "hinge" turn, where both skis are used to make a turn much like a two-part city bus that bends in the middle as it goes around a street corner.

In the sneak-a-mark variation of the hinge turn, you switch lead skis before you turn, and, continuing your rebel ways, keep most of your weight on the back foot as you switch. Sneak the new front ski out and around your rear tip and toward the next turn. Tip it slightly on edge and slowly weight it. Once it starts to turn and respond, move more of your weight onto it as the turn progresses. As you gain experience with this turn, you will know how much weight to place on each ski and when to weight each ski during the turn to match the conditions.

The sneak-a-mark is especially useful in unpredictable snow. It can be a savior when you are skiing with a heavy pack and do not want to suffer through repeated face plants made worse as your pack drives you into the snow. It can also be used in deeper snows and in tight terrain, but sneak-a-marks are too slow and are too tenuous for skiing at speed or on steep slopes.

Step and Jump Teles. The step tele is a quicker version of the hinge tele. It is very useful in tight trees and other terrain where you need to make a lot of turns in a short distance to control your speed. It works best if the snow is not too deep.

The step tele is a dance set to a one-two rhythm. To start a step tele, move your rear ski from behind to beside you and into a wedge position with your other ski (there we go, breaking another rule). Move over and onto this ski, which will become the front ski of the next turn. This is the one count. Pick up your other foot and step it into place as the back ski of your next telemark. Move your weight to between your feet as you set the second ski onto the snow. This is the two count.

You can literally walk yourself down steep slopes with this one-two rhythm if you always step your rear ski into a wedge position for the first count. Dick Hall calls this "never crossing the line." The line he refers to goes through your toes when you stand in a wedge facing the fall line. It is possible to make step teles while stepping forward of this line, but you will pick up speed with each and every turn. Eventually it gets too hard to keep up with everything if you step across the line and most skiers explode in a tangle of limbs, skis, and poles.

Jump teles are the quickest hinge turns. They are basically the same as step teles, but you jump off your front ski while moving your rear ski into the wedge position. The wedge actually happens in the air during the jump and then you land across the slope in the new telemark position and the new turn. Step turns follow a one-two rhythm set to a regular beat: one-two, one-two, one-two. Jump teles follow the same one-two rhythm but are syncopated: one-two—one-two—one-two—. The rear ski still begins to move across the hill and into the wedge position before the front ski moves, but the old front ski comes off the snow before the new front ski lands. Both the step and jump tele are most easily learned on a flat shelf above a moderate slope. Establish the rhythm on the shelf and then maintain that rhythm as you move onto the slope. To control your speed, remember to not cross the line.

The Tele Hop. In the step and jump teles, each ski lands back on the snow at different times and at slightly different angles to the slope. When the snow is deep and resistant, this will cause each ski to make a slightly different turn. The tele hop avoids this problem, because you hop off both skis and land on both skis at the same time.

To master the tele hop, start in a traverse on a moderate slope. Most skiers tend to want to jump off the front foot instead of both feet at the same time, so break this habit by starting with a one-two hop off your rear foot at first.

Take it step by step and lift just your front tip off the snow as you traverse without hopping, jumping, or switching lead skis. Try to eventually get the entire front ski off the snow. If you are balanced between your feet, it should be easy to shift all your weight temporarily onto the rear ski. If this seems impossible, review the drills in the *Telemark Stance* and *Keep Both Feet Beneath You* sections. When you can lift the front ski, hop into the air off your rear foot after lifting the front ski off the snow. Do not switch lead skis during the hop quite yet. After you hop, land back on the snow on both feet at the same time.

Once you have mastered this move, try switching lead skis while your skis are still in the air. Once again, land on both feet at the same time. Then hop and add a little turn before landing again on both skis simultaneously. Complete the turn after you land so you are traversing across the slope in the opposite direction.

When you are sure that you will not cheat by hopping off your front foot, switch from starting the hop by lifting your front ski to hopping off both feet. Turn your skis more while they are off the snow and tip your skis from one set of edges to the next before you land. Said another way, hop from the end of one turn directly to the end of the next turn.

To make a quicker tele hop, get your front ski out of the way and into the end of the next turn quickly by opening and swinging your front knee (the downhill knee) across the slope as you hop. In essence you are making a reverse wedge in the air. After opening your tips in the air, retract the ski you swung across the slope to become the rear ski of your next turn and close the reverse wedge by bringing what was your rear ski parallel to that ski. Land in the telemark position on both skis at the same time with your weight between your feet.

Remember to rise out and away from the slope instead of straight up in the air whenever you hop or jump. This is the secret to freeing your skis from the snow and turning them completely across the slope. Rising out will also keep you from ending up on your heels when you land. Jumping and hopping takes some effort, but there is no need to get your skis way above the snow. Once you find the rhythm with jump and hop turns, you will also be able to use the rebound of the skis to help you rise out and lift the skis up in the snow.

TURNING IN CHALLENGING CONDITIONS

When skiing in the backcountry, challenging conditions are almost a given. What follows are some tips to help you match your turns to the conditions you encounter.

BREAKABLE CRUST

The sneak-a-mark can work in breakable crust that is not too thick and fairly consistent. Set the front ski out and ease onto it as it breaks through. In thicker and stronger crust conditions, you may find that this tenuous approach may keep you on top of the crust and gaining speed for too long before you break through and begin to turn. In these conditions, get aggressive. Pick your rear ski up out of the last turn, high step it forward, and smash it through the crust. After it breaks through, immediately weight your rear ski to keep it below the crust as you complete the turn. This is hard work—you may want to take off a layer or two of clothing before you ski an entire slope like this.

Jumping off both skis, turning in the air, and then smashing through the crust with your skis relatively parallel but in a telemark stance will actually take less effort than the high step approach if you time your jump with the rebound of your skis. This is easier to do on beefier equipment. The downside to this approach is when you do not break through upon landing and find yourself on top, living in dread of where and when you might break through.

A more subtle way to deal with this turn-resistant condition is the small/tall approach. As you turn across the fall line at the end of a turn, get small (pull your skis up as you flex at the ankles, knees, and hip). This will make your skis light and you will begin your next turn on top of the crust. As your tips swing toward the bottom of the hill, stand up hard to get tall and to push your skis through the crust and bow them into the turn. This takes good timing and faith that your skis will penetrate the crust at the bottom of the turn.

Regardless of your approach, speed is not your friend when skiing breakable crust. Be cautious and bail out on your uphill hip if you get caught accelerating on top of the crust. Avoid forward falls.

TRAILS

Snow will often stay on trails after it has melted from the surrounding terrain. This is opportunity skiing—go straight when you have to, turn where you can, and drag your poles, grab some brush, sit down, or otherwise bail out when all else fails. One trick is to turn your tips uphill and off the trail when you find any snowy patch along the trail and sideslip to scrub speed until the snow runs out. Another way to scrub speed is to run up a streambed that the trail switchbacks into if it is holding extra snow. Unless you know for sure what lies ahead, keep your speed very contained while skiing down a trail. If you do grab brush, branches, or saplings to slow down or turn make sure they are more flexible than you are to avoid ripping your shoulder out of joint. Always bail out sooner rather than later.

ICE

In resistant conditions like breakable crust and crud, a lot of movement is often needed to help your skis turn. On ice the opposite is true—every movement must be precise because there is no room for error. In a parallel turn widening your stance increases the side-to-side stability that is needed on ice. Splitting your feet from front to back in a telemark stance makes things worse. Use parallel turns while skiing on icy slopes.

On lighter weight gear in the backcountry, turns on ice are mostly skidded turns, especially at the end. Be gentle on your edges and balanced over your feet so that you can stay with your skis as they skid through the bottom of the turn. Keep your torso facing downhill and across your skis, your hands well out in front, and pinch sideways at the waist to remain over your feet.

Use the less icy patches for any quick and sudden direction changes that you need to make. Sudden edge sets can give you a quick and temporary platform to move from at times, but do not rely on them to start every turn.

STEEPS

Icy steeps are once again parallel terrain, but in softer snow steeps can be negotiated with the telemark. Regardless of the turn you choose, the first requirement of skiing the steeps is to keep your eye on the ball, which in this case means always facing down the fall line with your head and chest.

The second prerequisite is to rise out at the start of every turn. Your spine should remain perpendicular to the slope at all times to prevent your body from moving uphill of your feet as you move into the next turn.

At the end of the turn, your hips will be pushed into the hill to make the edge bite into the snow. Remember to pinch sideways at your waist to keep your weight over your feet.

The trick to skiing the steeps is to keep your speed down. This means that you have to get your skis from the end of one turn to the end of the next one quickly. Jump, step, or hop turns are often the fastest way to go about this. Blocking pole plants (see the *Using Your Poles* section) will also help you to unleash the twist between your upper and lower body that will help get your skis around quickly at the start of each turn.

In parallel parlance, these quick turns are called windshield wipers (for obvious reasons) or bicycle turns. The bicycle reference refers to the fact that your uphill foot will often be at about knee height on your downhill leg as if you were pedaling a bicycle. Push down with your uphill leg as if you were pushing down on the pedal of a bike to rise out and into the next turn. Be sure to rise out and away from the hill and not directly up in the air. If you do push directly up, you will be way behind your feet and skis when you come back to earth. Keeping your spine perpendicular to the slope automatically takes care of this detail.

The steeper the hill is, the less you have to push off to make your skis light and easy to flip around. In both parallel and telemark turns, when you do touch back to earth, pull up on the foot and ski that is uphill. This will ensure that you land with enough weight on your downhill ski to make it bite into the snow. Tucking the uphill ski under you as you settle into the next turn also helps you keep your spine perpendicular to the slope.

Bicycle turns work in the tele, but you have more movements to accomplish with your feet and legs as you flip from one direction to the next. For the quickest and most secure turns, choose parallel turns on steep terrain.

CRUD

Crud refers to deeper snows that are not powdery. This type of snow tends to trap your skis and makes it hard to get a turn started. The easiest way to help your skis turn in crud is to get small at the start of each turn and then tall in the middle. Getting small helps pull your skis up and out of the crud at the start of each turn, making it easier to turn and guide your skis into the fall line with your feet and legs. After your tips start moving downhill, extend your legs and push into the snow to add pressure on your skis that will help bow your skis into the next turn. After they turn, your skis will rebound from being bowed as you get small again to start the next turn. To practice this small-tall maneuver, start out by heading straight down to get some speed while small, then press your skis into the snow (get tall) to make them turn across the fall line. Relax your legs as the skis turn across the hill to let the rebound of the ski "boing" the ski back toward you as you get small at the start of the next turn. Change edges, push out with your legs again to press the skis into the snow and turn back across the fall line, then relax and "boing" into the next turn.

Sidecut does little for you in crud, so ski on the bases of your skis and feather your skis on to their next set of corresponding edges at the beginning of each turn to avoid slicing into the snow and getting stuck. Your goal is to bend the ski like a banana and then ride that curve through the goo. Keep your speed up by not turning too far across the hill with each turn so you can plane up in the thick stuff, just like a water skier being pulled by a boat.

POWDER

Deep powder is wonderful stuff, but it can be hard to ski for the opposite reason as crud—sometimes there is little or no resistance from the snow. In deep and light powder, you again need speed to plane your skis up into the snowpack. Keep your skis close together (both side-to-side and front-to-back) to use the combined surface area of both ski bases as a platform from which to move from one turn to the next.

As when skiing in crud, avoid edging your skis too much or you will slice into the snow and lose too much speed. Turning too far across the hill should also be avoided or the next turn will be difficult.

To get a feel for powder skiing, traverse across a medium steep slope. Keep your feet underneath you and start to bounce on your skis, trying to bring both ski tips up and out of the snow at the same time, regardless of whether you are practicing parallel or telemark turns. Once you can bounce and bring both tips out of the snow together, add a turn at the end of the bounce.

Experience in powder will allow you to feel how much speed and up-and-down movement is needed to create the resistance in the snow to turn your skis. Once you get a sense for building a platform in each turn, then the bounce will come from your skis as they rebound out of one turn and into the next, floating in between. Once you've mastered this floating feeling, you'll be on a lifelong hunt for powder.

Glossary

A position Tips of the skis closer together than the tails of the skis.

Alpine Skiing Skiing with equipment that attaches the boot to the sole in such a way that the heel cannot lift. Also called *downhill skiing.*

Base The bottom of the ski.

Base Structure A shallow pattern ground, cut, or pressed into the base to enhance glide.

Binder Wax A specially formulated wax that is heated into the grip zone of the base to make the grip wax of the day more durable.

Camber The arch of a ski seen beneath the middle of the ski as it lies base down on a flat surface.

Carved Turns In a carved turn, the tips of the skis always point to where the skis are going and the tails follow the same track as the tips.

Center of Gravity A point where an object could be supported in any position and remain in equilibrium against the pull of gravity.

Center of Mass A point where the entire mass of an object can be considered to be concentrated. The center of mass is a more useful and more accurate concept to use when describing or analyzing movement as non-gravitational forces affect a body in motion.

Classic Skiing—techniques used for forward propulsion on skis derived from walking and running. Also called *traditional skiing.*

Core Used in this text to refer to the center of mass of a skier which is located somewhere near the belly button.

Core Muscles Abdominal and lower back muscles that stabilize and support the trunk and create flexion and extension of the waist.

Cork A block of natural cork or synthetic material used to smooth wax and press it into the ski base with heat from friction and pressure.

Corresponding Edges The right or left edges of each ski. A skier on corresponding edges presses the big toe edge of one ski and the little toe edge of the other into the snow.

Cross-lateral Movement Simultaneous movement of the opposite arm and leg used in walking, running, and the diagonal stride.

Diagonal Poling Use of the pole opposite of the gliding ski to create additional forward motion of the skier. Called single sticking when used without foot or leg motions.

Diagonal Skate A skating technique that combines diagonal poling with skating—the opposite pole is planted as the skier skates onto each ski. Also called diagonal V-skate and a gliding herringbone.

Diagonal Stride The primary technique of classic or traditional skiing where the skier strides from ski to ski with a cross-lateral motion and then glides on each ski between strides. Poles are used to help push the skier forward. Also called kick and glide.

Double Poling Simultaneous use of both poles to propel the skis and the skier forward.

Extension Opening of a body joint. When you extend your ankle, the angle between your shin and your foot "opens" or grows larger.

Fall Line The shortest path from the top to the bottom of a slope.

Flex or Flexion Closing of a body joint. When you flex your ankle, the angle between your shin and your foot "closes" or becomes smaller.

Forward-falling stance Flexing forward from the ankles to create and/or keep up with the forward motion (glide) of the skis.

Freestyle Skiing See *skating*.

Glide Wax Wax and other preparations applied to the ski base to help the skis slide more easily in various snow and weather conditions.

Gliding Wedge A wedge position with the skis relatively flat to the snow surface.

Grip When a ski stops and does not slide back as the skier moves forward.

Grip Wax Wax and other preparations applied to the ski base to make the skis grip when a skier presses down and back on the grip zone.

Grip Zone The middle of a classic ski where the waxless pattern is located or grip wax is applied.

Hard Shell A shell usually of woven synthetic yarns. A coating may or may not be applied or laminated to the inner surface of the fabric to prevent wind and/or water from penetrating.

Hard Wax A type of grip wax sold in a short cylindrical container used in crystalline snow conditions.

Herringbone Technique used to climb straight up a hill on the inside edges of the skis with the tips farther apart than the tails. The resultant track resembles the skeleton of a fish, hence the name.

Hot-waxing Applying glide wax by melting it into the base of the ski with a hot iron.

Javelin Tip Forebody of a ski that is narrower than the rest of the ski.

Kick A term used to indicate both grip and the body motion that creates grip and moves the skier forward onto the next ski.

Kick Double Pole Sequence of one forward stride or kick combined with one double pole.

Kick Zone See *grip zone.*

Klister A type of grip wax sold in a toothpaste-like tube that resembles very sticky jelly. Klister is used when above-freezing temperatures or force has destroyed the snow crystals' sharp edges.

Layering A combination of different garments, each with a specific function, used to stay warm and dry.

Lead Ski The ski in front; usually refers to the front ski while in the telemark position.

Marathon A long ski race usually open to anyone. No distance is specified to qualify as a marathon, but most are from 50 to 100 kilometers in length. Also called a loppet.

Marathon Skate A skating technique with one ski aligned with the overall direction of travel. The pole and leg timing and overall body motions are similar to the V-1.

NNN New Nordic Norm, the boot and binding system from the Norwegian manufacturer Rottefella.

No Poles Skating A skating technique using just the legs. Also called free skating or V-skating.

Nordic Center A cross-country ski area with parking, some sort of indoor facility, and machine-groomed trails.

Nordic Skiing Skiing on equipment that attaches the boot to the ski only at the toe, leaving the heel free; hence the alternate name: freeheel skiing.

Offset skate International name for the V-1 skate.

One skate International name for V-2 skate.

Opposing edges The edges beneath the skier's big toes. A skier on opposing edges presses the big toe edges of both skis into the snow.

Parallel Position Skis side by side like the lines on a legal pad.

Parallel Turn Turn with the skis in a parallel position and the feet side by side.

P-tex (Polyethylene) Base material used on all modern skis.

Pulks Sled pulled behind a skier, usually containing a child and connected to the skier with rigid arms attached to a waistbelt.

Push-off Moving forward from one ski to the next by extending at the waist, knee, and ankle.

Ready stance The basic stance of skiing, shared by a tennis player awaiting the next serve, a basketball player ready for a rebound, and wrestlers circling at the start of a match.

Shape Another word for *sidecut.*

Shell The outer piece of clothing in a layering system; it resists penetration by wind and water from the outside while allowing air and moisture to flow to the outside.

Sidecut The shape of the ski as seen from above or below. A ski with an hourglass shape turns more easily while a ski with no shape goes straight more easily.

Sideslip Movement on the skis that is not aligned with the direction that the tips (or the tails) are pointing.

Skate Position Tails of the skis kept closer together than the tips of the skis to form a V position. Also used in the herringbone.

Skate Turn Pushing off from each ski to maintain or increase speed while making a step turn.

Skating Also called skate skiing, free technique and freestyle skiing—moving forward by angling at least one ski away from the overall direction of travel and pressing the edge of that ski into the snow to create resistance to move forward against. See skate ski position and skating body position.

Skating Body Position Feet turned out to match the V of the skate ski position by rotating the entire leg outward at the hip joint while the pelvis and core remain facing forward and inside of the ski tips.

Skidded Turns In a skidded turn, the skis move forward and sideways at the same time. The tips do not point in the overall direction of travel during the turn.

SNS Salomon Nordic System, the boot and binding system from the French manufacturer Salomon.

Snowplow A technique used to increase the resistance of the snow against the skis by pressing the big toe edges of both skis into the snow surface from a wedge position.

Soft Shell A shell (usually knit from synthetic fibers) that resists penetration by water and wind from the outside while allowing water vapor to escape from within. Soft shells are functionally windproof but are not waterproof.

SPF Sun Protection Factor. A sunscreen with an SPF of eight allows you to stay out eight times longer than you could without sunscreen. In practical use, waterproof sunscreens with a SPF of at least 25 should be used while skiing in the sun and reapplied every four hours to be effective.

Step Turn Changing directions by picking up one ski at a time, realigning it with where you want to go, and then placing it back into the snow as you step forward and onto it.

Striding Short for the diagonal stride. Also used as an alternate term for all classic techniques.

Telemark Body Position Weight on both feet with the skis in the telemark position. The front foot is equally weighted from heel to toe, the front knee is over the front toes, the rear thigh is vertical or angled slightly forward, and the rear foot is weighted through the ball of the foot. The rear heel is raised.

Telemark Position The tip of one ski is drawn back to between the tip and toe binding of the other. Skis may be convergent (one tip pointing at the other ski) or in parallel position.

Telemark Turn Turn with the skis in the telemark position and the skier in the telemark body position when the tips are pointing downhill.

Three-pin or 75mm Boot and Binding A toe binding and matching boot with a sole that is 75mm wide at the toe. Three holes in the toe of the boot mate with three pins on the plate of the binding.

Traditional Skiing See *classic skiing*

Two Skate International name for the V-2 Alternate skating technique.

Unweighting Reducing the pressure of the snow against the ski(s) by strategic use of terrain and/or the storage and release of energy in the flex of the ski and/or flexion and extension of the skier.

V-1 A skating technique that combines one double pole with every other skate. The poles are planted, in an asymmetrical or offset position to avoid planting one of the poles between the skis, just as the skier skates onto one ski.

V-2 A skating technique combining a double pole with every skate. The poles are planted after the skier has skated onto each ski.

V-2 Alternate A skating technique with timing and body motions similar to the V-2 except the skier poles with only one of the skates. Often called the Gunde or open field skate during the historical development of the skating techniques.

Waist The mid-section of a ski. The waist of a ski with sidecut will be narrower than either the tip or the tail.

Waterproof-Breathable Vapor-permeable barriers applied to fabrics and garments that block water and snow from penetrating from the outside while allowing perspiration from the inside to escape.

To function as designed, waterproof-breathable garments require an environment outside of the garment that is colder and drier than inside.

Wax Substances applied to the ski base to make the skis grip or slide on the snow and to protect the base of the ski.

Waxable Ski A classic ski that needs grip wax to grip.

Waxless Pattern A pattern placed in the grip zone on the base of a ski that resists slippage without using grip wax to the rear while allowing the ski to glide forward.

Waxless Ski A classic ski that uses a waxless pattern to provide grip.

Wedge Position Ski tips closer together than the tails place the skis in an A position. The outside or forward edges of the skis are tipped up and off the snow surface to varying degrees depending on the purpose of the wedge position.

Wedge Turns Turns made with the skis in a wedge position.

Weighting Increasing the pressure of the snow against the ski(s) by strategic use of terrain and/or the storage and release of energy in the flex of the ski and/or flexion and extension of the skier.

Wind Shell Shell that prevents penetration by the wind but not by water while allowing perspiration to pass to the outside more easily than waterproof-breathable or waterproof shells.

Index

About the Author

Steve Hindman has taught cross-country skiing since 1980 and was a member of the Professional Ski Instructors of America National Nordic Demo Team from 1992-2004. He has written instruction and travel articles for various magazines, contributed to ski instruction manuals, and has been the instructional editor at *Cross-Country Skier* magazine since 2002.

Steve started a cross-country ski rental shop in Glacier, WA on the way to Mt. Baker in 1981. That led to the creation of a cross-country ski area just up the road and eventually an outdoor retail store in Bellingham, WA. He ran a backcountry ski guide service and taught touring and telemark skiing as well as sea kayaking through his shop and for other organizations. After liquidating the retail business he spent several summers guiding road bike tours.

Steve is currently the manager of the adult programs at the Ski and Snowboard School at Stevens Pass, WA and teaches throughout the Northwest at various cross-country and telemark ski camps and clinics. When the snow melts, he is forced to ride his road and mountain bikes and paddle his kayak in and around Bellingham, WA where he lives with his wife Sue.

THE MOUNTAINEERS, founded in 1906, is a nonprofit outdoor activity and conservation club, whose mission is "to explore, study, preserve, and enjoy the natural beauty of the outdoors...." Based in Seattle, Washington, the club is now the third-largest such organization in the United States, with seven branches throughout Washington State.

The Mountaineers sponsors both classes and year-round outdoor activities in the Pacific Northwest, which include hiking, mountain climbing, ski-touring, snowshoeing, bicycling, camping, kayaking, nature study, sailing, and adventure travel. The club's conservation division supports environmental causes through educational activities, sponsoring legislation, and presenting informational programs.

All club activities are led by skilled, experienced instructors, who are dedicated to promoting safe and responsible enjoyment and preservation of the outdoors.

If you would like to participate in these organized outdoor activities or the club's programs, consider a membership in The Mountaineers. For information and an application, write or call The Mountaineers, Club Headquarters, 300 Third Avenue West, Seattle, WA 98119; 206-284-6310. You can also visit the club's website at *www.mountaineers.*org or contact The Mountaineers via email at *clubmail@mountaineers.org.*

The Mountaineers Books, an active, nonprofit publishing program of the club, produces guidebooks, instructional texts, historical works, natural history guides, and works on environmental conservation. All books produced by The Mountaineers Books fulfill the club's mission.

Send or call for our catalog of more than 500 outdoor titles:

The Mountaineers Books
1001 SW Klickitat Way, Suite 201
Seattle, WA 98134
800-553-4453
mbooks@mountaineersbooks.org
www.mountaineersbooks.org

The Mountaineers Books is proud to be a corporate sponsor of The Leave No Trace Center for Outdoor Ethics, whose mission is to promote and inspire responsible outdoor recreation through education, research, and partnerships. The Leave No Trace program is focused specifically on human-powered (nonmotorized) recreation.

Leave No Trace strives to educate visitors about the nature of their recreational impacts, as well as offer techniques to prevent and minimize such impacts. Leave No Trace is best understood as an educational and ethical program, not as a set of rules and regulations.

For more information, visit *www.LNT.org,* or call 800-332-4100.

MORE TITLES YOU MIGHT ENJOY FROM THE MOUNTAINEERS BOOKS

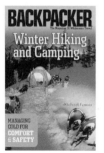